Text Summarization in Digital Libraries

Shiyan Ou

Text Summarization in Digital Libraries

Development and Evaluation of a Multi-document Summarization Method for Research Abstracts

VDM Verlag Dr. Müller

Impressum/Imprint (nur für Deutschland/ only for Germany)
Bibliografische Information der Deutschen Nationalbibliothek: Die Deutsche Nationalbibliothek
verzeichnet diese Publikation in der Deutschen Nationalbibliografie; detaillierte bibliografische
Daten sind im Internet über http://dnb.d-nb.de abrufbar.
Alle in diesem Buch genannten Marken und Produktnamen unterliegen warenzeichen-, marken-
oder patentrechtlichem Schutz bzw. sind Warenzeichen oder eingetragene Warenzeichen der
jeweiligen Inhaber. Die Wiedergabe von Marken, Produktnamen, Gebrauchsnamen,
Handelsnamen, Warenbezeichnungen u.s.w. in diesem Werk berechtigt auch ohne besondere
Kennzeichnung nicht zu der Annahme, dass solche Namen im Sinne der Warenzeichen- und
Markenschutzgesetzgebung als frei zu betrachten wären und daher von jedermann benutzt
werden dürften.

Coverbild: www.purestockx.com

Verlag: VDM Verlag Dr. Müller Aktiengesellschaft & Co. KG
Dudweiler Landstr. 99, 66123 Saarbrücken, Deutschland
Telefon +49 681 9100-698, Telefax +49 681 9100-988, Email: info@vdm-verlag.de
Zugl.: Singapore, Nanyang Technological University, Diss., 2006

Herstellung in Deutschland:
Schaltungsdienst Lange o.H.G., Berlin
Books on Demand GmbH, Norderstedt
Reha GmbH, Saarbrücken
Amazon Distribution GmbH, Leipzig
ISBN: 978-3-639-18083-1

Imprint (only for USA, GB)
Bibliographic information published by the Deutsche Nationalbibliothek: The Deutsche
Nationalbibliothek lists this publication in the Deutsche Nationalbibliografie; detailed
bibliographic data are available in the Internet at http://dnb.d-nb.de .
Any brand names and product names mentioned in this book are subject to trademark, brand or
patent protection and are trademarks or registered trademarks of their respective holders. The use
of brand names, product names, common names, trade names, product descriptions etc. even
without a particular marking in this works is in no way to be construed to mean that such names
may be regarded as unrestricted in respect of trademark and brand protection legislation and
could thus be used by anyone.

Cover image: www.purestockx.com

Publisher:
VDM Verlag Dr. Müller Aktiengesellschaft & Co. KG
Dudweiler Landstr. 99, 66123 Saarbrücken, Germany
Phone +49 681 9100-698, Fax +49 681 9100-988, Email: info@vdm-publishing.com

Printed in the U.S.A.
Printed in the U.K. by (see last page)
ISBN: 978-3-639-18083-1

Acknowledgements

I would like to express my wholehearted gratitude to all those who helped me with their guidance and support whilst writing this book.

First of all, I am particularly indebted to Dr. Christopher Khoo Soo Guan who taught me much of what I know about research, clear thinking, and effective writing. His sound, conscientious advice has been continuous throughout the writing of the book. I must also thank Dr. Dion Goh Hoe Lian who broadened my perspectives and gave me constructive comments with the creation of the text.

I am very grateful to Professor Schubert Foo Shou Boon, Dr. Abdus Sattar Chaudhry, Dr. Theng Yin Leng, and other faculty members in the Division of Information Studies, School of Communication and Information, Nanyang Technological University (NTU), for their valuable suggestions and constant supports.

Many thanks also go to my colleagues in the Computational Linguistics Research Group, Research Institute in Information and Language Processing, University of Wolverhampton, UK. It has been a wonderful experience working with them.

Finally, I owe much to my family for their love and support without which I could not have finished this book.

Table of Contents

List of Tables

List of Figures

Chapter 1

Introduction

1.1 Introduction

This work aims to develop a method for automatic summarization of a set of research abstracts that may be retrieved by a digital library system (or other information retrieval systems) in response to a user query. Automatic summarization has attracted attention both in the research community and commercial organizations as a solution for reducing information overload and helping users to scan a large number of documents to identify documents of interest (Mani & Maybury, 1999). It is an important function that should be available in large digital library systems, information retrieval systems and Web search engines, where the retrieval of too many documents and the resulting information overload is a major problem for users.

Information retrieval systems and Web search engines attempt to address the problem of information overload by ranking documents retrieved by their likelihood of relevance, and displaying titles and short abstracts to give users some indication of the document content. The abstracts may be constructed by humans or automatically generated by extracting the first few lines of the document text (called lead sentences) or extracting the most important sentences in the document.

However, the user has patience to scan only a small number of document titles and abstracts, usually within the range of 10 to 30 (Jansen, Spink & Saracevic, 2000; Spink & Xu, 2000). To help the user identify relevant documents from a larger number of records, some search engines group the retrieved records into folders or categories (e.g. Northern Light search engine[1]). These categories may be pre-created, and the records assigned to them by human indexers, or by automatic categorization techniques. The categories may also be constructed dynamically by clustering the documents

---

[1] http://www.northernlight.com

retrieved, e.g. Grouper, an interface to the results of the HuskySearch meta-search engine (Zamir & Etzioni, 1999).

A related approach is to dynamically construct a multi-document summary of the documents retrieved. While single-document summarization is a well-developed field, especially in the use of sentence extraction techniques, multi-document summarization has begun to attract attention only in the last few years (National Institute of Standards and Technology, 2002). Multi-document summarization is capable of condensing a set of related documents, instead of a single document, into one summary. A multi-document summary has several advantages over the single-document summary. It provides a domain overview of the subject area indicating common information across many documents, unique information in each document, and cross-document relationships (relationships between pieces of information in different documents), and it can allow users to zoom in for more details on aspects of interest.

This work is in the area of multi-document summarization. However, instead of summarizing from the original document content, the focus is on summarizing from the abstracts of the documents, in effect treating the abstracts as documents. This work focuses on informative research abstracts since such research abstracts (e.g. dissertation abstracts, and abstracts of medical articles) often have a clear structure and provide a summary of the research findings. In this work, dissertation abstracts in the domain of sociology are selected because of the recent interest in constructing digital libraries of dissertations (Moxley, 2001), especially in academic institutions (e.g. Networked Digital Library of Theses and Dissertations[2]). Furthermore, little work has been done in the domain of sociology since most summarization research has been with news articles, and scientific and technical articles.

Dissertations are a rich source of information on new and emerging research fields (Herther, 2000). There is a ready supply of student dissertations in universities. However, the access to full-text dissertations is often restricted by institutional policies and copyright concerns, whereas dissertation abstracts are often freely available (e.g. ProQuest Digital Dissertations). A dissertation abstract is a high-quality informative research abstract providing substantial information on the research objectives, research methods and results of dissertation projects. It is relatively long (about 300-400 words), and browsing too many of such abstracts result in information overload. Therefore, it is helpful to summarize a set of dissertation abstracts to assist users in grasping the central ideas in the group of research studies and the relations between the different studies. Dissertation abstracts have

---

[2] http://www.ndltd.org

a relatively clear and standard structure. The language is more formal and standardized than in other corpora, e.g. news articles, and is thus easier to analyze automatically.

Most research on automatic summarization has been carried out with news articles, and some news summarization systems have been developed, e.g. Newsblaster[3] (Mckeown et al., 2002) and NewsInEssence[4] (Radev, Blair-Goldensoh; Zhang & Raghavan, 2001). Summarization research on scientific and technical articles has been carried out to a less extent, mainly in the field of science and engineering, e.g. chemistry papers (Pollock & Zamora, 1975), research papers on crop agriculture (Paice & Jones, 1993), and medical articles (Elhadad & McKeown, 2001). Little work has been done in the field of humanities and social science. Edumulason (1969) developed a summarization system for a heterogeneous corpus including physical science, life science, information science and humanities. Farzindar and Lapalme (2004a & 2004b) constructed single-document summaries of legal documents. However, no work has been done on multi-document summarization of sociology dissertation abstracts.

The sociology domain is selected for this work because much of sociology research adopts the traditional quantitative research paradigm of looking for relationships between concepts operationalized as variables. Sociology dissertation abstracts are also well-structured and have the classical research report structure with five standard sections such as *background, research objectives, research methods, research results* and *concluding remarks* (see Section 3.2). Many other domains, such as psychology, medicine, crop agriculture and chemistry, adopt this research paradigm and report structure. Although some sociology research is carried out using the qualitative research paradigm, focusing on description and explanation, many of these studies also seek to identify relationships between concepts representing events, behaviors, attributes, and situations. This work focuses on the quantitative research paradigm and research report structure (e.g. five standard sections) to summarize a set of related sociology dissertation abstracts.

1.2   What is Multi-document Summarization?

Mani (2001a) characterized automatic summarization as *"to take an information source, extract content from it, and present the most important content to the user in a condensed form and in a*

---

[3] http://newsblaster.cs.columbia.edu
[4] http://lada.si.umich.edu:8080/clair/nie1/nie.cgi

manner sensitive to the user's or application's needs." Stein, Strzalkowski and Wise (2000) regarded automatic summarization as *"the process of creating a shorter representation of an original information source"*, and indicated that *"the resulting summary is a (much) shorter text document that should contain the essential parts of the original."*

Different from single-document summarization, multi-document summarization condenses a set of related documents, rather than one document, into a summary. It is more useful than single-document summarization in digital libraries and Web search engines. For example, when a user submits a search query to an information retrieval system or Web search engine such as Google, thousands of related documents are retrieved, and displayed in decreasing order of probable relevance. Since the related documents are likely to contain repeated information or share the same background, their single-document summaries are likely to be similar to each other and thus cannot indicate unique information in individual documents. Moreover, browsing so many similar single-document summaries is tedious and time consuming, and it is hard to obtain an overview of the subject area. A multi-document summary is likely to be essential in such a situation (Goldstein, Kantrowitz, Mittal & Carbonell, 1999). It provides an overview of the topic by indicating what is similar and different in different documents and relationships between pieces of information across documents, and allows people to zoom in for more details on aspects of their interest.

Although multi-document summarization can be seen as an extension of single-document summarization (Mani, 2001b), it also can be much more. Since it combines and integrates information across documents, it performs knowledge synthesis and knowledge discovery, and can be used for knowledge acquisition. It provides a domain-overview of a subject area (based on a document set) and, if presented in a graphical or visual way, can support user browsing and information visualization. Multi-document summaries are useful in large digital libraries, especially in academic institutions, and can be used for knowledge discovery to identify connections between research results that are not obvious, and gaps in the field for future research.

Multi-document summarization has more challenges than single-document summarization in the issues of compression, redundancy, cohesion, coherence, and temporal dimension etc. (Goldstein, Mittal, Carbonell & Kantrowitz, 2000). Traditional single-document summarization approaches do not always work well in a multi-document environment. For example, if there are too many documents in a collection, simply concatenating the single-document summaries of individual documents will result in a very long multi-document summary containing lots of redundant information (Hahn & Mani, 2000).

In a set of related documents, many of them are likely to contain similar information and only differ in certain parts. Thus, an ideal multi-document summary should contain common information among most of the documents, plus important unique information present among the individual documents (Goldstein et al., 2000). In previous work (Mani & Bloedorn, 1999; Barzilay, Mckeown & Elhadad, 1999; Radev, 2000, Zhang, Blair-Goldensohn & Radev, 2002), the similarities and differences were identified at a low level based on similar words, phrases, sentences and their syntactic and rhetorical relations. It is desirable for the similarities and differences to be identified at a more semantic level.

Like most of the previous multi-document summarization approaches, this work focuses on the similarities and differences across documents to summarize a set of related dissertation abstracts. However, the identification of similarities and differences among sociology dissertation abstracts is focused on research concepts and their research relationships expressed in the text.

1.3   Research Objectives

The objective of this work is to develop a method for automatic construction of multi-document summaries of research abstracts, focusing on research concepts and their research relationships, in the context of digital libraries.

In sociological studies, concepts are used to identify elements of society and human social behavior (Macionis, 2000). A concept is a mental construct that represents a group of things which have common characteristics (Macionis, 2000). For example, *family* and *culture* represent concepts. Concepts are often operationalized as variables. A variable represents a specific concept investigated in a particular research study whose value can change from case to case (Macionis, 2000). For example, *income* is a numerical variable because a person's income can be assigned a numerical value. Variables also can be qualitative, which can represent attributes of target concepts or social phenomena, and can be described using text values (e.g. categories, themes, patterns) (Trochim, 1999). For example, *gender* is a qualitative variable that takes two categorical values "*male*" and "*female*". A research relationship refers to the correspondence between two research variables that are investigated in the sociological study (Trochim, 1999). In this work, the terms "*research concepts*" and "*research variables*" are used interchangeably. In dissertation abstracts, they are expressed as terms and are often indistinguishable.

5

Much of sociological research aims to explore research concepts and their research relationships (Macionis, 2000). In a set of dissertation abstracts on a specific topic, the same or similar concepts may be investigated by several dissertation studies. In each of these dissertation studies, different attributes of a specific concept or its relationship with other concept(s) may be examined using different research methods and in different contexts. Thus the similarities and differences across sociology dissertation abstracts are mainly reflected through research concepts and their research relationships investigated in the dissertation studies. In this work, a variable-based framework is proposed for information integration and organization. This framework covers four kinds of information – *research concepts* and *their research relationships, contextual relations* and *research methods*. It integrates each kind of information hierarchically and then organizes the four kinds of information based on the *main concepts* that were investigated in many dissertation studies. The framework has a hierarchical structure in which the summarized information is presented at the top level and the more detailed information given at the lower levels.

Based on the variable-based framework, a new summarization method is developed in this work. This is a hybrid summarization method involving both extraction and abstraction steps. It focuses on extracting research concepts and their research relationships from each dissertation abstract, integrating the information across different dissertation abstracts, organizing the integrated information according to the variable-based framework, and presenting it in a Web-based interface.

The summarization method developed in this work focuses on the following tasks:
(1) Automatic macro-level discourse parsing to segment a dissertation abstract into different sections and identify the *research objectives* and *research results* sections;
(2) Automatic information extraction based on the micro-level discourse structure (within sentences) to extract different kinds of information from a dissertation abstract;
(3) Automatic integration of information extracted from different dissertation abstracts based on the cross-document discourse structure;
(4) A presentation method to organize all kinds of information using a taxonomy and display them in a Web-based interface.

1.4 Significance of the Work

This work is possibly the first attempt to construct multi-document summaries of sets of related dissertation abstracts. No work was found in the literature on multi-document summarization of dissertations and dissertation abstracts as well as other kinds of informative research abstracts. Most of summarization research has been on news articles, and scientific and technical articles. Only a small amount of work has been done in the domain of humanities and social science.

The work focuses on research concepts and their research relationships. A variable-based framework is proposed to integrate and organize information extracted from different documents. In previous work, sentence extraction approaches have been extensively used in automatic summarization. Although some studies made use of cross-document rhetorical relations to identify similarities and differences across documents, no attention was paid to concepts and the relationships between them that were investigated by the researchers in the research studies.

Although the summarization method is developed based on dissertation abstracts in the field of sociology, it should be easy to extend it to other domains, such as psychology, medicine, crop agriculture, and chemistry, which adopt the same research paradigm of seeking to investigate research concepts and their research relationships and use a similar research report structure.

1.5 Organization of the Book

This book contains six chapters. Chapter 2 provides a review of the literature as it relates to automatic text summarization. The areas surveyed mainly include single-document summarization approaches, multi-document summarization approaches, and evaluation approaches. Chapter 3 proposes a variable-based framework for multi-document summarization. Chapter 4 describes the design and development of the summarization method used in this work. Chapter 5 reports the evaluation of the summarization method. Chapter 6 discusses this research in the context of existing work, and also presents future work. Finally, Chapter 7 outlines the principal trends of the area of automatic text summarization in the context of digital libraries.

Chapter 2

Literature Review

This chapter begins by reviewing the types and uses of text summaries. Next, it reviews the approaches for single-document summarization and multi-document summarization used in previous studies. These approaches can be divided into two categories – extractive approaches and abstractive approaches. Finally, various evaluation approaches for summarization are also surveyed here. These are of two types – intrinsic evaluation and extrinsic evaluation.

2.1 Types of Summaries

Research in automatic summarization has had a history of more than forty years since the early study by Luhn (1958). Summarization is used for different purposes and different users. For this reason, various types of summaries have been constructed.

2.1.1 Extracts vs. Abstracts

There is a distinct difference between abstracts and extracts. Mani (2001a) defined the two as follows:

- *"An extract is a summary consisting entirely of material copied from the input."*
- *"An abstract is a summary at least some of whose material is not present in the input, e.g. subject categories, paraphrase of content, etc."*

The summaries generated in this work are closer to an abstract. They not only contain terms extracted from original documents but also contain new texts generated to fuse the terms and normalize the surface expressions of relationships extracted from original documents.

9

2.1.2 Informative vs. Indicative vs. Evaluative Summaries

A summary can be indicative, informative, or evaluative (Hovy & Lin, 1998; Hahn & Mani, 2000; Kan, McKeown & Klavans, 2001; Afantenos, Karkaletsis & Stamatopoulos, 2005a):

- *An indicative summary* provides an indication of what the original document is about. It can help the user to determine whether the original document is worth reading or not, but the user has to consult the original for details.
- *An informative summary* reflects the contents of the original document and represents the contents in a concise way. It can be used as a substitute for the original document so that the user does not need to read the original.
- *An evaluative or critical summary* not only contains the main topics of the original document but also provides the abstractor's comments on the document contents.

The summary generated in this work is a hybrid of indicative and informative summaries. It is presented in a hierarchical structure, which provides indicative information at the top level and more detailed information at the lower levels.

2.1.3 Generic vs. User-focused Summaries

Another distinction to be made is between a generic summary and a user-focused summary (Hovy & Lin, 1998; Hahn & Mani, 2000; Afantenos et al., 2005a):

- *A generic summary* covers all major themes or aspects of the original document to serve a broad readership community rather than a particular group.
- *A user-focused or query-driven summary* favors specific themes or aspects of the original documents that are relevant to a user query to cater to special needs or interests of an individual or a particular group.

The summary generated in this work is a hybrid of generic and user-focused summaries. It provides general information at the top level but also allows users to explore more details of interest at the lower levels by clicking on hyperlinks.

2.1.4 General-purpose vs. Domain-specific Summarization Systems

A summarization system could be general-purpose or domain-specific (Hovy & Lin, 1998; Afantenos et al., 2005a):

10

- *A general-purpose summarization system* can be applied to different domains with almost equivalent performance. It extracts salient text passages by mainly depending on statistical features (e.g. keyword frequency) that are domain-independent.

- *A domain-specific summarization system* can only work well in a specific domain, and its performance becomes much worse when applied to other domains. It extracts salient text passages and/or reformulates them into a new text using various kinds of domain knowledge (e.g. knowledge of important terms in the subject area, text structure, and grammatical usage).

The summarization system developed in this work is specific for sociology dissertation abstracts. It can be extended to other domains which adopt the same research paradigm of seeking to investigate research concepts and their research relationships and use a similar research report structure.

2.1.5 Single-document vs. Multi-document Summaries

Depending on the number of documents being summarized at the same time, the resulting summary can be a single-document summary or a multi-document summary (Hovy & Lin, 1998; Hahn & Mani, 2000; Afantenos et al., 2005a):

- *A single-document summary* is a shorter representation of only one document;

- *A multi-document summary* is a shorter representation of a set of documents. In a document set, the documents not only repeat similar information but also contain unique information. Multi-document summarization has more challenges in the issues of redundancy, cohesion, coherence etc. than single-document summarization, since the summarized materials are extracted from different sources.

The summarization method developed in this work seeks to construct multi-document summaries of sets of sociology dissertation abstracts. The number of dissertation abstracts to be condensed into one summary can be specified by the user.

2.2 Approaches for Single-document Summarization

Summarization approaches for single documents can be broadly divided into extractive approaches and abstractive approaches. Extractive approaches extract salient text passages (typically sentences and paragraphs) from the source document and assemble them to form an extract. Abstractive approaches create grammatical and coherent new texts to paraphrase and replace salient information extracted from the source document (Hahn & Mani, 2000; Afantenos et al., 2005a).

Extractive approaches are usually domain independent. They do not require linguistic processing and knowledge bases. The weaknesses of extraction are that the resulting extracts may be redundant, not coherent and fluent, and thus hard to read. These weaknesses become more serious in multi-document summarization because the extracted text passages may come from different sources and have different writing styles (Hahn & Mani, 2000; Afantenos et al., 2005a). Abstractive approaches, on the other hand, are usually very knowledge-intensive, domain-dependent and expensive, but produce better summaries for a specific domain. They often require a sizable and complicated domain-specific knowledge base as well as involve natural language generation techniques. The strengths of text abstraction are in the conciseness and readability of the resulting abstracts (Hahn & Mani, 2000; Afantenos et al., 2005a).

Extractive approaches are of three types:
- *Statistics-based approaches* rank sentences depending on statistical features and extract the top ranked sentences.
- *Cohesion-based approaches* extract inter-connected sentences by detecting cohesive links between them.
- *Discourse-based approaches* analyze the discourse structure of the original document to determine the importance of text units, and then extract the most important text units.

The three types represent an increasing understanding of text and an increasing complexity in text processing (Aone, Okurowski & Gorlinsky, 1999).

Abstractive approaches are also of three types:
- *Sentence compression approaches* extract important sentences from the original document and compresses them into concise versions.
- *Knowledge-based approaches* construct a knowledge representation of the text and then transform the knowledge representation into fluent texts.
- *Concept generalization approaches* replace the specific concepts extracted from the original document with broader ones and convert them into fluent sentences.

2.2.1 Statistics-based Approaches

The earlier attempts at summarization typically were based on the extraction of significant sentences from a text. It made use of statistical and linguistic features to measure the significance of sentences thereby allowing the highest scoring sentences to be extracted. Well-known statistical features used in previous studies are as follows:

- **Frequent keywords:** Sentences are scored using the number of occurrence of high frequency non-stop words (Luhn, 1958; Edmundson, 1969; Paice, 1990; Kupiec, Pedersen & Chen, 1995).

- **Topic signatures:** Sentences are scored using the number of occurrence of the distinct terms from topic signatures. A topic signature is a list of related terms that are most likely to be associated with a particular topic (Hovy & Lin, 1999; Lin & Hovy, 2000; Lacatusu, Hickl, Harabagiu & Nezda, 2004).

- **Cue words:** The relevance of a sentence is often affected by the presence or absence of certain cue words. The cue words could be positive (e.g. *significant, greatest, important, definitely*) and negative (e.g. *impossible, hardly, unclear, perhaps*) (Edmundson, 1969; Paice, 1990).

- **Indicator phrases:** The presence of positive indicator phrases such as *"the aim of this article"*, *"the purpose of this paper"* often signal summary sentences (Rush, Salvador & Zamora, 1971; Kupiec et al, 1995; Teufel & Moens, 1997), whereas the presence of negative indicator phrases such as *"for example"* often signal non-summary sentences (Myaeng & Jang, 1999).

- **Title keywords:** Important sentences often contain non-stop words that appeared in the title, subtitles or headings of a document (Edmundson, 1969; Paice, 1990).

- **Sentence position:** Sentences occurring in some specific positions (e.g. at the beginning or end of a document, in the first or last sentences of paragraphs) and particular paragraphs (e.g. the first paragraph) in the text have a higher probability of being relevant (Baxendale, 1958; Edmundson, 1969; Paice, 1990; Kupiec et al., 1995). These privileged positions are often genre-dependent and can be determined automatically through training (Lin & Holy, 1997).

- **Sentence length:** Short sentences tend not to be included in extracts (Kupiec et al., 1995).

Each of the above features can be used individually. But most often, two or more features are used in combination with assigned weights to generate a final score which is used to determine the inclusion of the sentences in the extract. Edmundson (1969) used a subjective weighting to combine three features (cue words, title words and sentence position) to measure the significance of sentences. Kupiec et al. (1995) used a simple Bayesian classification function to combine some features (sentence length, sentence position, indicator phrases, and frequent keywords) to calculate the probabilities of sentences in an extract. In the Bayesian classification, the feature weights can be trained using a corpus.

Sentence extraction approaches are the simplest approaches for automatic summarization. This approach is domain-independent and does not employ domain knowledge in their use. It does not attempt to understand the meaning and structure of the text, and also does not involve any language processing tasks. However, a collection of separately extracted sentences often lack context. This sometimes result in unintelligible and even misleading extracts, due to a lack of cohesion and coherence as well as the presence of "dangling anaphors" (Stein, Strzalkowski & Wise, 2000). To solve the above problems, the cohesion-based approaches are developed to produce more readable and coherent summaries by extracting related sentences or paragraphs instead of separate sentences.

2.2.2 Cohesion-based Approaches

Cohesion is a device for linking together different parts of the text to fuse them as a whole. It can be identified at the surface level of the text, through the use of cohesive links, such as *lexical chains*, *co-reference*, and *word co-occurrence* (Halliday & Hasan, 1976). Cohesion-based approaches employ these cohesive links to extract internally linked text units (often paragraphs or related sentences), instead of separate sentences, to form a more fluent summary.

Lexical chain is defined as groups or sequences of semantically related words (Morris & Hirst, 1991). Barzilay and Elhadad (1998) used lexical chains as a source representation of the original text to build a summary. The terms occurring in the same lexical chain represent the same concept. For example, the concept of *network* is denoted by the terms "*network*", "*net*", and "*system*" in the same chain. They found that the concepts represented by strong lexical chains give a better indication of the central topic of a text than the most frequent words in the text. On the basis of lexical chains, the sentences that contain the terms representing the same concept were extracted from the text, instead of those containing high frequency separate words. Thus, the extracted sentences were more related and more central to the topic of a text, and thus resulted in a well-connected summary. Lexical chains are relatively easy to compute and do not rely on full text processing. This makes summarization techniques based on them rapid and robust. In comparison, the processing of co-reference relations described subsequently requires more complex techniques (Azzam, Humphreys & Gaizauskas, 1999).

14

Co-reference chain (e.g. anaphor link) is another kind of cohesive link, which is often used to identify inter-connected phrases, sentences, or passages. Anaphors are words such as pronouns, demonstratives and comparatives which can only be understood by referring to an entity appearing earlier in the text. The frequent presence of dangling anaphors is a big problem among a collection of extracted sentences. If an extracted sentence contains an anaphor without a previously mentioned referent, it is unintelligible or even misleading (Paice & Jones, 1993). Azzam et al. (1999) constructed sets of co-reference chains and selected the best chain to represent the main topic of a text using a variety of criteria. Then the sentences that contain one or more expressions occurring in the best chain were extracted for inclusion in the summary.

Word co-occurrence means the sharing of single words between text segments (often paragraphs) and can be used as a measure of the relatedness of text segments (McKeown, Klavans, Hatzivassiloglou, Barzilay & Eskin, 1999). A text relationship map (Salton, Singhal, Mitra, & Buckley, 1997; Mitra, Singhal & Buckley, 1997) is one of the methods used to depict how the paragraphs are related to each other. A text relation map is a graphical representation of textual structure, in which paragraphs are represented by nodes on a graph and related paragraphs are linked by edges. A vector similarity measure is then used to determine related paragraphs which contain similar words, i.e. word co-occurrence among paragraphs. Using the text relationship map, a document is decomposed into segments, namely a set of contiguous paragraphs that are linked internally, but largely disconnected from the adjacent text. The important nodes that address central information to the topic are identified on the map automatically using various algorithms, and the selected paragraphs are assembled in text order to form an extract. The evaluation results indicated that the agreement on the selected important paragraphs between the automatic method and human was 45.60% whereas the agreement between two humans was 45.81%.

Although cohesion-based approaches can create fluent summaries, the summaries lack coherence because they do not convey a full understanding of the text. There is a distinction between coherence and cohesion. Cohesion involves surface relations among text units, which create connectedness of the text, including *anaphor, ellipsis, conjunction* and *lexical relations* (Morris & Hirst, 1991; Mani, Bloedorn & Gates, 1998). In contrast, coherence involves higher-level relations such as *elaboration, cause* or *explanation* among text segments, which determine the global argumentative or narrative structure of the text (Mani et al., 1998; Barzilay & Elhadad, 1997).

2.2.3 Discourse-based Approaches

The construction of highly coherent summaries depends on an analysis of the discourse structure. This focuses on linguistic processing of the text to derive a discourse representation of the text used for determining important text units in a text (Spark Jones, 1993; Ono, Sumita & Miike, 1994). However, it is difficult to identify discourse structure since it requires complete understanding of the text and complex inference (Barzilay & Elhadad, 1997). Cohesion can be used as one of the surface signs to identify discourse structure of the text. The other signs include cue phrases, connectives, tense shifts etc. (Barzilay & Elhadad, 1997).

One of the most popular discourse theories is Rhetorical Structure Theory (RST) (Mann & Thompson, 1988). This theory defines rhetorical relation as a relation that holds between two non-overlapping text spans that are distinguished as *nucleus* and *satellite*. The *nucleus* expresses more important information than the *satellite* and is comprehensible independent of the *satellite*, but not vice versa. For example, for an *elaboration* relation that holds between two text spans, the text span representing basic information is considered a *nucleus*, and the other one representing additional information is the *satellite*. The rhetorical structure of the text can be represented as a binary rhetorical structure tree by recursively detecting the rhetorical relations between text spans whose sizes increase from the tree leaves to the tree root (Marcu, 1999a).

Many researchers (Mann & Thompson, 1988; Matthiessen & Thompson, 1988; Hobbs, 1993, Polanyi, 1993; Spark Jones, 1993) hypothesized that the nuclei of a rhetorical structure tree could be used as the components of the summary. Marcu (1997b and 1999a) carried out an experiment to test the hypothesis. He built a rhetorical structure tree of the original text using a rhetoric parsing algorithm and derived a partial ordering on the importance of all the text units depending on each elementary unit's role (*satellite* or *nuclei*) and depth in the tree structure. Then, a summary could be constructed by selecting the most important units in the partial ordering. His experiment results indicated that the discourse-based summarizer could determine the most important units in a text with a high recall (66%) and precision (68%) and outperformed the Microsoft Office 97 summarizer. Unfortunately, no evaluation was carried out to determine whether the discourse-based extracts have a better readability than the other types of extracts (Marcu, 1997b and 1999a).

Ono et al. (1994) used connective expressions to identify the rhetorical relations between sentences and between paragraphs. The rhetorical structure of the text was derived and represented by a binary tree. The relative importance of the sentences was determined based on the rhetorical relations between them, and the most important sentences were selected to generate a summary. The evaluation results indicated that the resulting summary contained 74% of the most important sentences for newspapers and 60% of the most important sentences for technical papers.

Rhetorical structure information has also been used as a complement to the traditional clustering-based summarization method where sentences were clustered based on their similarities and representative sentences extracted from each cluster as the components of the summary. Song, Jang and Myeng (2005) identified surface-level rhetorical relations using conjunctive and demonstrative rhetorical phrases and clustered adjacent sentences based on the rhetorical phrases connecting them. Two adjacent sentences connected by a joining rhetorical phrase (e.g. *therefore, in detail, like this*) were assigned to the same group, whereas those connected by a dividing rhetorical phrase (e.g. *however, on the other hand, contrary to this*) were assigned to different groups. After considering the rhetorical relationships between adjacent sentences, the sentences containing similar words were grouped using the traditional hierarchical or non-hierarchical clustering methods. Finally, all the sentences from the main cluster plus representative sentences from each of the other clusters were extracted to generate a summary. The evaluation results indicated that the clustering-based sentence extraction method with rhetorical structure information outperformed the feature-based sentence extraction method and component-based sentence extraction method (i.e. extracting important sentences from specific text components) (Myaeng & Jang, 1999). Moreover, the rhetorical structure information improved the precision of the important sentences in the summary by 8.3% over the pure hierarchical clustering, and 6.6% over the pure non-hierarchical clustering.

Although most previous work on discourse-based summarization followed Rhetorical Structure Theory (RST), Teufel and Moens (2002) used a different discourse model, namely *rhetorically defined annotation scheme*, to code the entire or parts of the source text of scientific research articles. In contrast to RST, the discourse model stresses the importance of rhetorical moves which are global to the argumentation of the text whereas the RST-type relations are more local. This annotation scheme consists of seven non-hierarchical labels, such as *background, other, own, aim, textual, contrast*, and *basis*. The extracted sentences were categorized into the seven categories according to their argumentative roles. These categories are useful to provide context information to interpret the extracted sentences. For example, an *"aim"* label reflects that the sentence expresses a main goal of the source text, and a *"contrast"* label indicates that the sentence reports a shortcoming in someone else's work. The summarization system can then use this information to generate more coherent template-like abstracts, for example, *"Main goal of the text: ..."*, *"Builds on work by: ..."* and *"Contrasts with: ..."*

17

A related idea is the *text component identification model* proposed by Myaeng and Jang (1999). They analyzed the thematic structure of the document and assigned the sentences into four text components – *background, main theme, document structure explanation*, and *future work* – to reflect different narrative roles of the sentences in the document. The text component information can be used to filter out parts of the text that are not likely to contain summary sentences, and focus the statistics-based sentence extraction to the important text components (e.g. *main theme*). The evaluation results indicated that 67% recall and 40% precision were obtained by selecting the sentences only from the *main theme* component to include in the summary.

Boguraev and Neff (2000) used linear discourse segmentation to enhance a salience-based sentence extraction summarizer for news stories. The segment-based discourse structure, which focuses on topic shifts, is a non-hierarchical narrative structure different from the hierarchical rhetorical structure. First, the document was segmented according to cue phrases, section heads, paragraph openers, cosine similarity between adjacent text blocks, etc. Then, the sentences that were representative of the main topic of the segment were selected from each segment and concatenated together to form the summary. The evaluation indicated that discourse segmentation improved the quality of the summaries, especially for short summaries whose size was equal or less than 10% of the size of the full length news stories. For example, the recall rate of the important sentences in the summary improved from 46.9% to 56.5% with the use of discourse segmentation for the very short four-sentence summaries.

To parse the discourse structure automatically, discourse parsing algorithms using various kinds of lexical and syntactic cues were developed by researchers, such as Kurohashi and Nagao (1994), Marcu (1997a), Hearst (1994), Le and Abeysinghe (2003). There has been an increasing interest in applying machine learning to discourse parsing, including supervised and unsupervised methods. Nomoto and Matsumoto (2000) used a C4.5 decision tree induction program to develop a model for parsing the discourse structure of news articles. Marcu (1999b) also used a C4.5 decision tree program to develop a rhetorical parser for constructing rhetorical structures of unrestricted texts. His experiment results indicated that the decision tree parser obtained a good performance close to human's for constructing discourse hierarchies and identifying *nucleus* and *satellite* text units but poor for identifying specific rhetorical relations. Although supervised learning gives reasonable results as above for discourse parsing, it requires a large training corpus and manual assignment of pre-defined category labels to training dataset.

A radical alternative was to derive the set of labels themselves using an unsupervised technique (e.g. clustering algorithm). Andernach (1996) and Andernach, Poel and Salomons (1997) used two different clustering algorithms, a Bayesian soft-clustering package and a Kohonen self-organizing map, for recognition of the dialogue structure. Moller (1997 and 1998) used a custom hierarchical clustering algorithm for dialogue structure parsing. However, in all of these works, the evaluation was incomplete so that the use of the unsupervised algorithms is not convincing (Clark, 2003). Marcu and Echihabi (2002) built an unsupervised Naïve Bayes classifier to recognize discourse relations, such as *contrast, explanation-evidence, condition* and *elaboration*, without relying on the presence of cue phrases. The use of unsupervised techniques is well motivated as an adjunct to a labeled classification task (Clark, 2003).

2.2.4 Sentence Compression Approaches

Sentence compression is a simple version of abstractive summaries. Angheluta, Mitra, Jing, and Moens (2004) developed a K.U.Leuven summarization system by applying two compression algorithms to the first sentence in each document or the important sentences that contain most of keywords (often topic terms) to create headline summary. The first *substring selection* compression algorithm selected the longest substring between two topic terms based on the parse tree of the sentences and removed determiners and auxiliaries from it. The second *statistical compression* algorithm eliminated sub-trees of the parse tree of the sentences. In the Document Understanding Conference 2004 evaluation[5], applying *substring selection* algorithm to the first sentence in the document obtained slightly better results than applying it to the most important sentence and applying the *statistical compression* algorithm to the first sentence or the most important sentence.

Zajic, Dorr and Schwardz (2004) also developed a system called Topiary to compress the first sentence of a news article and thus create a headline summary. First, unimportant constituents, such as low-content syntactic constituents, determiners, time expressions, *have* and *be* etc., were removed one by one from a parse tree of the sentence until a length threshold was reached. Then, the compressed sentence was augmented with the statistically selected topic terms to generate the summary. Topiary produced very good results in the Document Understanding Conference 2004 evaluation, and of course was much better than Angheluta's (2004) et al. K.U.Leuven system.

---

[5] Document Understanding Conferences (DUC), run by the National Institute of Standards and Technology (NIST), is a continuing evaluation in the area of text summarization.

Knight and Marcu (2000) treated sentence compression as a statistical problem. They parsed each sentence into a sequence of words in a specific order. Two algorithms, *a probabilistic noisy-channel model* and *a decision-based deterministic model*, were developed for sentence compression. Each algorithm was trained to learn some parameters using a corpus containing a set of sentence pairs. Each sentence pair consisted of an original sentence and its compressed version written by human. The trained algorithms were used to drop unimportant words from each original sentence, and the remained words were kept the original order and formed a short sentence.

2.2.5 Knowledge-based Approaches

This kind of approach involves performing a detailed semantic analysis of the source text, and constructing a knowledge representation of the meaning of the document. A set of domain-specific templates, frame, or scripts is normally pre-defined using domain knowledge to facilitate the analysis by extracting the information relevant to each slot of the template and filling it. When analysis is complete, the instantiated slots are used as the material to generate the fluent summary using some natural language generation techniques.

One of the earliest knowledge-based text summarization systems was the FRUMP system developed by DeJong (1982) for summarizing UPI (United Press International) newspaper stories. FRUMP employed sketchy scripts, which contained a set of pre-defined situations from earthquakes to labor strikes, to represent a topic and extracted information from news stories. The instantiated scripts were then used to generate summaries of the news stories.

Jacobs and Rau (1990) developed a system, named SCISOR, for conceptual information summarization, organization and retrieval of financial news. SCISOR analyzed linguistic structures of the texts and matched them to a conceptual framework, and then applied conceptual interpretation to generate the summary. This system applied domain knowledge to characterize specific conceptual knowledge of a text.

Paice and Jones (1993) extracted important concepts using a set of semantic frames from highly structured empirical research papers in the field of crop agriculture and filled them in various slots of a semantic frame to generate a summary.

Instead of using a pre-defined scheme to represent the text, Hahn and Reimer (1999) constructed a terminological knowledge representation of the texts using a text parser and transformed the knowledge representation into a text summary. First, each paragraph was represented using a terminological logic which focuses on concepts, properties and conceptual relations. Then, the salient items were chosen from the represented knowledge structures using salience operators and merged into a topic description for the paragraph. Finally, the topic descriptions of all the paragraphs were combined, using generalization operators, into a text graph which constitutes a summary at the representation level.

Lescovec, Milic-Frayling and Grobelnik (2005) created a novel semantic graph representation of a document by extracting elementary syntactic structure from each sentence in the form of logical triples, i.e. subject-object-predicate, and presenting the linguistic properties of the nodes in the triples. Using a machine learning classifier, some triples were selected from the semantic graph of the original document by grasping essential semantic relationships among concepts. The sentences represented by the selected triples were extracted to generate a summary. Vanderwende, Banko and Menezes (2004) used triples to construct a graph representation for a document set. They identified a set of triples based on the logical form analysis of each sentence and then linked these triples through their semantic relationships. Each node in the document graph was scored according to the number of the other nodes linking to it. Then the links between two nodes were scored based on the scores of the linked nodes. The important logical form fragments were selected from the document graph according to the scored nodes and links, and then merged together to generate a multi-document summary.

Unfortunately, constructing a knowledge representation of the text requires rich domain knowledge and deep understanding of text. Thus, this kind of approach is often knowledge-intensive, domain-dependent and expensive, but produces better summaries for a specific domain.

2.2.6 Concept Generalization Approaches

This kind of approaches involved extracting important concepts and generalizing them to capture the main content of a document.

Important concepts could be represented by different kinds of terms including noun phrases (Jones & Paynter, 2002), single-word and multi-word terms (Neff & Cooper, 1999), words (Buyykkokten, Garcia-Molina & Paepcke, 1999), and n-grams (Leuski, Lin & Stubblebine, 2003). The most common approaches for identifying important concepts were based on statistical criteria including TF*IDF (Neff & Cooper, 1999; Buyukkokten et al., 1999; Jones & Paynter, 2002), likelihood ratio suggested by Dunning (1993) (Leuski et al., 2003), term frequency (Kraaij, Spitters & Hulth, 2002). In addition, Amigo, Gonzalo, Peinado, Penas and Verdejo (2000) identified key concepts represented by noun phrases from sentences using the combination of statistical measures with shallow syntactic information (including the distance of phrase to the verb and syntactic functions of phrase in sentences).

Lin (1995) developed a new text summarization method using concept generalization. Concept generalization or fusion was to replace a collection of concepts with a higher-level unifying concept (Lin, 1995). The concepts which represent central ideas of the text were selected using a knowledge-based concept counting paradigm. Different syntactic categories and relations among concepts were distinguished using a part-of-speech tagger and syntactic parser. The concepts related with the selected concepts (called matching concepts) were identified by specifying appropriate syntactic categories and relations. For example, if a noun concept was selected, its accompanying verb was also identified. For a set of selected concepts, their matching concepts were generalized using a hierarchical concept taxonomy WordNet to obtain a list of "selected concepts + matching generalization" pairs as sentences.

The concept generalization method was also used in SUMMARIST, an automatic text summarization system developed by Hovy and Lin (1997). The system included three summarization steps: topic identification, concept fusion and summary generation. In the first step, the sentences that contain topic-related information were selected based on Optimal Position Policy in the text. In the second step, the concepts that represent central ideas of the topic were extracted from the selected sentences by counting concepts rather than words and generalizing them using WordNet. In the third step, the generalized concepts were input into the sentence planner and sentence generator to produce a well-formed and fluent summary.

Concept generalization can be performed at the semantic level or syntactic level. Lin (1995) and Hovy and Lin (1997) generalized concepts based on semantic relations among concepts such as instance, subclass, and part-of, etc. For example, *mainframe*, *workstation*, *PC* and *laptop* can be generalized into *computer*. Such generalization is accurate and sufficient but requires a thesaurus, ontology or knowledge base to provide an appropriate concept hierarchy for a specific domain. In contrast, the syntactic-level generalization is easy to realize but not very accurate, since it identifies similar concepts only according to their syntactic structures rather than their meanings. Bourigault and Jacquemin (1999) clustered term variants depending on some syntactic variations like internal insertion of modifiers, preposition switch and determiner insertion, and obtained a satisfactory precision rate of 93%~98% in comparison to human output. Ibekwe-SanJuan and SanJuan (2004a and 2004b) defined two types of syntactic variations – COMP and CLAS, for term clustering. The terms sharing COMP variations were clustered first, followed by clustering the terms sharing CLAS variations.

COMP referred to the variations that only affected modifier words in a term, for example:

- – Left-expansion: *academic library → uk academic library*
- – Insertion: *academic library → academic biology library*
- – Modifier substitution: *academic library users ↔ public library users*

CLAS referred to the variations that shared the same head word, for example:

- – Left-right expansion: *academic library → Canadian academic library privilege*
- – Right expansion: *academic library → future of academic library*
- – Head substitution: *directors of academic library ↔ future of academic library*

2.3 Approaches for Multi-document Summarization

Although Mani (2001b) defined multi-document summarization as an extension of single-document summarization to sets of related documents, Goldstein, Mittal, Carbonell and Kantrowitz (2000) indicated some important differences between single-document and multi-document summarization:

- The degree of redundancy becomes significantly higher in multi-document summarization than in single-document summarization, since some information is repeated in different documents in a collection;
- There is a time sequence in a group of related documents, typically in a series of news articles about an unfolding event;
- Since many documents are encapsulated into one summary, a higher compression rate is required in order that the resulting summary becomes concise and thematic;
- Co-reference resolution is more difficult when referents occur across documents;
- Cohesion and coherence is more difficult because the summarized information come from different sources and have different writing styles;
- In a group of related documents, each document does not only share similarities but also describe differences. Thus both similarities and differences should be included in the multi-document summary.

Given the above differences, single-document summarization methods do not work very well in multi-document summarization environment. Therefore, several new approaches were developed for multi-document summarization, focusing on reducing redundancy, ensuring cohesion and coherence, and identifying similarities and differences across documents (Afantenos et al., 2005a).

Multi-document summarization approaches also can be further divided into extractive approaches and abstractive approaches. The use of extractive approaches in multi-document summarization often requires a post-processing stage to cope with redundancy and ensure coherence and cohesion of the combined text units extracted from different source documents. In comparison, abstractive approaches seem more appropriate for multi-document summarization (Afantenos et al., 2005a). However, there is no pure abstractive approach that completely imitates human abstracting behavior. Current abstractive approaches in multi-document summarization are in reality hybrid methods – involving extractive techniques at the pre-processing stage to extract important information and then using abstractive techniques to convert the extracted information into concise and fluent new texts.

Extractive approaches are of two types:

- *Approaches based on single-document summaries* extract salient sentences from each document and then concatenate them by removing redundancy and ensuring cohesion and coherence.
- *Cross-document sentence extraction approaches* extract the most important sentences from different documents using various techniques and concatenated them by removing redundancy and ensuring cohesion and coherence.

Abstractive approaches are of four types:

- *Approaches based on similarities* extract repeated information across documents and then synthesize the similarities into new sentences.
- *Approaches based on similarities and differences* extract repeated information in many documents plus important unique information in some individual documents and then synthesize the similarities and differences into new sentences.
- *Template-based information extraction approaches* extract pieces of information to fill in various slots of the templates and then convert the instantiate slots into new sentences by comparing the similarities and differences between them.
- *Approaches based on cross-document structure* extract salient text units based on cross-document rhetorical relations between them and concatenate them together.

In addition, *approaches based on document set classification* summarize different types of document sets using different approaches.

2.3.1 Approaches Based on Single-document Summaries

The simplest approach for multi-document summarization is to treat multi-document summarization as an extension of single-document summarization to a document collection. This kind of approach involves analyzing and summarizing each document in the collection and then concatenating individual single-document summaries together to form a multi-document summary. However, simply concatenating summaries of each single document does not suffice because there may be too many summaries, and they may contain redundant information (Hahn & Mani, 2000). Therefore, only representative single-document summaries are selected as the components of the multi-document summary to reduce redundant information.

The GE multi-document summarizer (Stein et al., 2000) is a good example of this kind of approach. First, each document in a document set was summarized by extracting important inter-connected paragraphs. Then the single-document summaries on the same topic were grouped together. For each group, the most representative one was selected. Finally, all the selected single-document summaries were organized in a logical way to form a multi-document summary.

Fukumoto and Sugimura (2004) did not perform clustering of single-document summaries. Instead, they combined single-document summaries directly and then deleted unnecessary parts from them to reduce redundancy.

2.3.2 Cross-document Sentence Extraction Approaches

Statistics-based sentence extraction approaches can also be used in multi-document summarization. But the selection of important sentences is across documents. Since the component sentences are from different sources, the resulting multi-document summaries suffer from lack of cohesion and coherence, and contain more redundant information. Some revision has to be done to ensure cohesion and coherence as well as reduce redundancy.

(1) Sentence Extraction without Clustering

The DEMS summarizer (Schiffman, Nenkova & McKeown, 2002; McKeown et al., 2001a) summarized a set of news articles that were on different events by extracting the top-ranked sentences across documents. To determine sentence salience, some new strategies were created, i.e. occurrence of the lead words based on a lead-word lexicon derived from the first paragraph of each document in a large corpus, verb specificity based on the statistical association between subject nouns and verbs derived from a large corpus, and frequency of semantic groups derived from WordNet. These new strategies were combined together with the other traditional features such as sentence position and sentence length, for ranking sentences.

Furthermore, cohesive links, such as lexical chain and co-reference, were also used to identify related sentences across documents. Brunn, Chali and Dufour (2002) extracted internally linked important sentences using topical clues, a kind of lexical chain, from different documents to generate coherent summaries. The Multi-ERSS summarization system (Bergler et al., 2004) extracted noun phrases from all the documents and ranked them depending on the length of the cross-document co-reference chains containing the noun phrases and the length of the noun phrase itself. Then the sentences that contain the highest ranking noun phrases were extracted as the components of the summary. In the Document Understanding Conference 2004 evaluation, Multi-ERSS scored above average in all the participant systems but the linguistic quality is worse.

(2) Sentence Extraction Based on Document Clustering

Radev, Jing and Budzikowska (2000) and Erkan and Radev (2004) developed a multi-document summarization system of news articles called MEAD, using centroid-based sentence extraction. First, news articles on the same event were clustered using Topic Detection and Tracking (TDT). For each cluster, a centroid was produced using modified TF*IDF. A centroid was a set of words that were statistically important to a cluster of documents. The sentences that contain the words from the centroids were more relevant to the topic of the cluster. A linear combination of three features, i.e. centroid words, sentence position and first-sentence overlap, was used to calculate the significance of a sentence. The sentences with high rank were extracted from different documents of each cluster as the components of the multi-document summary. The extracted sentences were then arranged in chronological order of the documents and in text order to form the multi-document summary. At the same time, the sentences which contain the similar information with others were omitted, and the equivalent sentences which contain the same information were substituted for each other. A user study was performed to evaluate MEAD using a new evaluation scheme based on sentence utility (relevance of a sentence to the general topic of a cluster) and subsumption (repeated information across sentences). The evaluation results indicated that MEAD produced summaries that are similar in quality to the human summaries (Radev, Jing, Stys & Tam, 2004).

(3) Sentence Extraction Based on Sentence Clustering

As with MEAD, the XDoX system also produced high quality extraction-based summaries based on conceptual clustering (Hardy, Shimizu, Strzalkowski, Ting, Wise & Zhang, 2002). However, instead of the entire documents, one or more adjacent paragraphs were clustered by measuring their similarities based on n-gram matching. A representative paragraph was extracted from each cluster to form the summary. In the Document Understanding Conference 2001 evaluation, XDoX successfully outperformed the other participant systems on large document sets that contain multiple themes, and also worked well on small document sets with some parameter adjustments.

Instead of using conceptual clustering, Chali and Kolla (2004) clustered similar text segments based on the number of lexical chain members shared by them. Then the sentences, segments of sentences and clusters of segments were ranked with regard to the lexical chains. The top ranked sentences were selected from the top ranked segments from the top ranked clusters to include in the summary. In the Document Understanding Conference 2004 evaluation, the system performed well in quality questions according to the human evaluation.

The MultiGen summarizer (Barzilay, McKeown & Elhadad, 1999; McKeown et al., 1999; McKeown et al., 2001a) also clustered sentences according to their similarity. However, sentence clustering is not always accurate, and this affects the quality of the summary. To improve the clustering accuracy, Blair-Goldenshohn et al. (2004) simplified the sentences by removing their relative clauses and appositives first and then clustered the simplified sentences using the similar clustering method used in MultiGen. The experiment demonstrated that sentence simplification can result in more accurate sentence clusters. One representative sentence was selected based on TF*IDF from each cluster. The selected sentences were assembled in decreasing order of their cluster size, or decreasing order of TF*IDF for clusters with the same size, to form a fluent summary. In the Document Understanding Conference 2004 evaluation, the multi-document summarization system called Columbia's SC based on sentence simplification and sentence clustering outperformed the Columbia's DEMS-MG system which combined DEMS and MultiGen summarizers (McKeown et al., 2001a).

(4) Redundancy Removal Based on Maximal Marginal Relevance

To minimize redundancy and maximize the diversity in the extracted passages (i.e. phrases, sentences, segments, or paragraphs), the Maximal Marginal Relevance (MMR) metric was used by Carbonell and Goldstein (1998) and Goldstein et al. (2000). The metric is based on the assumption

27

that "a text passage has high marginal relevance if it is both relevant to the query and useful for a summary, while having minimal similarity to previously selected passages" (Goldstein et al., 2000, p.43). The extracted passages were re-ranked based on MMR and high rank passages were selected as the components of the summary (Goldstein et al., 2000).

Lin and Hovy (2001) developed an extraction-based multi-document summarization system NeATS for newspaper news articles. The individual techniques used in the system were not new, for example, ranking sentences based on sentence position, term frequency and topic signature; filtering out sentences based on stigma words, and using MMR for reducing redundancy. The system combined these individual techniques and applied them to the multi-document summarization. In addition, it also included the lead sentences of the documents containing the extracted important sentences to improve the coherence of the resulting summary. NeATS system did well in the Document Understanding Conference 2001 evaluation and was among the top two performers.

(5) Other New Methods for Sentence Extraction

Saggion and Caizauskas (2004) identified important sentences according to the similarity between each sentence and the centroid of the document set. The centroid is a vector of pairs of terms and weights, which was statistically important to the whole document set. It is different from Radev's et al. (2000) centroid that was for a cluster of similar documents in a document set (a document set may contain several document clusters). In addition, redundant information was identified by calculating n-gram (n=1, 2, 3, and 4) co-occurrences between two text segments. Their system obtained very good results for mean coverage according to the human evaluation in the Document Understanding Conference 2004 evaluation.

Fatma, Maher, Lamia and Abdelmajid (2004) did not seek to identify the most important sentences in a document set for inclusion in the summary. Instead, they considered the summarization process as an optimization problem by choosing the optimal summary from a set of random summaries. Their ExtraNews system randomly selected sentences from various documents in a set and concatenated them using crossover and mutation operator to form various summaries. These summaries were then evaluated and classified according to some statistical criteria such as length criteria, weight criteria and coverage criteria, to determine the best summary that maximized the information coverage and minimized the information redundancy. ExtraNews obtained the best results for readability and good results for redundancy according to the human evaluation in the Document Understanding Conference 2004 evaluation.

2.3.3 Approaches Based on Similarities

One characteristic of a group of related documents is the repetition of the same information albeit in different forms. Repeated information is a good indicator of its importance and can be used for the generation of a summary.

The MultiGen summarizer (Barzilay et al., 1999; McKeown et al., 1999, Mckeown et al., 2001a) identified and synthesized the similarities across documents to generate a concise summary for a set of news articles. First, similar sentences or paragraphs were identified and clustered across documents. However, these similar sentences or paragraphs usually include both common and distinct phrases. Extracting all similar sentences or paragraphs would produce a redundant summary, while extracting some similar sentences or paragraphs would produce a summary only covering some source documents. Therefore, MultiGen identified the common phrases among a set of similar sentences or paragraphs and used them to reformulate a new sentence as the component of the summary. In order to determine these common phrases, sentences were parsed and transformed to a dependency based representation, which emphasizes sentence features relevant for comparison and ignores those irrelevant features. Then, all the members in the set of similar sentences or paragraphs were compared in pairs to identify common phrases between them. The common phrases in a cluster were assembled in text order, added some additional information like entity descriptions and temporal reference, and converted into a fluent sentence using the FUF/SURGE sentence generator (Elhadad 1993; Robin 1994).

2.3.4 Approaches Based on Similarities and Differences

Summarization based on similarities ignores the fact that related documents not only contain common information but also different information. When similarities are dominant across documents, this is a feasible approach. But when there is a substantial amount of differences in individual documents, it is unavoidable that they will omit valuable and unique information. Thus both similarities and differences need to be considered in multi-document summarization.

Mani and Bloedorn (1999) described a graph matching method for summarizing similarities and differences in a pair of related documents. For each document, text items such as words, phrases, and proper names were extracted and represented in a graph. In the graph, each node stands for a word and the connections between different nodes represent specific relations between the words. The phrases and names could be formed from linking adjacent words. Given a topic, the salient

29

nodes related to the topic were identified by exploiting meaningful relations between text units based on an analysis of text cohesion. The idea is that words mentioned in the topic description should be considered important and nodes connected to many topic nodes are more salient than those that have little connectivity with topic nodes. Then, these salient nodes in different graphs were compared to find similarities and differences. Finally, a set of sentences or fragments (pieces of sentences) containing similar words or phrases and a set of sentences or fragments containing different words or phrases were extracted from source documents and concatenated into a summary covering both similarities and differences.

The advantage of identifying similarities and differences is that the similarities indicate salient information in the document set, whereas the differences indicate unique information about each document.

2.3.5 Template-based Information Extraction Approaches

Template-based information extraction is also used in multi-document summarization. But the information needs to be extracted from different documents rather than a single document to fill in various slots of predefined templates. Then, the similarities and differences extracted from different templates are synthesized together and converted into fluent sentences using some natural language generation techniques. This kind of approach seems very complicated by involving information extraction and natural language generation techniques, but is expected to produce coherent and relevant summaries.

The SUMMONS system (McKeown & Radev, 1995) summarized a set of news articles on the same event in the terrorism domain using a set of templates developed for the forth Message Understanding Conference (MUC, 1992). Each template represents the information extracted from one or more news articles. The instantiated slots in different templates were combined using different content planning operators based on the relations between two templates. For example, when the two templates agree on the facts, the *agreement* operator was used; when the two templates report conflicting information, the *contradiction* operator was used. The combined pieces of information were polished and converted into fluent sentences using the FUF/SURGE sentence generator (Elhadad 1993; Robin 1994). The strength of SUMMONS was to summarize the similarities and differences across documents and highlight how the perception of an event changes over time.

The RIPTIDES system (White, Korelsky, Cardie, Ng, Pierce & Wagstaff, 2001) combined template-based information extraction and sentence extraction to summarize a set of news articles on natural disasters. First, a set of instantiated templates produced by an information extraction system was merged into an event-based structure by grouping similar facts and converted into a fluent summary using natural language generation techniques. Then, the sentences that contain other potentially relevant information not currently found in the templates were extracted and added into the template-generated summary as its complements. RIPTIDES allowed users to specify their preferred slots in the templates and their preferred sentences to generate a user-focused multi-document summary. In comparison to SUMMONS, RIPTIDES focused more on the most relevant current information on an event, and can handle larger documents sets.

The GISTEXTER system (Harabagiu & Lacatusu, 2002) used information extraction templates for multi-document summarization in a different way from SUMMONS and RIPTIDES. It extracted the sentences containing text pieces mapped from the template slots, rather than text pieces themselves, as the components of the summary. These sentences extracted from different documents were incrementally added to create the summaries of different length, based on their mapping from the template slots. In the Document Understanding Conference 2002 evaluation, GISTEXTER achieved a high precision and recall while matching against a human reference summary, and produced very good results for coherence and organization.

2.3.6 Approaches Based on Cross-document Structure

The approaches based on discourse structure can also be used in multi-document summarization. Because Rhetorical Structure Theory (RST) was limited to a single document, Radev (2000) introduced a Cross-document Structure Theory (CST), which was used to describe the rhetorical structure of sets of related documents and present a reasonable equivalent to RST for multi-document summarization.

Cross-document Structure Theory (CST) makes use of a multi-document graph to represent text simultaneously at different levels of granularity, i.e. words, phrase, sentences, paragraphs, and documents (see Figure 2-1). Each graph consists of smaller sub-graphs for each document. It has two types of links: one type represents inheritance relationships among elements within a single document such as words → sentences → paragraphs → documents; a second type of link represents cross-document rhetorical relationships among text units, such as *identity* (the same text appears in more than one location), *equivalence* (two text spans have the same information content), *cross-*

reference (the same entity is mentioned), *contradiction* (conflicting information) and *historical background* (information that puts current information in context).

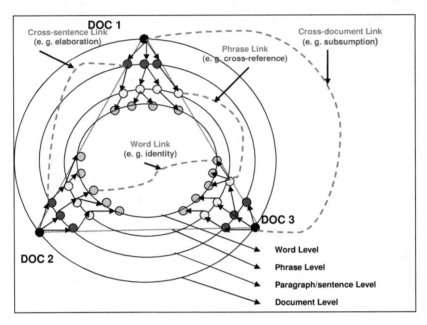

Figure 2-1. Sample multi-document graph (Radev, 2000, p.78)

Whereas Marcu (1997a) relied on cue phrases to identify rhetorical relations in a single document, it is difficult to find a common phrase to indicate a particular cross-document relationship (link) in different documents. This is because separate documents, even when they are related to a common topic, are generally not written in a unified style. Zhang, Otterbacher and Radev (2003) developed a binary classifier to determine the existence of cross-document relationships between sentence pairs extracted from various documents. Features at three linguistic levels, i.e. lexical features, syntactic-level features, and semantic-level features, were considered.

Zhang, Blair-Goldensohn and Radev (2002) carried out an experiment to test whether the use of cross-document relationships can improve the quality of extractive summaries. In their experiment, the baseline summaries were created using a sentence extraction system MEAD (Erkan & Radev, 2004). Next, the baseline summaries were modified by replacing low salience sentences with other sentences that increase the total number of some specified cross-document relationships included in the summary. Then, the modified summaries were compared against the baseline summaries. The experiment results indicated that most cross-document relationships, e.g. *equivalence* and *contradiction*, can have a positive effect on the quality of the extractive summaries, though two cross-document relationships, *historical background* and *description*, have no contribution to, or even worsen, the summaries.

However, Afantenos (2004) indicated that Radev's (2000) Cross-document Structure Theory (CST) has two problems. Unlike Rhetorical Structure Theory (RST) which assumes a coherent text, CST lacks a coherent environment because multiple documents are usually written by different authors, with different writing styles, for different purposes, and in different contexts. The second is that CST focuses more on rhetorical relations that exist between text units in documents, such as *words*, *phrases*, *sentences*, *paragraphs*, or even *documents*, rather than meanings represented by them, such as *event*.

Instead, Afantenos, Doura, Kapellou and Karkaletsis (2004) and Afantenos, Liontou, Salapata and Karkaletsis (2005b) proposed identifying cross-document relations existing between topic-specific messages in a set of event-based news sources. Unlike text units in Radev's (2000) work, a message was a topic-specific template, similar with those used in the Message Understanding Conference (MUC, 1992), which represents the main entities involved in an event (see Figure 2-2).

> **- Performance (entity, in_what, time_span, value)**
> entity   : TEAM, PERSON
> in_what   : offense, defense, general, etc.
> value   : bad, good, moderate, excellent
> time_span : TIME
> comment   : entity had value performance in_what during time_span

> **- Satisfaction (entity 1, entity 2, value)**
> entity 1, entity 2   : TEAM, PERSON
> value   : low ... high
> comment   : entity 1 had value satisfaction from entity 2

Figure 2-2. Two messages on "football match" (Afantenos et al., 2004, p. 416)

The messages in different news sources were connected by cross-document relations, which can be general rhetorical relations, similar to Radev's (2000) CST and Mann and Thompson's (1988) RST, or topic-specific relations. The cross-document relations were divided into synchronic relations and diachronic relations. The synchronic relations concentrate on identifying the similarities and differences between different news sources, such as *identity, elaboration, contradiction, equivalence, etc.*

The diachronic relations concentrate on identifying the similarities and differences through time in the same news source, such as *continuation, stability, positive or negative graduation,* etc.

Afantenos et al. (2004 and 2005b) used an information extraction system to extract a set of messages from multiple news sources. Using synchronic relations, the messages across different news sources were connected for creating the summary focusing on the similarities and differences between news sources. Using diachronic relations, the messages within the same news source were connected for creating the summary focusing on the evolution of an event. A natural language generation system was used to process the messages and the relations connecting these messages within or across news sources to generate a fluent query-based summary. For example, the following summary indicates the evolution of an event through time:

"Georgenas's performance for the first two rounds of the championship was almost excellent. In the third round his performance deteriorated and was quite bad." (Afantenos et al., 2004, p. 418)

2.3.7 Approches Based on Document Set Classification

Sometimes, the document sets being summarized are quite different, for example, a set of news articles that all describe the same event, a set of news articles that describe a series of evolving events, and a set of news articles that describe different but related events (e.g. different bombing events). It is not suitable to process different types of document sets using a uniform summarization method. Thus the document sets were classified into different types, and each document set was summarized using its appropriate method.

Columbia's DEMS-MG multi-document summarization system (McKeown et al., 2001a) combined two summarizers - DEMS (see Section 2.3.1[1]) and MultiGen (see Section 2.3.4). DEMS was used to summarize the document sets with news articles on different events, whereas MultiGen was used to summarize the document sets with news articles on the same event. In DEMS-MG, a router was used to recognize the type of the input document set based on its content (one event or multiple events) and decide which summarizer to use. In the Document Understanding Conference 2004 evaluation, DEMS-MG did very well on the human evaluation, including mean coverage and all the quality questions.

The CRL/NYU summarization system (Nobata & Sekine, 2004) categorized document sets based on how these should be summarized. A Support Vector Machine (SVM) was applied to document set classification, using some features such as time span of the document set, frequency and document frequency of named entities (e.g. *event, location, organization, person, and product*), and so on. For different types of document sets, different rules were used to identify important sentences based on sentence position, sentence length and TF*IDF. For example, important sentences often appeared in the beginning of each document in one type of document set, whereas important sentences were scattered among documents in another type. In the Document Understanding Conference 2004 evaluation, CRL/NYU did well in mean coverage and most of the quality questions except for the same entity question.

Fukumoto and Sugimura (2004) constructed a multi-document summary by combining single-document summaries and deleting unnecessary parts from them. To determine the unnecessary information, the document sets were automatically classified into three types - one topic, multi-topic and others, based on named entities and high frequency nouns. For different types of document set, different strategies were used to delete the unnecessary parts: (1) for one topic document sets, the unnecessary parts were similar parts between single-document summaries; (2) for multi-topic document sets, the unnecessary parts were different parts between single-document summaries; and (3) for the other document sets, the unnecessary parts were identified based on TF*IDF scores used for single-document summarization.

2.4   Evaluation Approaches

Evaluation methods have long been of interest to text summarization researches, with extensive evaluations being carried out as early as the 1960s (Edmunson, 1969). Approaches for evaluating text summarization can be divided broadly into two types (Jones & Galliers, 1996):

- **Intrinsic evaluation:** the quality of summaries is judged directly, such as analyzing them according to some criteria (e.g. conciseness, readability and understandability), or comparing them to "ideal" summaries.
- **Extrinsic evaluation:** the quality of summaries is judged indirectly depending on how well the summaries can help users complete some tasks, such as finding documents relevant to the user's need and answering some questions related to the original documents.

2.4.1 Intrinsic Evaluation

In some studies, intrinsic evaluations were performed by direct human judgment of grammaticality, cohesion, coherence, organization, and coverage of stipulated "key/essential ideas". Minel, Nugier and Piat (1997) had human assessors grade the readability of summaries based on the presence of dangling anaphors, "choppiness" of the text, presence of tautological sentences, etc. Brandow, Mitze and Rau (1995) asked professional news analysts to assess the acceptability of the summaries generated by an automatic summarizer ANES and "lead summaries" that displayed the first portion of the texts up to the target length of the summaries, using content and readability guidelines established in advance, and unexpectedly found that "lead summaries" outperformed the summaries generated using sophisticated NLP techniques significantly. Paice and Jones (1993) characterized each source document in terms of its focal concepts and non-focal concepts and measured the summary's coverage of these concepts using a set of statistics. Saggion, Radev, Teufel, Lam and Strassel (2002) determined the acceptability of the summaries based on good spelling, grammar, clear indication of the topic of the source document, impersonal style, and whether the summaries are concise, readable and understandable.

Most intrinsic evaluations were performed by comparing the machine-generated summary against an "ideal" summary. Edmunson (1969) selected 200 documents in chemistry and compared the abstracts produced by professional abstractors with the outputs of four extraction methods. Kupiec et al. (1995) calculated the percentage of sentence matches and partial matches between the machine-generated summary and a human- generated summary.

The main problem with matching a machine-generated summary against an "ideal" summary was that there was no single correct summary (Edmunson 1969; Paice 1990; Hand, 1997). There could be a number of ways for humans to create abstracts for a given document. In addition, there have been several reports on the low agreement among human coders in extracting important sentences (Rath, Resnick & Savage, 1961; Salton, Singhal, Mitra & Buckley, 1997). Of course, there was better agreement for the most important sentences than other sentences, and the amount of agreement in the sentence extracts was related with the summary length (Jing, Barzilay, McKeown & Elhadad, 1998). Johnson, Paice, Black and Neal (1993) proposed matching a template of manually generated key concepts with the concepts included in an abstract, but again, there was no single correct template of key concepts. Furthermore, the matching of concepts was a fuzzy problem too. To reduce the subjectiveness of the "ideal" summary, Jing et al. (1998) proposed to create an "ideal" summary by merging summaries from multiple human coders, using methods such as majority opinion, union, or intersection.

Precision, recall and *F-measure* are used to measure the degree of match between the machine-generated summary and the "ideal" summary (Firmin & Chrzanowski, 1999). But these measures only consider sentence identity rather than sentence content to carry out the comparison, and are mainly applicable to machine-generated extracts but not applicable to abstracts (Saggion et al., 2002). Therefore, content-based evaluation methods that measure similarity between summaries based on *cosine similarity, unit overlap* and *longest common sequences*, were proposed to reduce the problems with precision and recall, and were expected to be applicable in principle for both extracts and abstracts (Saggion et al., 2002; Mani, 2001c).

Although most intrinsic evaluations still depend on manual judgments, some tools have been developed to support the judging process in the Document Understanding Conferences (DUC). The DUC, sponsored by the National Institute of Standards and Technology, started in 2001 in the United States. In the DUC conferences, large-scale intrinsic evaluations were carried out by asking human assessors to compare system-generated summaries to be evaluated against the reference summaries created by humans. In the DUC 2001 and 2002, human assessors used an evaluation program SEE[6] to judge both the content and the quality of summaries manually. SEE decomposed a system-generated summary and a reference summary into a list of units (often sentences) and displayed them in separate windows. Then human assessors identified the matches between summary pairs by examining unit by unit and computing the overlap as precision and recall scores. In the DUC 2004, an automatic evaluation package, ROUGE[7] was used to measure the similarity between a system-generated summary and a reference summary by automatically counting the number of overlapping units between them. ROUGE includes four measures: ROUGE-N is a recall-related measure counting n-gram co-occurrences; ROUGE-L is a LCS-based F-measure counting the longest common subsequence (LCS) among pairs of sentences from two summaries, ROUGE-W is similar with ROUGE-L but counting the weighted LCS; and ROUGE-S is a skip-bigram-based F-measure counting co-occurring word pairs in their sentence order (Lin, 2004). Since ROUGE measures consider both word-level and sentence-level overlap, it is expected to be more accurate than the traditional *precision, recall* and *F-measure* which only consider sentence-level overlap. The evaluation

---

[6] Summary Evaluation Environment: see http://www.isi.edu/~cyl/SEE/
[7] Recall-Oriented Understudy for Gisting Evaluation: see http://www.isi.edu/~cyl/ROUGE/

results indicated, ROUGE measures achieved very good correlation of more than 90% with human judgment in single-document summarization and good correlation (less than but sometimes close to 90%) in multi-document summarization (Lin, 2004). However, ROUGE focuses more on the overlap of units (n-gram, word sequences and word pairs) in form and does not consider the meaningful relations among them, such as *inclusion, synonymy, entailment* etc. It still can not compute the matches between two summaries very accurately.

2.4.2 Extrinsic Evaluation

Extrinsic evaluations are attractive because they are based on objective evaluation measures. Most tasks, designed and used in extrinsic evaluations, fall under two main types:

- Relevance assessment task
- Reading comprehension task (question & answering task)

In the task of relevance assessment, human subjects are presented with a document (full text or summary) and a topic, and asked to determine the relevance of the document to the topic. Time and accuracy (often precision and recall) are used to evaluate the performance of the summarization system. The real-world activity represented by this task is that of a human conducting full-text search using an information retrieval system who must determine quickly and accurately the relevance of a retrieved document. There have been numerous extrinsic evaluations involving relevance assessment task. Tombros and Sanderson (1998) selected 50 queries from TREC (Text REtrieval Conference, 2004) collection of topics and used a classic document ranking system employing TF*IDF term weighting scheme to retrieve documents using each query, and then asked human subjects to identify as many relevant documents as possible from the ranked retrieved document list for a query in 5 minutes according to the summary of each document. The recall values using the summaries were compared to those achieved using a typical information retrieval output.

Jing et al. (1998) and Mani and Bloedorn (1999) both followed the summarization evaluation proposal under TIPSTER III (Hand, 1997). They selected four queries from the TREC (Text REtrieval Conference, 2004) collection of topics and used SMART system to retrieve documents. Then, they asked human subjects to determine whether each retrieved document was relevant or irrelevant to the query according to its full-text or summary. Brandow's et al. (1995) evaluation is similar with the above studies, except the leading-text summaries were also used for this purpose.

In reading comprehension task, human subjects are asked to answer multiple-choice questions using full-texts or summaries. Thus a human's comprehension based on the summary can be objectively compared with that based on the full-text. If reading a summary allows a human to answer questions as accurately as reading the full-text, it means that the summary is highly informative. Morris, Kasper and Adams (1992) carried out a question-answering task using four multi-choice GMAT reading comprehension exercises under different conditions, i.e. given a full-text, given an extract, given an abstract, and given no text (depending on guess). However, the number of exercises in this study was very small, and the exercises being summarized tended to be very short. The reading comprehension task was also used to evaluate an event-based summarizer SumGen for summarizing output logs from a battle simulation and business news about joint venture (Maybury, 1995). The human subjects were asked to fill in answers to questions according to full-texts or summaries, for example, names, participants, time and duration of all missions appeared in battle simulation, or type, partners, and status of all joint ventures mentioned in business news.

The largest extrinsic evaluation to date is the TIPSTER Text Summarization Evaluation (SUM-MAC). It is the first large-scale evaluation effort of summarization systems, and differs from earlier extrinsic evaluations in task details and methodology. Although the SUMMAC evaluation also included an intrinsic acceptability test, its main focus was on extrinsic evaluation, based on tasks which modeled real-world activities typically carried out by information analysts in the U.S. government. In the SUMMAC evaluation, three main tasks were performed (Mani et al., 1998):

- **The adhoc task:** How well can humans determine whether a full text is relevant to a query just from reading the summary? It is used to evaluate indicative, user-focused summarization systems.

- **The categorization task:** How well can humans categorize a summary compared to its full text? It is used to evaluate generic summarization systems.

- **The question-answering task:** How well can humans answer questions about the main thrust of the source text from reading just the summary? The correct answers to these questions represent the "obligatory" aspects of a topic.

Mani (2001c) pointed out that the choice of an intrinsic or extrinsic method depends on the goals of the developers and the users of the summarization system. In general, at the early development stages of the system, intrinsic evaluation is recommended focusing on evaluating the summarization components. As the system becomes more developed, extrinsic evaluation is more suitable, focusing on the test of the whole system involving "real" users. However, Alonso (2005) indicated that extrinsic evaluation is not considered a valid method for evaluation since there is bias in the nature of the summaries to the task-based final application, and moreover it is costly. In previous studies, intrinsic evaluation was used extensively (e.g. Edumunson 1969; Paice, 1990; Kupiec et al., 1995; Salton et al., 1997).

In comparison to single-document summaries, evaluation of multi-document summaries is more difficult. Currently, there is no widely accepted procedure or methodology for evaluating multi-document summaries (Schlesinger, Conroy, Okurowski & O'Leary, 2003; Radev et al., 2004). Most of the tasks used in extrinsic evaluations (e.g. relevance assessment task) were designed for evaluating single-document summaries. Moreover, it is more difficult to obtain uniform reference summaries, since human differed greatly from each other in summarizing multiple documents (Schlesinger et al., 2003).

2.5 Summary and Conclusion

Summarization approaches can be divided broadly into extractive and abstractive approaches. Extractive approaches are easy to implement. But the resulting summaries often have redundant materials and lack cohesion and coherence. These weaknesses become more serious in multi-document summarization because the extracted sentences are from different sources, have different writing styles, often contain repeated information, and lack context. Therefore, abstractive approaches seem more appropriate for multi-document summarization (Afantenos et al., 2005a).

In contrast to extractive approaches, abstractive approaches are more complicated to implement because they require extensive domain knowledge to interpret source texts and generate new texts. But they can produce more coherent summaries and obtain a higher compression rate. Real abstractive approaches that completely imitate human abstracting behavior are difficult to achieve with current natural language processing techniques (Goldstein et al., 1999). Current abstractive approaches are in reality hybrid approaches involving both extraction and abstraction techniques.

Multi-document summarization mainly focuses on similarities and differences across documents. Thus information comparisons among documents are required using shallow or deep approaches. Shallow approaches extract text passages based on statistic and linguistic features, and remove repeated information by vocabulary overlap comparisons (Mani & Bloedorn, 1999). Deep approaches extract text passages based on statistic and linguistic features or pre-defined templates, and synthesize them using concept generalization (Lin, 1995; Hovy & Lin, 1997), summary operators (McKeown & Radev, 1995; Hahn & Reimer, 1999), and rhetorical relations (Radev, 2000; Zhang et al., 2002; Afantenos et al., 2004 and 2005b). Deep approaches are more promising for constructing multi-document summaries, since they involve information synthesis and inference to some extent to produce a coherent and concise summary.

This work did not use purely extractive approaches. Instead, a hybrid summarization method involving both extraction and abstraction techniques was developed in this study. Like most of the previous studies for multi-document summarization, this method focused on similarities and differences across documents. However, the identification of similarities and differences was based more on meaningful research concepts and their research relationships expressed in the text, instead of words, phrases or sentences and their rhetorical relations used in the previous studies (Mani & Bloedorn, 1999; Barzilay et al., 1999; Radev, 2000; Zhang et al., 2002).

The summarization method involved extraction of research concepts and their research relationships from different dissertation abstracts as well as integration across dissertation abstracts using concept generalization and relationship normalization and conflation. To identify more important research information to be extracted from each dissertation abstract, the discourse structure of dissertation abstracts both at the macro-level and micro-level was analyzed in this study. At the macro-level, a dissertation abstract was segmented into several sections, each of which contains a specific kind of information. It was similar with the *rhetorically defined annotation scheme* proposed by Teufel and Moens (2002) and the *text component identification model* proposed by Myaeng and Jang (1999). All these three structures are non-hierarchical, consisting of several categories or text components that reflect different narrative roles of sentences in the document. At the micro-level (within sentences), four kinds of information – *research concepts* and *their research relationships, contextual relation concepts* and *research method concepts* were focused. The micro-level discourse structure was different from Mann and Thompson's (1988) Rhetorical Structure Theory (RST) which focuses on rhetorical relations between text units. To identify similar information, unique information and relationships between pieces of information from different dissertation abstracts, the cross-document discourse structure among different dissertation abstracts was also analyzed. Different from Radev's (2000) Cross-document Structure Theory (CST), the cross-document discourse structure used in this work was an extension of the micro-level discourse structure in a set of dissertation abstracts. It focused more on common concepts and the relationships involving the common concepts that were investigated by researchers in different dissertation studies.

In this work, concept generalization was performed based on syntactic variations among concepts rather than their semantic relations provided by a thesaurus. Relationship normalization and conflation was performed by normalizing different surface expressions for the same type of relationships using a standard expression and conflating them into one sentence. The text generation involved in this work was simple. The new sentences were generated using pre-defined templates rather than real natural language generation techniques, for integrating concepts extracted from original documents and normalizing different surface expressions of relationships extracted from original documents. To sum up, the summarization method developed in this work focused more on extracting research concepts and their research relationships from different dissertation abstracts, integrating similar concepts and their relationships across dissertation abstracts using concept generalization and relationship normalization and conflation, and presenting the integrated information in a Web-based interface.

After building a summarization system, it is important to evaluate its effectiveness and usefulness. Evaluation approaches can be divided broadly into intrinsic evaluation and extrinsic evaluation. Since extrinsic evaluations are expensive and hard to design, most of existing evaluations are intrinsic. Furthermore, there is a lack of procedures and methodologies for evaluating multi-document summaries (Schlesinger et al., 2003). The existing types of tasks for extrinsic evaluations (e.g. relevance assessment task, categorization task) are mainly for evaluating single-document summaries, and not appropriate for evaluating multi-document summaries.

Therefore, intrinsic evaluation was more suitable for this work. This was done at two evaluation levels: (1) accuracy and usefulness of each important summarization step; and (2) overall quality and usefulness of the final summaries. The evaluation of each important summarization step was accomplished by comparing the system-generated output against human coding. More than one human codings were used since there is no single "gold standard". The user evaluation of the final summaries was carried out using a questionnaire to record users' assessments. The quality of the system-generated summaries was judged directly by human subjects, rather than compared against "ideal" summaries. This is because it is time-consuming and mentally strenuous work for human abstractors to create reference multi-document summaries. It is like writing a literature review. The usefulness of the summaries was also judged directly in this study, rather than based on a specific task. It is difficult to design a reasonable task (e.g. research-related work or general understanding of a topic) which can reflect real-world applications to evaluate the usefulness of the summary accurately.

Chapter 3

A Variable-based Framework

3.1 Introduction

To understand a text, it is important to analyze its discourse structure and identify how discourse units are combined and what kind of relations they have to one another (Kurohashi & Nagao, 1994). In text summarization, discourse-based approaches have been employed often, focusing on the narrative structure (global and non-hierarchical structure) and rhetorical structure (local and hierarchical structure). Teufel and Moens (2002) used a linear discourse model called *rhetorically defined annotation scheme*, which consisted of seven categories, such as *background*, *aim*, *own*, *contrast*, *textual*, *basis*, and *other*, to code the sentences extracted from scientific articles. The seven categories reflected different argumentative roles of the sentences and provided some context information to explain the extracted sentences included in the summary. Boguraev and Neff (2000) identified linear discourse segments according to their topic shifts and selected representative sentences from each segment to generate the summary. Ono et al. (1994) and Marcu (1997b and 1999a) used the hierarchical rhetorical structure to determine the relative importance of text units (clauses or sentences) and selected the most important text units to generate the summary.

In this work, I carried out a manual analysis of the discourse structure of dissertation abstracts both at the macro-level (between sentences or segments) and micro-level (within sentences) to identify which segments of dissertation abstracts contain more important information and further, which kinds of information can be extracted from specific segments in each dissertation abstract. At the macro-level, the sentences in each dissertation abstract were categorized into several non-hierarchical categories or sections. Each section contains a specific kind of information such as *research objectives* and *research results*. At the micro-level, the discourse analysis was more semantic. It focused on research concepts and the relationships investigated in the dissertation research.

43

This was different from the Rhetorical Structure Theory (Mann & Thompson, 1988) which focused on rhetorical relations existing between text units (clauses or sentences). In addition to single-document discourse analysis of individual dissertation abstracts, the cross-document discourse structure of a set of dissertation abstracts was analyzed to identify similar information, unique information, and cross-document relationships among the dissertation abstracts. Radev (2000) proposed the Cross-document Structure Theory (CST) which focused on rhetorical relations between text units across documents at different levels of granularities, such as words, phrases, sentences, and paragraphs. Afantenos et al. (2004) and Afantenos et al. (2005b) proposed identifying cross-document rhetorical relations existing between topic-specific messages across documents. Different from the granularities in Radev's work (2000), the topic-specific messages are instantiated templates representing the main entities involved in an event. In this work, I proposed identifying research concepts or research variables across different dissertation abstracts and combining all the variables associated with a common variable.

A variable-based framework was then proposed to integrate and organize the similarities and differences among different dissertation abstracts. This framework focused more on research concepts and their research relationships investigated in different dissertation studies.

This chapter describes:

(1) the macro-level discourse structure of dissertation abstracts;

(2) the micro-level discourse structure of dissertation abstracts;

(3) the cross-document discourse structure of a set of dissertation abstracts; and

(4) the variable-based framework to integrate various kinds of information extracted from different dissertation abstracts and organize them together.

3.2 Macro-Level Discourse Analysis

A sample of 300 abstracts were selected, using a random number table, from a set of 3214 dissertation abstracts indexed under sociology, PhD degree and year of publication 2001 in the Dissertation Abstracts International database, and the macro-level discourse structure of each abstract was analyzed.

The macro-level discourse structure of dissertation abstracts is well-known to researchers and PhD students. Nevertheless, I manually analyzed and identified the category of each sentence, and found that the sentences in most of the abstracts (about 85%) could be subsumed under five categories - *background, research objectives, research methods, research results* and *concluding* remarks. Not every abstract contained all of the five categories. The 85% abstracts were considered to have a clear structure containing the above five sections. I shall refer to these abstracts as structured abstracts.

An example of a structured dissertation abstract containing these five sections is given in Figure 3-1, and described in detail below:

- **Background:** This section introduces the general area of the research problem, explains why it is an important or interesting problem, and identifies studies that are related to the current study.
- **Research objectives:** This section includes research objectives, questions, hypotheses, and the adopted theoretical framework. The expected results are sometimes indicated. This section may also provide definitions or explanations of concepts.
- **Research methods:** This section outlines how the study was carried out. It can be decomposed into three subsections: *research design, sampling* and *data measure and analysis.*
- **Research results:** This section reports the results of the data analysis (found in the *statistical results* subsection) and research conclusion (found in the *research findings* subsection).
- **Concluding remarks:** This section presents recommendations, future work, or implications of the research results.

As shown in Figure 3-1, each section in the example structured abstract comprises one or more sentences and contains a specific kind of information. The *research objectives* and *research results* sections in structured abstracts are hypothesized to contain more important information relating to the key research ideas of the dissertation study. It is considered that research concepts and their research relationships are most likely to occur in the *research objectives* and *research results* sections.

The remaining 15% of the abstracts were difficult to segment into the five standard sections. Two kinds of unstructured abstracts were found in most of them. Some of the abstracts describe qualitative research findings including situations, phenomena and facts (see example in Figure 3-2). Others were found to report the research in a different way – indicating the contents of each chapter (see example in Figure 3-3). These 15% of the abstracts were considered unstructured. Although unstructured abstracts are different from the structured abstracts in organization, they also report research concepts and sometimes even research relationships. In most of the unstructured abstracts, the research objectives are clearly discernable, as illustrated by the underlined sentences in Figure 3-2 and 3-3. Thus, for unstructured abstracts, the research objective sentences were also hypothesized to contain the more important concepts.

An evaluation of this hypothesis for structured and unstructured abstracts is reported in Section 5.2.

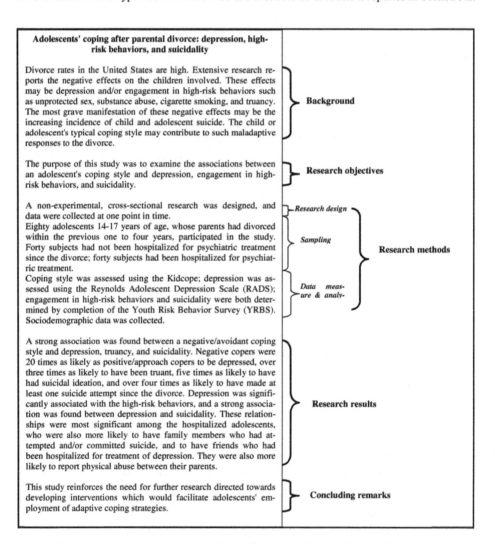

Figure 3-1. An example structured dissertation abstract having five standard sections

---

Cultural conflicts and common interests: The making of the sugar planter class in Louisiana, 1795—1853

In this dissertation, I focus on two themes; the first being the manner in which a particular planter class emerged to dominate one of the wealthiest and most slave labor-intensive regimes in nineteenth-century North America. The second theme addresses the ways in which ethnic and cultural differences affected relations between the members of that class. At the end of the eighteenth-century, a series of dramatic events transformed the economy and society of lower Louisiana. In 1795, a newly patented granulation process installed sugar as a profitable staple crop for the region, and created a small French Louisianian planter class. At the same time, transfer of the once French colony from Spain back to France, and violent revolutions in France and Haiti left Louisiana diversely populated with residents of French, Spanish, Caribbean, and African heritage. With the Louisiana Purchase of 1803, Anglo-Americans joined the mixture, installing a new government and igniting ethnic conflict between the Anglo-American politicians and the old Creole leaders. As the political leaders wrangled over rules of governance, Anglo-American migrants flocked to lower Louisiana eager to profit from the lucrative cane crop. Although dissent emerged in the political arena in the early nineteenth century, French Louisianian planters and Anglo-American newcomers ignored their ethnic differences, those of language, religion, and custom, and found consensus in their shared efforts to build and fortify a slave-driven sugar plantation economy. At the end of the 1820s, a new group of migrants arrived in lower Louisiana, Anglo-Americans with extensive capital garnered from businesses and plantations they owned elsewhere in the United States. These newcomers sought to expand rather than build their fortunes with Louisiana sugar and created plantations and slave forces of enormous size. The planters already in residence, both Creole and Anglo, scrambled to match the scale of the new operations. The diverse members of the sugar planter class viewed sugar cultivation as both a capitalist venture and as a means to fortify their social status. Many invested in modern technologies and labor management techniques to boost profit margins, but they used those profits to reinforce their role as masters of a pre-modern society. This dissertation examines how a planter class emerged in the Louisiana parishes of Ascension, Assumption, Iberville, St. James, and St. Mary governed by a process common to all plantation societies and yet altered by the unique circumstances of Louisiana sugar country.

- *The underlined sentences are research objectives.*

Figure 3-2. An example unstructured abstract mainly describing qualitative research findings

---

The old charities and the new state: structures and problems of welfare in Italy (1860-1890)

This work analyses the evolution of the Italian legislation on charities from 1860 to 1890.

The first two chapters broadly discuss the themes of poverty and welfare reform, and the attitudes of the leaders of the Risorgimento to poor relief and social justice.

The third chapter focuses on the origins and evolution of the Piedmontese charity legislation which was extended to the entire Peninsula upon unification.

Chapters four and five explore the characteristics of the charity systems in force in Central and Southern Italy before the unification--to evaluate the efficacy of the Piemontese legislation in those contexts--and look into the interim legislation on charities introduced in 1859 and 1860 by the provisional governments. Some attention is also paid to the provisions to relieve poverty during the process of political unification.

Chapter six focuses on the general attitude of the new State towards poverty and assistance and gives an account of the origins and parliamentary debate of the act of 3 August 1862. This was modelled on the Piedmontese act of 1859, but contained various alterations which relaxed central and peripheral control.

Chapter seven gives an account of the implementation of this Act, describes the attempts made in the 1870s by the central authorities to bring the charities to heel, analyses the bill proposed by Nicotera in 1877, the response of the charities in the welfare congresses of 1879 and 1880, and the mini-reform proposed by Depretis in 1880.

Chapter eight is devoted to the analysis of both the methods followed by the Royal Commission set up in 1880 to inquire into the charities, and its results. Particular attention is paid to the structure of the charity system.

Chapter nine analyses the Act of 17 July 1890 and broadly assesses its implementation. Chapter ten attempts some general conclusions.

- *The underlined sentences are research objectives.*

Figure 3-3. An example unstructured dissertation abstract indicating the contents of each chapter

3.3   Micro-level Discourse Analysis

In addition to the macro-level discourse analysis, I also carried out a content analysis, including conceptual analysis and relational analysis (Weber, 1990), on the same sample of 300 dissertation abstracts, to identify the micro-level discourse structure of dissertation abstracts.

Quantitative sociology research usually focuses on research concepts operationalized as research variables and their relationships. Qualitative research does not usually operationalize concepts as variables. It focuses on description and explanation of human behaviors or social phenomena. However, many of these studies also seek to identify relationships between concepts representing events, behaviors, attributes, and situations. Thus, sociology research can be divided into three types (Trochim, 1999):

- **Descriptive Research:** one or more target concepts are investigated to identify attributes of interest;

- **Relational Research:** two or more variables are investigated at the same time to see if there is any relationship between them;

- **Causal Research:** one or more variables are manipulated by the researcher to see how they cause or affect one or more outcome variables.

In causal research, one or more variables are designated as the *dependent variables* (DV) while another group of variables are designated as the *independent variables* (IV). *Dependent variables* are the variables that the researchers are interested in explaining or predicting, while *independent variables* are variables that affect or are used to predict the *dependent variables*. In relational research however, variables are not distinguished as dependent and independent variables. Sometimes, a third variable, known as *mediator variable* or *moderator variable,* comes in between the two variables. A *mediator variable* is one that explains the relationship between the two other variables (Baron & Kenny, 1986). A *moderator variable* is one that influences the strength of a relationship between two other variables (Baron & Kenny, 1986).

The *research objectives* and *research results* sections are usually focused on research concepts and their research relationships. The main types of semantic relations and associated concepts found in these two sections are represented in linear conceptual graph notation (Sowa, 1984) as follows:

- **Descriptive Research:** [concept] → (attribute. *) → [*]

- **Relational Research:** [variable 1] → (relation with. *) → [variable 2]

- **Causal Research:** [independent variable] → (effect on. *) → [dependent variable]

In conceptual graph notation, concepts are represented in square brackets and relations are represented in round brackets with arrows indicating the direction of the relation. An asterisk indicates that the subtype of the *relation, effect* or *attribute* is unknown and is to be determined in the research study. Relational research aims to investigate *correlations* between two variables, whereas causal research aims to investigate *cause-effect relationships* between two variables. Different from relational and causal research, descriptive research does not investigate any relation between variables, rather seeks to identify and describe attributes (i.e. specific values) of the variables investigated.

While many studies aim to explore relationships directly, some studies explore relationships in the context of a *framework, model, theory, hypothesis* etc., or in the *perception* or *attitude* of a target population. For example, "The purpose of this qualitative, descriptive study was to examine *mothers' perception of* how their children are affected by exposure to domestic violence." I call this a *contextual relation.* Some types of contextual relations found in sample dissertation abstracts are given in Table 3-1.

Table 3-1. Some types of contextual relations found in sample abstracts

Types of contextual relations	Example
Perception	The purpose of this research is to assess the *perception* of public school districts' human resources directors regarding the effects of ......
Model	This research posits a theoretical *model* of school crime based on family, home, economics and demography, in association with ..., exacerbated by ....
Hypothesis	My *hypothesis* was "as structural strain increase in the United States, the cultural moves from sensate (material) to ideational (spiritual)."
Attitude	The study also wished to discover teachers' *attitudes* about the impact that domestic violence has on children.
Theory	The present study has used attachment *theory* as its theoretical basis for making an investigation of three phenomena relevant to adult life in a foreign culture ...
Framework	..., my dissertation develops a new conceptual *framework* for investigating social information processing...
Context	The research presented in this dissertation represents an exploratory investigation of the extent to which visiting friends and relatives (VFR) tourism can be viewed in the *context* of transnationalism and transnational identities.

The following sentence is an example taken from the *research objective* section. I visually identified important concepts found in the sentence and then the semantic relations between these concepts according to indicator phrases. The relations between concepts found in the micro-level discourse structure were represented using a conceptual graph notation.

The sentence is:

- *The purpose of this research is to assess the perception of public school districts' human resources directors regarding the effects of serious school violence on teacher retention and recruitment.*

The important concepts found in the sentence are:

- *public school districts' human resources directors*
- *serious school violence*
- *teacher retention and recruitment*

Thus the concepts and their main semantic relation found in the sentence are represented as follows:

- *[Independent variable: serious school violence] → (effect on. *) → [Dependent variable: teacher retention and recruitment] .... [#1]*

Likewise, a contextual relation found in the sentence is represented as:

- *[Person: public school districts' human resources directors] → (perceive) → [#1]*

In a research study, certain concepts and their relationships are investigated using one or more research methods. Three types of information – *research design*, *sampling*, and *data measurement and analysis* – are usually found in the *research methods* section of abstracts. *Research design* clarifies what type the study this is, such as *experiment, survey, interview, field work, observation, case study etc. Sampling* describes who participate in the study, how many cases were in the sample, how they were selected, and whom or what they represented. *Data measurement and analysis* indicates what types of data measures were used and what types of statistical analyses were performed, such as *content analysis, regression analysis, bivariate analysis*, or *multivariate analysis*, etc. In addition, research methods are sometimes mentioned casually in the *research objectives* and *research results* sections. For example, *"Findings from this sample 317 undergraduate women indicated that there were no statistically significant differences in the prevalence of sexual violence reported based on sorority membership."* Some aspects of research methods found in the sample dissertation abstracts are given in Table 3-2.

Table 3-2. Some aspects of research methods found in sample abstracts

Aspects of research methods	Subtypes	Example indicator phrase
Research Design	Quantitative Research	quantitative method, quantitative study, quantitative result, quantitative approach, quantitative design, quantitative methodology, quantitative investigation, quantitative data, quantitative analysis, quantifiable measure, quantitative finding
	Field work	field observation, field work, field note, field method, field study, field research, fieldwork
	Experiment	experimental study, experimental data, experimental research, experimental design, experiment
Sampling	--	convenience sampling, random sampling, stratified sampling, snowball sampling, purposive sampling, cluster sampling, non-probability sampling, probability sampling
Data Measurement & Analysis	Regression Analysis	regression model, regression result, regression method, regression equation, regression coefficient, regression analysis, regression technique
	Statistical Analysis	statistical result, statistical technique, statistical test

To sum up, from the micro-level discourse analysis, four kinds of important information can be extracted from sociology dissertation abstracts:

- **Research concepts:** often operationalized as research variables, including dependent variables, independent variables, mediating variables, and moderator variables.

- **Research relationships between concepts:** including correlations, cause-effect relationships and descriptive attributes.

- **Contextual relations:** including framework, model, theory, context, etc., or perception, attitude, insight, etc. of a target population.

- **Research methods:** including research design, sampling, and data measurement and analysis method

An example of information manually extracted from 10 dissertation abstracts on the topic of "school crime" is given in Table 3-3.

Table 3-3. Information extracted from 10 dissertation abstracts on the topic of "school crime"

Doc ID	Dependent variable	Relationship	Independent variable	Contextual relation	Research method
1	teacher retention and recruitment	was not affected by	serious school violence	in the perception of public school districts' human resources directors	• Qualitative, issues-oriented case study • Archival records • Survey • In-depth interviews
	districts' future plans regarding teacher retention and recruitment	was not affected by	different school districts		
2	parameters of legal authority of officers	had a balance between	need for school security /safety and safeguarding the constitutional rights of students as US citizen	–	Formal analysis of case law on 48 relevant cases published from 1974-1997
3	types of school violence	were	theft, personal attack, sexual assault, bully behavior, alcohol, graffiti, drugs, weapons	perceived by students, staff , and a Gang Abatement Task Force	• Archival data found in school incident reports • National Crime Victimization Survey • Principal/School Disciplinary Survey
	prevalence of school violence	was	student tardiness and absenteeism		
4	differences in reporting school crime	were affected by	different schools	–	• A 67 item, 5 category questionnaire • Safe Schools Program
5	school size	was related with	student extracurricular activity participation	–	• 36 schools from across North Carolina • Multiple regression analyses • Bivariate correlation procedures
		was not significantly related with	school dropout rate		
		was not significantly related with	rate of school crime and school violence		
6	school delinquency	was affected by	students' commitment	in a theoretical framework	• Secondary data analysis on a sample of urban public high schools drawn from HSES • Data from 1990 Census of Population and Housing
		was not affected by	school restructuring		
		was affected by	level of socioeconomic deprivation in the surrounding community		
7	school crime	was strongly associated with	• school district size • school district density	in a theoretical model of school crime	• A sample of 50 public school districts in Texas • School crime reporting experiment • Bivariate analysis
8	serious school crime	was not significantly related with	• ethnicity • minority culture classes • per-pupil expenditure • disadvantageness	–	• Representative High School and Beyond Survey (1980-1984) • Bivariate and multivariate analysis • 889 high school principals
		was strongly related with	• disorder • lack of parent/student engagement		
		was affected by	different administrators		
9	frequency of criminal incidences	was affected by	school district size	–	A sample of 50 Texas public school districts
		was affected by	school district type		
	category of criminal incidences	was not related with	areas of the school campus		
	types of criminal incidences from repeated offenders	were	simple assault, disorderly conduct, intimidation, etc.		
10	school crime rate	was associated with	• principal tenure • student attendance • teacher attendance • student mobility • district-wide changes • grade structure shifts • abolition of corporal punishment	–	• Official records of the Cleveland Public Schools • Longitudinal correlational design • Analysis of variance in an ex post facto study • Multiple regression

3.4 Cross-document Discourse Analysis

In a set of dissertation abstracts on a specific topic, the same or similar concepts are often investigated in different dissertation projects. These investigations may be in different contexts, from different perspectives, focus on relationships with other different concepts, and use different methods. To understand the cross-document discourse structure of a set of dissertation abstracts, I analyzed the research concepts and their research relationships in sets of related abstracts to identify what is common information, what is unique information, and how common and unique information is linked in different abstracts.

The cross-document discourse structure was manually analyzed for five research topics – *school crime, juvenile crime, domestic violence on children, women's studies and recreation*. The five research topics were haphazardly selected. Each topic was used as a search query to retrieve a set of dissertation abstracts from the Dissertation Abstracts International database. For each topic, only 10 dissertation abstracts were retained.

The cross-document discourse analysis involved the following steps:

(1) Comparing all the research concepts extracted from a set of dissertation abstracts to identify similar concepts among them;

(2) Identifying the relationships involving these similar concepts extracted from the micro-level discourse structure of different dissertation abstracts;

(3) Comparing these relationships to identify the same types of relationships;

(4) Normalizing different surface expressions for the same type of relationships using a standard expression;

(5) Conflating the normalized relationships together by replacing the similar concepts with a broader concept.

An example of the cross-document discourse analysis for the 10 dissertation abstracts on the topic of "school crime" (see Table 3-3) is shown as follows.

The following five similar concepts relating to *"school crime"* were found in five of the dissertation abstracts:

- D4: *differences in reporting school crime*
- D5: *rate of school crime*

53

- D7: *school crime*
- D8: *serious school crime*
- D10: *school crime rate*

In the five dissertation abstracts, the following relationships of "*school crime*" with other different concepts were investigated:

- D4: <u>*Differences in reporting school crime*</u> *was affected by different schools and administrators.*
- D5: *School size was not significantly related with* <u>*rate of school crime*</u>.
- D7: <u>*School crime*</u> *was strongly associated with school district size and density.*
- D8: <u>*Serious school crime*</u> *was strongly related with disorder and parent/student engagement.*
- D10: <u>*School crime rate*</u> *was associated with student attendance, teacher attendance, etc.*

Among the five relationships involving "*school crime*", one is a positive cause-effect relation, one is a negative correlation, and three are positive correlations. For each type of relationship, different surface expressions were normalized using a simple, standard expression as follows:

- Positive cause-effect relation is kept untouched as "*was affected by*".
  - D4: *Differences in reporting school crime* <u>*was affected by*</u> *different schools and administrators.*
- Negative correlation is normalized as "*was not related with*".
  - D5: *School size* <u>*was not related with*</u> *rate of school crime.*
- Positive correlation is normalized as "*was related with*".
  - D7: *School crime* <u>*was related with*</u> *school district size and density.*
  - D8: *Serious school crime* <u>*was related with*</u> *disorder and parent/student engagement.*
  - D10: *School crime rate* <u>*was related with*</u> *student attendance, teacher attendance, etc.*

The normalized relationships can be conflated together by replacing the similar concepts "*serious school crime*" and "*school crime rate*" with the common broader concept "*school crime*". Thus, all the relationships involving "*school crime*" are integrated as follows:

- For the "*school crime*" variable,
  - *It was related with* <u>*school district size and density*</u>, <u>*disorder*</u>, <u>*parent/student engagement*</u>, <u>*student attendance*</u>, <u>*teacher attendance*</u>, *etc.*
  - *It was not related with* <u>*school size*</u>.
  - *It was affected by* <u>*different schools and administrators*</u>.

In the cross-document structure of a set of dissertation abstracts, the similarities and differences across documents are mainly reflected through research concepts and their research relationships.

Similar concepts may be investigated in different dissertation studies. These similar concepts can be generalized by a common broader concept. Each dissertation study may focus on the research relationships of the common concept with other different concepts. These research relationships can be integrated to provide an overview of all the variables associated with a common variable.

3.5 A Variable-based Framework for Multi-document Summarization

To integrate similarities and differences among different dissertation abstracts, a variable-based framework was proposed. It is based on research concepts and their research relationships that are the focus of the dissertation study, but also includes other research-related information. The framework contains four kinds of information:

- **Main concepts:** The common concepts investigated by most of the dissertation abstracts in a document set.

- **Research relationships between concepts:** For each main concept, the attribute values or relationships with other concepts investigated in different dissertation abstracts.

- **Contextual relations:** The context in which the research concepts and their relationships are situated, usually the perception of a group of people or a theoretical framework or model.

- **Research methods:** One or more research methods used to explore the attributes of concepts or their relationships.

The central elements of the framework are the *main concepts* that were investigated by most of the dissertation abstracts in a document set. In this framework, each kind of information is integrated across dissertation abstracts and the four kinds of information are combined and organized around the *main concepts*. This has a hierarchical structure in which the summarized information is given at the top level and the more detailed information is at the lower levels. Similar concepts extracted from different dissertation abstracts are clustered and summarized by a broader concept called *main concept*. For a specific concept, its attribute values or research relationships with other concept(s) are given, together with the contextual relations and research methods used in the dissertations. All the relationships involving the same *main concept* are combined and summarized using a simple, standard expression. The contextual relations and research methods are summarized using simple, uniform terms.

Figure 3-4 shows some of the information which was extracted from 10 dissertation abstracts on the topic of "school crime", and integrated and organized using the variable-based framework.

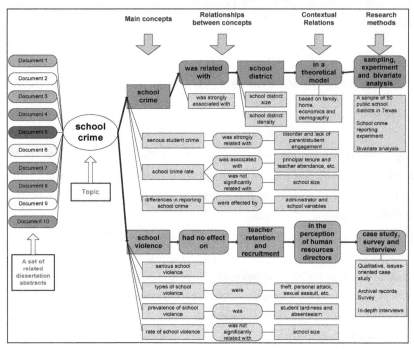

Figure 3-4. Integrated and organized information across 10 dissertation abstracts on the topic of "school crime" using the variable-based framework

In Figure 3-4, two main concepts are presented: "*school crime*" and "*school violence*". "*School crime*" was investigated in 5 documents, while "*school violence*" was investigated in 3 documents.

"*School crime*" included three sub-level concepts:
  – *Serious student crime*
  – *School crime rate*
  – *Differences in reporting school crime*

"*School violence*" included four sub-level concepts:
  – *Serious school violence*
  – *Types of school violence*
  – *Prevalence of school violence*
  – *Rate of school violence*

For *"school crime"*, the following relationships were investigated:

- School crime *was strongly associated with* school district including school district size and density.
- Differences in reporting school crime *were affected by* school and administrator variables.
- School size *was not significantly related with* school crime rate.
- Serious student crime *was strongly related with* disorder and lack of parent/student engagement.
- School crime rate *was associated with* principal tenure and teacher attendance, abolition of corporal punishment etc.

The above five relationships could be integrated as follows:

- For the main concept "school crime",
  - It was related with *school district, principal tenure and teacher attendance, abolition of corporal punishment, disorder and lack of parent/student engagement* etc.
  - It was not related with *school size.*
  - It was affected by *school and administrator variables.*

For *"school violence"*, the following relationships were investigated:

- Serious school violence *had no effect on* teacher retention and recruitment.
- Types of school violence *were* theft, personal attack, sexual assault, etc.
- Prevalence of school violence *was* student tardiness and absenteeism.
- Rate of school violence *was not significantly related* with school size.

The above four relationships could be integrated as follows:

- For the main concept "school violence",
  - It had no effect on *teacher retention and recruitment;*
  - It was not related with *school size;*
  - It was *theft, personal attack, sexual assault, student tardiness and absenteeism.*

Some relationships were investigated based on a contextual relation and using some research methods. For example,

- The relationship between "school crime" and "school district" was investigated *in a theoretical model* based on *family, home, economics and demography.* The research methods used are:
  - *a sample of public school districts in Texas,* summarized as *" sampling";*
  - *school crime reporting experiment,* summarized as *"experiment";*
  - *Bivariate analysis.*

57

- The relationship between "school violence" and "teacher retention and recruitment" was investigated *in the perception of human resources directors*. The research methods used are:
  - *qualitative, issues-oriented case study,* summarized as *"case study";*
  - *archival records survey,* summarized as *"survey";*
  - *in-depth interviews,* summarized as *"interview".*

3.6 Operationalization of the Variable-based Framework

The variable-based framework can be operationalized in different ways to generate summaries in different formats. In terms of the hierarchical structure of the variable-based framework, the summary was presented in an interactive Web-based interface with three levels – the summarized information is presented at the top level, the specific information extracted from each dissertation abstracted is presented at the second level, and the original dissertation abstracts are presented at the third level. The three levels are presented on different screens linked by hyperlinks. The summarized information at the top level is presented in the main window and viewed as the main summary. The user can click on the hyperlinks to access the more detailed information at the lower levels.

How to present a multi-document summary in fluent text and in a form that is useful to the user is an important issue. For sentence extraction approaches, the sentences are extracted from the original documents. For abstraction approaches, the sentences extracted from the document text are compressed in some way (e.g. Knight & Marcu, 2000), or the phrases extracted are reformulated into new sentences using sophisticated natural language generation techniques (e.g. McKeown et al., 1999). These extracted sentences and newly created sentences have to be arranged in a particular order that will make sense to the user. Most of studies usually arranged them in the same order as in the document text or in a chronological order to generate a summary. Some studies also organized the sentences in other formats to facilitate user reading and understanding. For example, Farzindar and Lapalme (2004a) presented the extracted sentences in a tabular format that was divided by such themes as *decision data, introduction, context, juridical analysis*, and *conclusion* found in legal text. Although sentence-oriented presentation is extensively used in summarization, a few studies have presented concepts (terms) in addition to sentences as the summary. Aone, Okurowski, Gorlinsky and Larsen (1999) presented a summary of a document in multiple dimensions through a graphical user interface. A list of keywords (i.e. person names, entity names, place names and others) was presented in the left window for quick and easy browsing. The full text was presented in the right

58

window, in which the extracted summary sentences were highlighted. Ando, Boguraey, Byrd and Neff (2000) identified multiple topics in a set of documents and presented the summary by listing several terms and two sentences that were most closely related to each topic.

In this work, a simple presentation design was adopted for the main summary presented in the main window (see Figure 3-5). The contextual relations, research methods and research concepts extracted from the documents are presented as concept lists, whereas the normalized and conflated relationships are presented as simple sentences. The concept-oriented presentation is concise and useful for quick information scanning, but it also has the potential to confuse users. A comparison between the concept-oriented presentation and the sentence-oriented presentation was performed in the user evaluation and reported later in Section 6.5.

As shown in Figure 3-5, the four kinds of information (i.e. *research concepts* and *relationships*, *contextual relations* and *research methods*) are organized separately in the main window. This design can give users an overview for each kind of information and is also easy to implement.

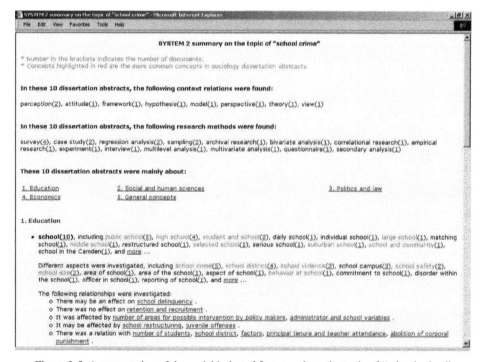

Figure 3-5. A presentation of the variable-based framework on the topic of "school crime"

Contextual relations and research methods found in the dissertation abstracts are presented first because these kinds of information are usually quite short and may be overlooked by users if presented at the bottom of the summary. However, presenting them in this way has the disadvantage that they are presented out of context. Contextual relations and research methods are closely related to specific research concepts and relationships investigated in the dissertations, and provide details of how the concepts and relationships are studied. In future work, new presentation formats that integrate contextual relations and research methods with their corresponding research concepts and relationships can be developed.

Research concepts extracted from the dissertation abstracts are organized into broad subject categories (determined by a taxonomy). A list of subject categories can give users an initial overview of the range of subjects covered in the summary and help them locate subjects of interest quickly. Under each subject category, the extracted concepts are presented as concept clusters – each cluster is labeled by a 1-word term called a main concept. For each main concept, a concept list is presented, giving a list of related terms found in the dissertation abstracts. The concept list is divided into two subgroups – one for subclass concepts and another for facet concepts. The important concepts in the sociology domain (as determined by a taxonomy) are highlighted in red.

After the concept list, the set of relationships associated with the main concepts are presented as a list of simple sentences, each of which represents a type of relationship normalized.

As an example, the two concepts *"school crime"* and *"school violence"* shown in Figure 3-4 are presented in Figure 3-6. *"School crime"* is listed in the category of *"crime"* whereas *"school violence"* is listed in the category of *"violence"*. Thus, the 2-word concepts *"school crime"* and *"school violence"* are generalized by the broader 1-word concepts *"crime"* and *"violence"*. The number of documents indicated in parentheses is clickable and is linked to a list of summarized documents sharing the given concept in a pop-up window.

In this work, a simple concept-oriented presentation format was adopted. More sophisticated presentation formats can be designed in future. Although there is a large body of literature on how to write good single-document summaries, not much is known about how to write good multi-document summaries and literature reviews (summarizing a set of documents is like writing a literature survey). More studies are needed to find out how good literature reviews are written and structured in different situations (e.g. for different purposes and users).

60

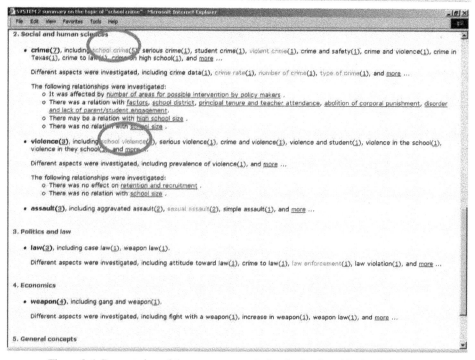

Figure 3-6. Presentation of the two concepts "school crime" and "school violence"

3.7 Summary and Conclusion

This chapter describes a variable-based framework for multi-document summarization of disserta-tion abstracts. The framework was proposed according to the single-document discourse analysis both at the macro-level and micro-level as well as the cross-document discourse analysis of a set of dissertation abstracts. At the macro-level, most of the dissertation abstracts were divided into five sections - *background, research objectives, research methods, research results*, and *concluding re-marks*. The *research objectives* and *research results* sections were hypothesized to contain more important research information. At the micro-level, four kinds of information can be extracted from the specific sections of dissertation abstracts - *research concepts* and *their research relationships, contextual relations* and *research methods*. In the cross-document discourse structure, the similari-ties and differences across different dissertation abstracts were mainly reflected through research concepts and their research relationships. Thus, the framework contains the four kinds of information and combines and organizes them around research concepts often operationalized as variables.

This variable-based framework was used for integrating and organizing extracted information from different abstracts and thus summarizing a set of dissertation abstracts. It has a hierarchical structure in which the summarized information is presented at the top level and more detailed information given at the lower levels. It presents a full map of a specific topic by integrating research concepts and their research relationships as well as contextual relations and research methods extracted from different dissertation abstracts using a hierarchical structure and organizing them based on the main concepts. The framework has two advantages – it gives an overview of a subject area by presenting the summarized information at the top level; and it also allows users to zoom in to more details of interest by exploring the specific information at the lower levels. This framework provides a way to summarize a set of dissertation abstracts that is different from the traditional sentence extraction approaches.

A simple presentation design was adopted for this work as one way to operationalize the variable-based framework. The presentation format designed focuses on the concepts extracted and organizes four kinds of information separately. However, relationships are presented in simple sentences. More sophisticated presentation formats can be designed in the future.

Chapter 4

Design and Development of Summarization Method

4.1 Overview

Based on the variable-based framework, an automatic summarization method was developed for constructing multi-document summaries of a set of sociology dissertation abstracts on a topic. The summarization system was implemented on the Microsoft Windows platform using Java 2 programming language and Microsoft Access database. But the system can be migrated easily to a Unix platform. The system has a blackboard architecture with five modules as shown in Figure 4-1. Each module accomplishes one summarization step. The five modules are:

(1) **Data Preprocessing**: Preprocess the original dissertation abstracts and divide the abstract text into sentences and further word tokens.

(2) **Macro-level Discourse Parsing**: Parse the macro-level discourse structure of each dissertation abstract to identify which sections contain more important research information.

(3) **Information Extraction**: Extract *research concepts* and *their research relationships*, *contextual relations* and *research methods* from the micro-level discourse structure of each dissertation abstract.

(4) **Information Integration**: Integrate each kind of information extracted from different dissertation abstracts.

(5) **Information Presentation**: Combine, organize and present the four kinds of information in a Web-based interface.

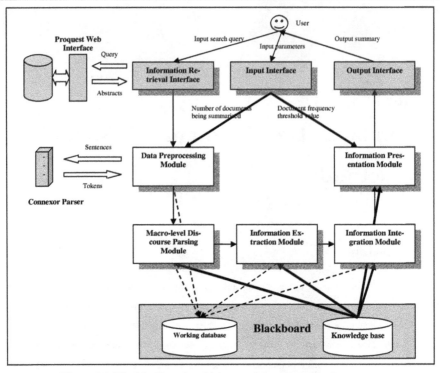

Figure 4-1. The blackboard architecture of the summarization system

The system includes three user interfaces – an information retrieval interface, an input interface and an output interface.

The information retrieval interface (see Figure 4-2) is for users to enter a search query and retrieve dissertation abstracts from an online database. The search query is input in the *keyword* field while the *subject* field is restricted to "sociology" and the *degree* field is restricted to "PhD". The interface connects with the Dissertation Abstracts International database via ProQuest Web-based Interface[8] and retrieves a set of PhD sociology dissertation abstracts related to the search query. The retrieved documents are downloaded as a set of HTML files.

---

[8] http://wwwlib.umi.com.ezlibproxy1.ntu.edu.sg/dissertations/gateway

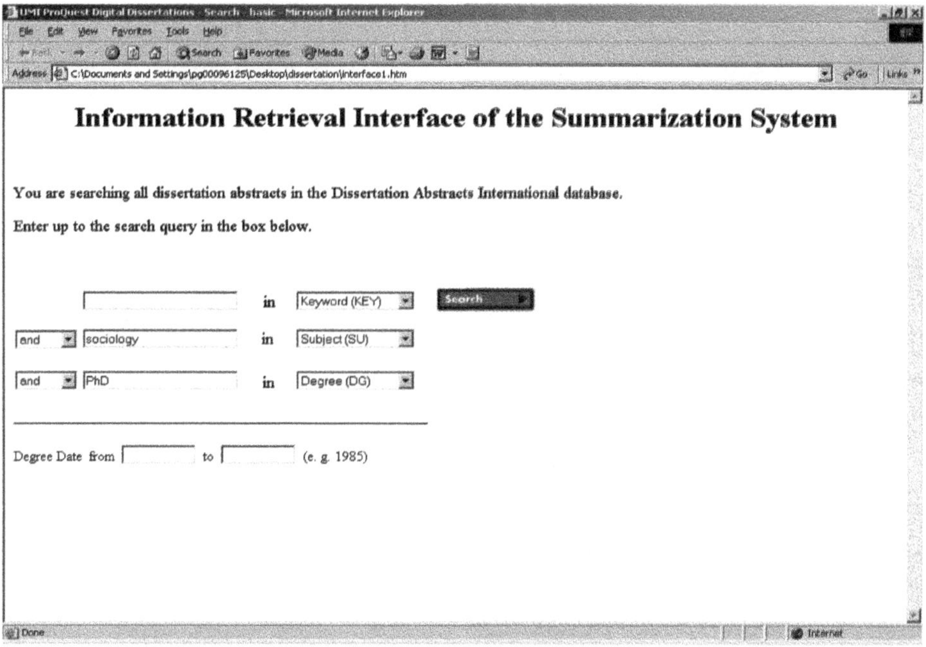

Figure 4-2. Information retrieval interface of the summarization system

The input interface (see Figure 4-3) is for users to input the parameters that will be used in the summarization process. One parameter is the maximum number of the dissertation abstracts to download and condense into a summary. The default value is 200. If too many dissertation abstracts (e.g. 1000 records) are retrieved on a topic, the document set is divided into several smaller subsets and each subset is summarized separately. Another parameter is the compression rate in terms of the number of the words. The default value is 20% of all the original dissertation abstracts in the document set. This value will determine the length of the generated summary.

The output interface is for presenting the final summary to users. It is an interactive Web-based interface that allows users to interact with the summary using hyperlinks to zoom in and explore details of interest.

65

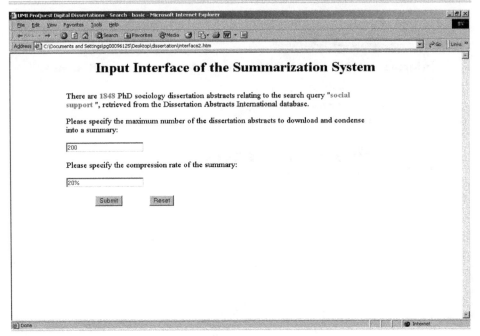

Figure 4-3. Input interface of the summarization system

This chapter describes the design and development of the summarization method which comprises four main steps:

(1) Develop an automatic macro-level discourse parsing method to divide a dissertation abstract into five sections and identify the *research objectives* and *research results* sections;

(2) Develop an automatic information extraction method to extract four kinds of information - *research concepts* and *their research relationships*, *contextual relations* and *research methods*;

(3) Develop an automatic information integration method to integrate each kind of information extracted from different documents;

(4) Develop a presentation method to combine and organize the four kinds of information and display them in a Web-based interface.

A macro-level discourse parsing method was developed to parse a dissertation abstract into five sections - *background, research objectives, research methods, research results*, and *concluding remarks*, using decision tree induction and cue phrases. A decision tree classifier was developed to assign each sentence in an abstract to one of the five sections according to sentence position in the document and presence of indicator words in the sentence. Then the categorization for the *research*

66

objectives and *research results* sections was improved using more reliable cue phrases, such as *"The purpose of the study was to ..."*, *"The results indicate that ..."* found at the beginning of sentences.

An information extraction method was developed to extract *research concepts* and *their research relationships, contextual relations,* and *research methods* from the micro-level discourse structure using term extraction and pattern matching. At the linguistic level, *research concepts, contextual relations* and *research methods* appear as nouns or noun phrases. A list of syntactic rules specifying the possible sequences of part-of-speech tags in a noun phrase was defined and used to identify sequences of contiguous words that were potential noun phrases. The terms relating to research methods and contextual relations were identified using indicator phrases. The terms relating to research concepts were selected from the *research objectives* and *research results* sections. To extract the *relationships between concepts,* linguistic patterns indicating various kinds of relationships were constructed containing two or three slots. The terms in the text that matched with the slots in a pattern represented the research variables connected by the relationship. Pattern matching was performed to identify the text segments in the sentences that matched with each relationship pattern.

An information integration method was developed to integrate similar concepts and their research relationships extracted from different documents using concept generalization and relationship conflation. Similar concepts were identified and clustered according to their syntactic variations. Terms of different word lengths which follow specific syntactic variation rules were considered term variants and represented similar concepts at different generalization levels, for example, "*abuse* → *sexual abuse* → childhood *sexual abuse* → survivor of *childhood sexual abuse* → woman *survivor of childhood sexual abuse* → adult *woman survivor of childhood sexual abuse*"*. The concept integration method linked shorter term variants to longer term variants to form a hierarchical term chain and thus derived a group of similar concepts from the nodes of the chain. Concepts at the lower level can be generalized by the broader concepts at the higher level. Chains sharing the same root node were combined to form a hierarchical cluster tree which represented a cluster of similar concepts sharing the same cluster label. The concepts at the higher levels in a cluster were selected and integrated together using a new sentence. Similar research method terms and contextual relation terms were identified based on indicator phrases and normalized using uniform terms. For example, "*qualitative design*", "*qualitative study*", and "*qualitative method*" were normalized as "*qualitative research*". For a cluster of similar concepts, their relationships with other concepts were integrated together to provide an overview of all associated variables connected by various types of relationships. Each type of relationship (e.g. *correlation* and *cause-effect relation*) was identified using a group of patterns. For the same type of relationships, linguistic normalization was carried out to normalize the different surface expressions using a standard expression and to conflate them. For example, "*school size is not significantly related with school crime rate*" and "*there is no relationship between school size and school dropout rate*" were transformed and conflated into "*school size is not related with school crime rate and school dropout rate*".

A presentation method was developed to combine and organize the four kinds of information, and present them in a Web-based interface to generate an interactive summary viewable through a Web browser. A template was used to combine and format the four kinds of information. A taxonomy was used to filter out non-concept terms, highlight important concepts in the domain, and categorize main concepts into different subjects. The Web-based interface has three levels which are connected through hyperlinks - the summarized information is presented at the top level, specific information extracted from each document is presented at the second level, and the original dissertation abstract is presented at the third level.

In the subsequent sections, each part of the summarization method is described in detail. Each part is hypothesized to contribute to the quality of the final summaries and is evaluated in the work.

4.2 Macro-Level Discourse Parsing

This section reports the development of a macro-level discourse parsing method. A preliminary analysis of 300 dissertation abstracts found that most of dissertation abstracts have a clear structure containing five sections – *background, research objectives, research methods, research results* and *concluding remarks* (see Section 3.2). Each section contains one or more sentences. In this work, discourse parsing was treated as a text categorization problem, i.e. assigning each sentence in a dissertation abstract to one of the five categories or sections.

Previous studies have made use of surface cues, supervised learning and unsupervised learning for automatic discourse parsing. Various surface cues have been used in discourse parsing: Kurohashi and Nagao (1994) used cue words, synonymous words or phrases, and similarity between two sentences; Hearst (1994) used lexical frequency and distribution information; and Le and Abeysinghe (2003) used syntactic information, cue phrases and other cohesive devices. In this work, I found that only some sentences in dissertation abstracts contain a clear cue phrase at the beginning. Thus the cue phrase method is not applicable for categorizing all the sentences. Instead, a supervised learning method, decision tree induction, was selected for discourse parsing, using high frequency word tokens in sentences and sentence position as features. Decision tree induction has been used for discourse parsing by many researchers such as Marcu (1999b) and Nomoto and Matsumoto (2000). It is easy to perform and easy to understand, and can be converted to a set of simple rules that is easy to be incorporated in other computer programs. Finally, the cue phrases found at the beginning of some sentences was used as a complement to improve the categorization of these sentences.

The next section reports the development of the decision tree classifier for sentence categorization and the use of cue phrases found at the beginning of sentences to improve the categorization.

4.2.1 Development of a Decision Tree Classifier

To categorize each sentence in dissertation abstracts into one of the pre-defined categories or sections, decision tree induction, a supervised machine-learning method, was applied to word tokens found in sentences to construct a decision tree model.

A sample of 300 abstracts was selected using a random table from the set of 3214 dissertation abstracts indexed under *sociology, PhD* degree and *year of publication 2001* in the Dissertation Abstracts International database (the same sample used in Chapter 3). The sample abstracts were partitioned into a training set of 200 abstracts used to construct the classifier, and a test set of 100 abstracts to evaluate the accuracy of the constructed classifier. Each sentence in the abstracts was manually assigned to one of the five predefined categories. To simplify the classification problem, each sentence was assigned to only one category, though actually some sentences could arguably be assigned to multiple categories or no category at all. Some of the abstracts were found to be unstructured and difficult to code into the five categories. There were 29 such abstracts in the training set and 16 in the test set. The unstructured abstracts were deleted from the training set.

In each sentence, stop words which are usually *determiners, prepositions, pronouns,* conjunctions, *numbers, negative particles* and *infinitive particles* were identified according to their part-of-speech tags and deleted from the sequence of word tokens. Word frequency was calculated for each unique word token in base form (lemma), and only words above a specific threshold value were retained in the work. Different threshold values were explored. Each sentence was converted into a vector of term weights. Binary weighting was used, i.e. a value of "1" was assigned to a word if it occurred in the sentence, "0" otherwise. The dataset was formatted as a table with sentences as rows and base-form word tokens as columns.

A well-known decision-tree induction algorithm, C5.0 (Quinlan, 1998), was used in the work. 10-fold cross-validation was used to estimate the accuracy of the decision trees built using the training sample, while reserving the test sample to evaluate the final model.

Preliminary experiments (using 10-fold cross-validation) were carried out to determine the appropriate parameters used in the model-building. The number of minimum records per branch was set at 5 to avoid overtraining. To make it easier to incorporate the output model into other computer programs later, the resulting model was specified to be a ruleset. The C5.0 algorithm has a special method called *boosting* to improve its accuracy rate (Quinlan, 1998). It constructs several models rather than just one. The first model is constructed in the usual way. It usually makes mistakes on some cases in the data. Thus the second model is constructed by paying more attention to these mis-classified cases. Then the third one is constructed to focus on the second model's errors. The process continues for a pre-determined number of trials. Finally, cases are classified by applying all the models to them, using a weighted voting procedure to combine the separate prediction into one overall prediction. Boosting usually can improve the accuracy of a C5.0 model but also requires longer training time to construct multiple models. However, in this work, boosting was found to contribute little to the accuracy of discourse parsing, and was not employed in the final experiments.

In this work, three models were investigated:
- Model 1 made use of high frequency word tokens found in the sentence.
- Model 2 made use of both high frequency word tokens and sentence position in the abstract. The position of the sentence was normalized by dividing the sentence number by the total number of sentences in the abstract.
- Model 3 took into consideration indicator words found in other sentences before and after the sentence being categorized, in addition to the features used in Model 2. These indicator words were extracted from Model 1 and Model 2.

(1) Model 1 : Using Words Present in the Sentence as Attributes

Model 1 used high frequency words present in the sentences as the attributes to build the decision tree. The accuracy of Model 1 with pruning severity of 90%, 95% and 99% were estimated using 10-fold cross validation for various word frequency threshold values. The results are reported in

Table 4-1. The threshold value determines the number of attributes used in the model. The pruning severity determines the extent to which the constructed model will be pruned. A large tree is first grown to fit the data closely and is then "pruned" by removing parts that are predicted to have a relatively high error rate (Quinlan, 1998). A higher pruning severity value leads to a more concise decision tree, whereas a smaller one leads to a more accurate tree. However, a tree that is either extremely accurate or concise may result in a higher error rate when applied to new data. Thus, three kinds of pruning severity (90%, 95% and 99%) were investigated when constructing Model 1.

The results showed that Model 1 obtained the best estimated accuracy of 58%, with a word frequency threshold value of 35 and pruning severity of 95%. The high word frequency threshold of 35 indicates that only high frequency words are useful for categorizing the sentences. In fact, only a small number of indicator words were selected by C5.0 algorithm to develop the decision tree (e.g. 20 indicator words were used in the best model).

Table 4-1. Estimated accuracy of Model 1 for various word frequency threshold values

Word frequency threshold value	Number of words input	Pruning Severity		
		90%	95%	99%
>5	1463	53.7	53.9	53.9
>10	876	54.4	54.4	53.7
>20	454	56.4	55.6	56.3
>35	242	57.5	**57.9**	56.2
>50	153	56.5	56.4	55.5
>75	75	51.6	51.0	50.7
>100	44	51.1	50.8	50.1
>125	30	50.7	50.7	50.7

- The values are estimated accuracy using 10-fold cross validation.
- The bold figure indicates the highest accuracy.

After the final decision tree for Model 1 was built, it was applied to the test sample of 100 abstracts (including 16 unstructured abstracts). The accuracy rate obtained was 50%. When the 16 unstructured abstracts were removed from the test sample, the accuracy rate became 61%. This means that some kind of preprocessing to filter out the unstructured abstracts can help to improve the categorization accuracy substantially.

(2) Model 2 : Adding Sentence Position as Attributes

For Model 2, I investigated whether sentence position was helpful in predicting categories of sentences. The normalized sentence position was used as an additional attribute to build Model 2. It is calculated using the following formula:

- $$\frac{the\ sentence\ ID}{the\ total\ number\ of\ sentences\ in\ the\ dissertation\ abstract}$$

As with Model 1, a word frequency threshold of 35 was used. The estimated accuracy values using 10-fold cross validation for various pruning severity values are given in Table 4-2.

Table 4-2. Estimated accuracy of Model 1 and Model 2 for various pruning severity

Word frequency threshold values	Number of words input	Sentence position as an additional attribute	Pruning severity				
			80%	85%	90%	95%	99%
>35	242	No (Model 1)	57.0%	57.9%	57.5%	57.9%	56.2%
		Yes (Model 2)	66.5%	66.4%	65.1%	66.6%	65.1%

- *The values are estimated accuracy using 10-fold cross validation.*

With sentence position as an additional attribute, the estimated accuracy obtained by Model 2 increased substantially. Clearly, sentence position was important in identifying which category or section a sentence belongs to. A general sequence for the five sections in a dissertation abstract is: *background → research objectives → research methods → research results → concluding remarks.*

Pruning severity did not have much effect on the accuracy of both Model 1 and Model 2. I selected 95% as the appropriate pruning severity because the size of the decision tree was smaller, and over-training was avoided.

Using 95% pruning severity and 242 high frequency words occurring in more than 35 sentences as well as normalized sentence position as attributes, I constructed the final decision tree classifier for Model 2. I applied Model 2 to the test sample of 84 abstracts (not including 16 unstructured abstracts). The accuracy rate obtained was 72%, much better than 61% for Model 1 (see Table 4-3).

Table 4-3. Comparison of sections assigned by Model 1 and Model 2

Section ID	Number of sentences	Model 1 correctly classified	Model 2 correctly classified
1	173	12 (6.94%)	123 (71.10%)
2	183	98 (53.56%)	102 (55.74%)
3	189	80 (42.33%)	94 (49.74%)
4	468	426 (91.03%)	410 (87.61%)
5	29	16 (55.17%)	17 (58.62%)
Total	1042	634 (**60.84%**)	746 (**71.59%**)

(3) Model 3 : Adding Indicator Words in Surrounding Sentences as Attributes

The dissertation abstract is a continuous discourse with relations between sentences. Surrounding sentences before and after the sentence being processed can help to determine the category of the sentence. For example, if the previous sentence is the first sentence in the *research results* section, then the current sentence is likely to be in *research results* section as well. Furthermore, sentences which are easy to classify, because they contain clear indicator words, can be used to help identify the categories of other sentences that do not contain clear indicator words. For example, the *research results* section often contains the clear indicator words *"reveal" and "show"*. Subsequent sentences will amplify on the results but may not contain a clear indicator word.

To test this assumption, I extracted indicator words from the decision tree of Model 1 and Model 2 (see Table 4-4). For each sentence, I then measured the distance between the sentence and the nearest sentence (before and after) that contains each indicator word. Table 4-5 illustrates this. Sentence #13 in document #4 is being processed. The indicator word *"study"* is found in sentence #4 (9 sentences earlier) and sentence #7 (6 sentences earlier), as well as in sentence #14 (1 sentence after).

Table 4-4. Indicator words found in Model 1 and Model 2

	Model	Number of words	Indicator words
Common words	Model 1 & 2	13	complete, conduct, data, dissertation, examine, explore, future, implication, interview, investigate, participate, reveal, test
Unique words	Model 1	7	literature, purpose, population, question, qualitative, reform, survey
	Model 2	12	access, age, analysis, form, method, participant, perception, scale, second, show, status, study

Table 4-5. Indicator words in surrounding sentences

Doc ID	Sentence ID	Neighboring sentence ID	Indicator word	Distance	Location
4	13	4	study	-9	before*
4	13	7	analysis	-6	before
4	13	14	study	1	after*

- *"Before" means that the indicator word is in the sentence before the one being processed;*
- *"After" means that the indicator word is in the sentence after the one being processed.*

Next, I used the surrounding indicator words as additional attributes (distance as the attribute values) in 3 ways:

- Sentence position of indicator words *before* the sentence being processed;
- Sentence position of indicator words *after* the sentence being processed;
- Sentence position of indicator words both *before and after* the sentence being processed.

The test results for Model 3 using 84 structured test abstracts are shown in Table 4-6. It was found that only indicator words *before* the sentence being processed can contribute to the categorization accuracy, by obtaining the best result of 74.5%.With indicator words *after* the sentences being processed, the result (68.6%) is even worse than that for Model 2 (71.6%).

Table 4-6. Test results for Model 3 based on the test sample of 84 structured abstracts

Section ID	Number of sentences	Model 2 correctly classi-fied	Model 3 correctly classified		
			With all indicator words	Only with before indicator words	Only with after indicator words
1	173	123(71.10%)	140 (80.92%)	138 (79.77%)	117 (67.63%)
2	183	102 (55.74%)	89 (48.63%)	96 (52.46%)	90 (49.18%)
3	189	94 (49.74%)	99 (52.38%)	99 (52.38%)	74 (39.15%)
4	468	410 (87.61%)	426 (91.03%)	426 (91.03%)	418 (89.31%)
5	29	17 (58.62%)	17 (58.62%)	17 (58.62%)	16 (55.17%)
Total	1042	746 (**71.59%**)	771 (**73.99%**)	776 (**74.47%**)	715 (**68.62%**)

4.2.2 Categorization Using the Decision Tree Classifier

Although the accuracy of Model 3 (74%) is a little better than that of Model 2 (72%), Model 3 required more effort to prepare the data. Therefore, Model 2 was selected to be used as the classifier to parse the macro-level discourse structure of dissertation abstracts in the summarization system developed in this work. A set of IF-THEN categorization rules was extracted from Model 2. Some of these rules are shown in Table 4-7. The rule antecedents ("IF" part) include the normalized sentence position and single indicator words, whereas the rule consequent ('THEN" part) indicates the predicted section or category. For each rule, its confidence value is calculated as follows:

- *1+ number of record in which the rule antecedents and consequent are both true*
  2+ number of record in which the rule antecedents are true

A higher confidence value means a more reliable rule.

During the categorization process, each dissertation abstract was preprocessed and segmented into sentences. For each sentence, its position in the document was normalized. Each sentence was then converted into a vector of term weights. The terms are those indicator words used in Model 2. Binary weighting was used, i.e. a value of "1" was assigned to an indicator word if it occurred in the sentence, otherwise "0". The dataset was formatted as a table with sentences as rows and the normalized sentence position and indicator words as columns. Then the rules extracted from Model 2 were applied to each sentence. If a sentence matches multiple rules and is assigned more than one category, the category assigned by the rule with the highest confidence value is retained as its final predicted category.

74

Table 4-7. Example rules found in Model 2

Section ID	Section label	Categorization rule
1	Background	if N_SENTEN_P <= 0.444444 then 1 (836, 0.355)* …
2	Research objectives	if STUDY = 1 and N_SENTEN_P <= 0.444444 and PARTICIPANT = 0 and DATA = 0 and CONDUCT = 0 and PARTICIPATE = 0 and FORM = 0 and ANALYSIS = 0 and SHOW = 0 and COMPLETE = 0 and SCALE = 0 then 2 (172, 0.733) …
3	Research methods	if DATA = 1 and TEST = 0 and EXAMINE = 0 and METHOD = 0 and ASSESS = 0 and EXPLORE = 0 then 3 (93, 0.613) …
4	Research results	if REVEAL= 1 and IMPLICATION = 0 then 4 (44, 0.932) if SHOW = 1 then 4 (57, 0.842) if IMPLICATATION = 0 then 4 (2030, 0.41) Default section is 4
5	Concluding remarks	if IMPLICATION = 1 then 5 (33, 0.788) if FUTURE = 1 and N_SENTEN_P > 0.444444 then 5 (36, 0.694)

- *The first number in the bracket is the number of the records to which the rule applies;*
- *The second number in the bracket is the confidence value of the rule;*

4.2.3 Improvement to the Categorization Using Cue Phrases

In the *research objectives* and *research results* sections of a dissertation abstract, some sentences, especially the first sentence of the section, often begin with a clear cue phrase, such as *"The purpose of this study was to investigate ..."*, *"The results indicated that ..."* . Sentences containing such phrases could be categorized more accurately than using the decision tree classifier. A list of cue phrases for identifying *research objectives* and *research results* sentences were manually derived from the 300 sample dissertation abstracts. Example cue phrases for *research objectives* are given in Table 4-8. Example cue phrases for *research results* are given in Table 4-9.

Some cue phrases are similar and can be represented by a small number of linguistic patterns. A pattern is a sequence of tokens, representing a series of contiguous words in the text. The token can be a specific word, group of synonyms, or wildcard. It can be set as mandatory or optional. Each token can be constrained with a part-of-speech tag. Example patterns of cue phrases found at the beginning of *research objective*s or *research results* sentences are listed in Table 4-10.

Table 4-8. Example cue phrases for identifying *research objectives* sentences

ID	Example cue phrase
1	*The purpose of this study was to investigate* the relationship between school size and the variables of school dropout rate, rate of school crime and violence and student extracurricular activity participation.
2	*My purpose here is to answer* the following question: What are the effects of restructuring on school delinquency?
3	*This study examined* school administrator differences in reporting school crime based upon selected school and administrator variables.
4	*The present study aimed to fill* this gap by reviewing 108 files of at risk children.
5	*This study was designed to understand* the subjective experience of women who had been abused as teens, and generate ideas about what might make it difficult to leave an abuser.
6	*Using primary and secondary sources, this study discusses* the impact of China's political, legal and social changes on juvenile crime.
7	*In this study, I examine* the effects of team composition based on task- and team- related knowledge, skills, and abilities (KSAs) on internal processes and outcomes of production teams.

Table 4-9. Example cue phrases for identifying *research results* sentences

ID	Example cue phrase
1	*Results indicate* the attitudes of Tennessee physicians are highly polarized over the issues of euthanasia and assisted death.
2	*Multiple regression analyses indicated* that parenting quality moderated the relationship between exposure to community violence and academic functioning.
3	*The analyses showed* competition, followed by collaboration, cooperation, accommodation, and avoidance, to be the most likely response regardless of other variables.
4	*Key findings are that* alcohol policies reduce youth drinking, specifically higher beer taxes reduce youth alcohol use.
5	*This research found that* the employees who received the enhanced training outperformed the employees who received the standard training at a statistically significant level.
6	*The results of this study suggest that* trust among African American families is not influenced by either family background or school background characteristics.
7	*It is suggested that* female exploitation is caused by their undocumented worker status, occupational segregation by sex, and a lack of marketable skills for employment in the non-ethnic labor market.

Table 4-10. Example patterns of cue phrases found at the beginning of *research objectives* or *research results* sentences

ID	Cue phrase pattern	Example cue phrase
1	The (<A>) purpose of the study be to <V>	– The main purpose of the study was to investigate – The objective of the research was to examine – The second goal of the project was to explore
2	This (<A>) study aim to <V>	– This study aims to address – This research seeks to answer
3	The result of the study indicate	– The findings of the study suggests – The results of the research indicates – The analysis of the study shows
4	This study be designed to <V>	– The study was designed to discuss – The research was conducted to examine

- *The tokens in round brackets are optional;*
- *The tokens in angle brackets are wildcard constrained with part-of-speech tags;*
- *The underlined tokens have synonyms*

The following groups of synonyms were used in the patterns:

- Purpose: *aim, goal, objective, intent, focus, significance*
- Study: *research, dissertation, project, work, thesis, paper, report*
- Aim (to): *seek (to), propose (to), wish (to)*
- Result: *finding, analysis*
- Indicate: *show, suggest*
- The: *this*
- Design (to): *conduct (to)*

A simple pattern matching program was developed to identify the sentences that match with each pattern at the beginning of the sentence. The final evaluation of the macro-level discourse parsing using both the decision tree classifier and cue phrases is reported in Section 5.2.

4.3 Information Extraction

This section reports the development of an automatic information extraction method involving term extraction and relationship extraction. A preliminary analysis of dissertation abstracts found that four kinds of information can be extracted from each dissertation abstract – *research concepts* and *their research relationships, contextual relations* and *research methods* (see Section 3.3). *Research concepts, contextual relations* and *research methods* can be expressed as single-word or multi-word terms.

In previous studies, automatic term extraction have used three kinds of methods – rule-based methods, statistics-based methods, and hybrid methods. Bourigault and Jacquemin (1999) extracted noun phrases according to their shallow grammatical structure. Nakagawa (2000) and Nakagawa and Mori (2002) extracted compound nouns depending on the statistics about the relation between a compound noun and its component single nouns. Sui et al. (2002) extracted closely related fragments through calculating the statistical association between the component words in candidate terms and filtering illegal terms according to the grammatical structure rules of terms. In this work, the rule-based method was used to extract single-word and multi-word terms according to syntactic rules for term formation. Since the language used in dissertation abstracts is formal and regular, the syntactic rules of terms are easy to construct.

The more important concepts in the dissertation abstracts were then identified. Statistical measures were extensively used in previous studies, including term frequency (Kraaij, Spitters & Hulth, 2002), TF*IDF (Jones, Lundy, & Paynter, 2002), and likelihood ratio (Leuski, Lin & Stubblebine, 2003). In addition, Myaeng and Jang (1999) used discourse structure to identify the segments that are likely to contain more important information. Since term frequency was often low in a dissertation abstract because of the short length of dissertation abstracts, it did not work well in this work. Instead, concepts were taken from specific sections of each dissertation abstract (*research objectives* and *research results* sections), and document frequency in the set of dissertation abstracts was used to identify the more important concepts.

The subsequent sections describe how the terms relating to research concepts as well as contextual relations and research methods were extracted from sentences using term extraction, and then relationships between variables were extracted using pattern matching.

4.3.1 Term Extraction

Concepts, expressed as single-word or multi-word terms, usually take the grammatical form of nouns or noun phrases (National Information Standard Organization [NISO], 2003):

- Common nouns, such as *school, family, culture, history*
- Verbal nouns (or nominalized verbs), such as *parenting, nursing*
- Noun phrases, which are multi-word terms occurring in two forms:
    - Adjectival noun phrases which are pre-modified by an adjective, such as *social science, public administration, school crime, adopted children*;

– Prepositional noun phrases which are post-modified by a prepositional phrase, such as *ability of the organization, history of European*.

In the summarization process, only nouns and noun phrases were extracted. Adverbs such as *"very"* or *"highly"* are deleted. Initial articles are deleted. For example, *"the arts"* is reduced to *"art"*, and *"the state"* to *"state"*.

After data preprocessing involving sentence breaking and sentence parsing, a sequence of word tokens in base form was obtained from each sentence in each document. Different numbers of contiguous words (i.e. 2, 3, 4 and 5 words) were extracted from each sentence to construct n-grams (*n* is the number of words). Some linguistic features were used to distinguish between terms and non-terms among the n-grams. One important feature was the syntactic pattern of the candidate terms. In this work, a list of syntactic rules was constructed for recognizing terms of 1, 2, 3, 4, and 5 words (see Table 4-11 for examples).

Table 4-11. Example syntactic rules for recognizing single-word and multi-word terms

ID	Part of speech tag					Example term
	1	2	3	4	5	
1	N					teacher
2	N	N				preschool teacher
3	A	N				young child
4	N	PREP	N			ability of organization
5	N	N	N			teacher training program
6	A	N	N			early childhood classroom
7	N	INFMARK	V	N		ability to speak English
8	N	PREP	A	N		effectiveness of early childhood
9	N	PREP	PRON	N		size on their nature
10	N	N	PREP	N		child ability of reading
11	A	N	PREP	N		parental ability of reading
12	N	N	N	N		preschool teacher training program
13	A	N	N	N		early childhood teacher input
14	N	PREP	A	N	N	effectiveness of early childhood teacher

Using the syntactic rules, terms of different number of words were extracted from the same part of a sentence. These terms represent concepts at different levels of generality (narrower or broader concepts). For example, in the sentence *"The present study assessed the effectiveness of preschool teachers of India with respect to their interactions with young children and their parents"*, the extracted terms of different word lengths are as follows:

- 1-word terms: *effectiveness, preschool, teacher, India, child, parent*
- 2-word terms: *preschool teacher, young child*
- 3-word terms: *effectiveness of preschool, teachers of India*
- 4-word terms: *effectiveness of preschool teacher, preschool teachers of India, child and their parent*
- 5-word terms: *young child and their parent*

The longest terms often, but not always, represent the full terms in the sentence. To identify the full terms in a sentence, the terms of different word lengths extracted from the same part of a sentence were compared, and terms which cannot be covered by other terms were retained, e.g. *"effectiveness of preschool teacher"*, *"preschool teacher of India"*, and *"young child and their parent"*. Then the terms which overlap in sentence position were combined to generate a full term which represents a more specific full concept in the text, e.g.

- *"effectiveness of preschool teacher"* + *"preschool teacher of India"* → *"effectiveness of preschool teacher of India"*.

After the full terms were extracted from the whole text, the research method terms and contextual relation terms were identified from them. In addition to the *research methods* section, information about research methods can sometimes be found in the *research objectives* and *research results* sections. Thus, the extraction of research method terms cannot be limited to the *research methods* section only. Instead, a list of indicator phrases, derived manually from the 300 sample dissertation abstracts (see Table 3-1 and Table 3-2 in Section 3.3), was used to identify the research method and contextual relation terms from the full terms throughout the whole text.

After removing the *research method* terms and *contextual relation* terms as well as all cue phrases (e.g. *"this study suggests"*) and common phrases (e.g. *"dissertation"*, *"research"*, *"result"*) from the full terms, *research concept* terms were selected from specific sections of the abstract. The *research objectives* and *research results* sections in structured abstracts and the *research objectives* section in unstructured abstracts are hypothesized to contain more important research information (see Section 3.2). Thus the full terms extracted from the *research objectives* + *research results* sections were considered *research concepts* to be extracted. An evaluation was performed to compare the accuracy of important concept extraction from three combinations of the sections – research *objective* section, *research objective* + *research results* section, and all sections. In the evaluation (reported in Section 5.2.3), the F-measure obtained for extracting the most important concepts from the *research objectives + research results* sections was significantly higher than that from the whole text and thus confirmed the above hypothesis.

Finally, the document frequency of the *research concept* terms, *research method* terms and *contextual relation* terms in a document set were calculated and the terms with higher document frequency were retained for multi-document summarization.

4.3.2 Relationship Extraction

Extraction of relationships between variables involves looking for certain linguistic patterns that indicate the presence of a particular relationship. The linguistic patterns used in this work were regular expression patterns, each comprising a sequence of tokens, with each token representing one of the following:

- A single word in the text, converted to a base form (i.e. lemma);
- A group of synonyms, each of which has been converted to a base form;
- A wildcard which can match with one or more words in the sentence;
- A slot to be filled in by a term representing a variable.

The tokens that are not slots are called indicator words which signal the occurrence of a relationship. Each indicator word can be constrained with a part-of-speech (POS) tag, e.g. "N", "V", and "ADV". In a pattern, some indicator words can be set as mandatory whereas others can be optional. In this way, the patterns are more general and flexible to match more relationship expressions in the text. The following is an example of a pattern that describes one way that cause-effect relationship can be expressed in the text:

Token	[slot: IV]	have	*	(*)	(*)	(and)	(*)	effect/influence/impact	on/in	[slot: DV]
POS	—	V	DET	ADV	A	CC	A	V	PREP	—

- *IV indicates independent variable;*
- *DV indicates dependent variable;*
- *POS indicates part-of-speech.*

The tokens in square brackets (e.g. *[slot: IV]* and *[slot: DV]*) represent slots to be filled by terms in the text. The slots indicate which part of a sentence represents the independent variable (IV) and which part represents the dependent variable (DV) in a cause-effect relationship. The tokens in round brackets (e.g. *(and)*) represent optional words, whereas the tokens without any brackets represent mandatory words. The wildcard tokens (e.g. *) only require matching their part-of-speech tags. The specific word tokens require matching both the words themselves and their part-of-speech

81

tags. The specific word could be a single word (e.g. *have*) or a group of synonyms (e.g. *effect/influence/impact*).

The pattern matches the following example sentences, where the extracted independent and dependent variables are underlined.

*(1) Changes in labor productivity **have a positive effect on** directional movement.*

*(2) Medicaid appeared to **have a negative influence on** the proportion of uninsured welfare leavers,*

*(3) Family structure **has a significant impact on** parental attachment and supervision.*

*(4) This support the hypothesis that ontogenic variables **have the greater impact in** predicting risk of physical abuse.*

A pattern matching program was developed to identify the text segments that match with the relationship patterns. Since the *research objectives* and *research results* sections are hypothesized to contain more important research information, the pattern matching was focused on these two sections to extract research relationships and their associated variables. A pattern typically contains one or more slots, and the research concept terms that match the slots in the pattern represent the variables linked by the relationship. Research concept terms had been extracted as nouns or noun phrases in an earlier processing step (reported in Section 4.3.1). For the slots at different locations in the patterns, the variables were extracted as follows:

− If the slot was located in the middle of the pattern, all the research concept terms between the *before-slot* indicator word and the *after-slot* indicator word were extracted as the variable;

− If the slot was located at the beginning of the pattern, the nearest research concept term before the first indicator word was extracted as the variable, ignoring other words between them.

− If the slot was located at the end of the pattern, the nearest research concept term after the last indicator word was extracted as the variable, ignoring other words between them.

This is a little different from the normal way of extracting the entire text string that matches the slots. This method can remove extraneous text from the variables. For example, in sentence #4, the *"ontogenic variables"* term are extracted as the dependent variable and the remaining string *"This support the hypothesis that"* is removed. In addition, the method can ignore extraneous text between the variable and the indicator words in the pattern and thus makes the pattern more general. For example, the example pattern can handle sentence #2 though there are two words *"appear to"* between the independent variable *"Medicaid"* and the first indicator word *"have"*. On the other hand, the method also makes errors when the target variable is not an exact research concept term. For example, in sentence #4, the extracted dependent variable is the term *"risk of physical abuse"* rather than the real one *"predicting risk of physical abuse"*. Furthermore, the variables extracted from the slots located at the beginning or the end of the pattern may be incomplete if more than one research concept term appears as variables. However, this case is not frequent since multiple short terms connected with connectives were usually extracted as a long term in this work. For example, in sentence #3, *"parental attachment and supervision"* was extracted as one term rather than several short terms such as *"parental attachment"* and *"supervision"*.

Based on an analysis of the research relationships found in the 300 sample dissertation abstracts, 126 relationship patterns were constructed manually by identifying the common indicator words found in these relationships. Example patterns are listed in Table 4-12. These 126 relationship patterns belong to nine types of semantic relations (e.g. cause-effect relationship and correlation). Detailed information on the types of relationships was reported in Section 4.4.3.

Table 4-12. Example relationship patterns

ID	Relationship pattern	Example sentence
1	[slot: IV] (not) play a (<ADV>) (<A>) (and) (<A>) role in [slot: DV]	*The results of this study suggest that family, environment, and sociopolitical factors all may play a role in the adopted patterns of acculturation for Mexican-Americans.*
2	[slot:V1] be find to be (<ADV>) relate with/to [slot:V2]	*General and proactive racial socialization were found to be negatively related to suidicality and positively related to reasons for living.*
3	There be (no) (<ADV>) (<A>) (and) (<A>) difference between [slot: V1] and [slot: V2]	*However, on the post-treatment Minor Infraction Report (MIR), there was significant differences between the experimental group and non-weighted control group, but there was no significant difference between the experimental group and control group.*
4	[slot: V1] be a (<A>) (and) (<A>) predictor of [slot: V2]	*Racism-related stress was a significant predictor of cultural incorporation.*
5	effect of [slot: IV] on [slot: DV] be mediated through Iby [slot: MV]	*The effect of family problems on SRB was mediated through emotional distress and drug involvement.*
6	[slot:V1] (not) have an (<A>) (and) (<A>) interaction with [slot:V2]	*Racial socialization did not have a significant interaction with academic achievement.*

4.4 Information Integration

This section reports the development of an automatic integration method using concept generalization and relationship normalization and conflation.

Previous studies have performed concept generalization using two approaches. The first approach is based on semantic relations among concepts (Lin, 1995; Lin & Hovy, 1997) and the second is based on syntactic variations among concepts (Bourigault & Jacquemin, 1999; Ibekwe-SanJuan & San-Juan, 2004a and 2004b). The first often requires a thesaurus, ontology, or knowledge base to provide a meaningful concept hierarchy. However, such thesaurus is sometimes unavailable and difficult to construct. This work focused on the second approach which was to generalize similar concepts according to the specific syntactic variations among them. It was easy to implement and did not require a thesaurus, though the generalization was not very accurate. Relationship normalization and conflation was performed by normalizing different surface expressions for the same type of relationships using a standard expression and conflating them into one sentence. In addition, similar *research method* concepts and *contextual relation* concepts were identified based on indicator phrases and were normalized using uniform terms.

Text generation involved in this work was very simple. The new sentences were generated using pre-defined templates rather than real natural language generation techniques, for integrating concepts extracted from original text and normalizing different surface expressions of relationships extracted.

The subsequent sections describe how the concept hierarchy was constructed and used for identifying similar concepts. Then, it describes how similar *research concepts*, *research method* concepts and *contextual relation* concepts were integrated. Finally, it describes how to normalize and conflate the same types of relationships.

4.4.1 Analysis of Concept Structure

To integrate similar concepts, I analyzed the structure of concepts (terms) that were extracted from the 300 sample dissertation abstracts using the term extraction method. Although term extraction and term integration were both based on the syntactic structure of the terms, the approaches taken were different – the former focused on the part-of-speech patterns of the multi-word terms, whereas the latter focused on the syntactic relations between the multi-word terms and their component terms.

The majority of the multi-word terms can be analyzed into the following two parts (NISO, 2003):

- **Head noun:** the noun component that identifies the broader class of things or events to which the term as a whole refers, for example, *cognitive ability, educated woman* ;

- **Modifier:** the part of the multi-word term that refers to a characteristic or logical difference, which narrows the denotation of the head noun by specifying a *subclass* or a *facet* of the broader concept represented by the head noun. For example, *cognitive* ability (a type of ability), *educated woman* (a subclass of woman), *woman's behavior* (an aspect of woman).

The component terms often refer to broader concepts than the full term. That is, a full concept is a narrower concept which may be composed of some broader concepts. I call these broader concepts *component concepts*. They can be identified by segmenting a full term into shorter terms of different lengths, e.g. 1, 2, 3, 4, 5-word terms. The terms with different number words represent the component concepts at different levels. The shorter terms represent broader component concepts whereas the longer terms represent narrower ones. There is a tangled hierarchy among the component concepts in a full concept.

Here is a full term (underlined) extracted from a research objective sentence using the term extraction method described in Section 4.3.1:

- *This research comprises two inter-related studies of adult women survivors of childhood sexual abuse.*

The concept can be segmented into 1, 2, 3, 4 and 5-word terms to identify its component concepts.
- 1-word terms: *adult, woman, survivor, childhood, abuse*
- 2-word terms: *adult woman, woman survivor, sexual abuse*
- 3-word terms: *adult woman survivor, childhood sexual abuse*
- 4-word terms: -
- 5-word terms: *adult woman survivors of childhood, survivors of childhood sexual abuse*

The tangled hierarchy of the component concepts and the full concept is shown in Figure 4-4.

The component concepts of a full concept have relations between them, distinguished by their logical roles or functions. They can be a *main concept*, a *facet concept*, or a *subclass concept*.

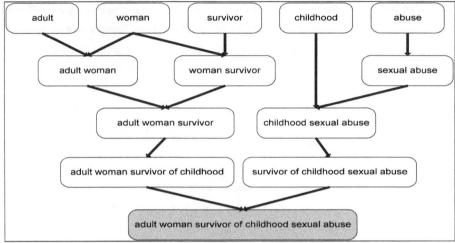

• *The concept in the shaded box at the bottom is a full concept.*

Figure 4-4. The tangled hierarchy of the component concepts and the full concept

A *main concept* is the broader concept represented by the head noun in the hierarchy. It can be of different types:

- a concrete object, such as *family, school, program*
- an abstract object, such as *tradition, culture, life*
- a person, such as *student, youth, woman*
- an organization, such as *institution, community, organization*
- an event or occurrence, such as *crime, revolution, abuse*
- an action, such as *parenting, participation, behavior*
- a process, such as *development, change, transition*
- a property or state of entities, processes, actions or events, such as *gender, age*
- a geographic area or country, such as *church, US, California*

A *facet concept* specifies one of the facets (aspects or characteristics) of the main concept. A facet refers to a property or state of an entity, action, process or event, for example, "*ability of the organization*", "*experience of woman*". But it also can be an action or a process itself, for example, "*teacher's behavior*", "*development of identity*".

In addition, there is a list of special facets, such as *number, size, level, rate, degree, type, and pattern*, which specifies a quality whereby the entity can be distinguished and measured quantitatively.

These facets are called *attributes.* An attribute cannot exist independently, but is dependent on a specific entity, action, process or action. For example, in the concept *"rate of school crime"*, *"rate"* is the attribute of an event *"school crime"*. The attribute may be unknown and needs to be investigated in the work. Attributes frequently used in sociology dissertation abstracts are listed in Table 4-13.

A *subclass concept* represents one of the subclasses of the main concept. One or more qualifiers are used to restrict or narrow the entities, actions, events or processes into a subclass. For example, the scope of *"crime"* is narrowed down by *"school"*, as in *"school crime"*. Any concept can be a qualifier to restrict or narrow down other concepts. It is hard to identify a comprehensive list of words (concepts) for qualifiers.

Table 4-13. Attributes frequently used in sociology dissertation abstracts

Attribute	Example concept
size	family size, size of organization
rate	female suicide rate, rate of crime
pattern	cultural pattern, pattern of interaction
type	household type, type of social capital
category	racial category , social category
level	community level, level of academic achievement
diversity	cultural diversity, diversity of woman
dimension	gender dimension, dimension of personality
role	leadership role, role of ethnic identity
score	achievement score, depression score
form	child form, form of belief
status	class status, status of the student
quality	job quality, quality of life
nature	nature of woman, social nature
degree	degree of conflict, degree of trauma
performance	academic performance, performance of expertise
function	function of age, family function

It is sometimes difficult to determine which component concept is the *main concept, facet concept* or *subclass concept.* The role of a component concept in a full concept depends on which noun is regarded as the head noun. Once the head noun (i.e. the main concept) is identified, the roles of the other component concepts can be determined. The full concept may be a more specific facet or subclass of the main concept. Given the tangled hierarchy of concepts (terms) in Figure 4-4, different nouns selected as head nouns give different vertical chains of component concepts. Each chain indicates hierarchical syntactic relations between component concepts. For example,

(1) If the head noun is *"abuse"*

- [abuse] –

      (subclass) → [sexual abuse] –

           (subclass) → [childhood sexual abuse] –

                (facet) → [adult woman survivor of childhood sexual abuse]

(2) If the head noun is *"survivor"*

- [survivor] –

    (subclass) → [woman survivor] –

        (subclass) → [adult woman survivor] –

            (subclass) → [adult woman survivor of childhood sexual abuse]

(3) If the head noun is *"woman"*

- [woman] –

    (subclass) → [adult woman] –

        (facet) → (adult woman survivor) –

            (facet) → [adult woman survivor of childhood sexual abuse]

- [woman] –

    (facet) → [woman survivor] –

        (subclass) → (adult woman survivor) –

            (subclass) → [adult woman survivor of childhood sexual abuse]

(4) If the head noun is *"adult"*

- [adult] –

  (facet) → [adult woman] –

      (facet) → [adult woman survivor] –

          (subclass) → [adult woman survivor of childhood sexual abuse]

(5) If the head noun is "childhood"

- [childhood] –

      (facet) → [childhood sexual abuse] –

           (facet) → [adult woman survivor of childhood sexual abuse]

The component concepts at different levels in a chain are considered a group of term variants, since they are syntactically related, i.e. the shorter terms are parts of longer terms sharing the same head noun. The term variants of different lengths represent similar concepts at different levels of generality. The top level represents the main concept whereas the bottom level represents the specific full concept. Thus, a full concept can be generalized by component concepts at different levels, and a lower-level component concept can be generalized by a higher-level component concept. The main concept is the broadest concept which can generalize all the other component concepts and the full concept itself.

Although any noun that is not a stop word, attribute word or indicator word can be used as the head noun in theory, only the high frequency ones were selected as the head nouns in the summarization. The threshold value of the document frequency for selecting the head nouns in a document set depends on the desired length of the final summary. For example, for 10 dissertation abstracts on the topic of *"childhood sexual abuse"*, the nouns with document frequency (df) equal to or above 6 were selected as the head nouns, including *"abuse"* (df=10), *"childhood"* (df=10), *"survivor"* (df=6) and *"woman"* (df=6), for generating a summary of size 20% of the total size of the 10 dissertation abstracts. Thus the four chains derived from the selected head nouns were selected to generalize the *"adult women survivors of childhood sexual abuse"* concept in four ways.

The hierarchy of component concepts provides a way to identify and integrate similar concepts extracted from different documents. The concepts that share the same component concepts are assumed to have meaning in common, and thus can be generalized by using the common component concept to replace them.

4.4.2 Concept Clustering and Generalization

An integration method was developed for clustering similar concepts and generalizing them based on their syntactic structure. It linked term variants of different lengths based on their syntactic variations to construct a hierarchal term chain, and generalized them using the broader terms at the higher level in the hierarchical chain. The concept integration method has three phases:

(1) Segment full terms
Full terms occurring in specific dissertation abstracts were segmented into 1, 2, 3, 4 and 5-word terms. For each n-word term (n=1, 2, 3, 4 and 5), its document frequency was counted. Stop words, attribute words and all indicator words were removed from the set of 1-word terms.

(2) Construct term chains

Starting from each frequent 1-word term, a list of term chains were constructed by linking it level by level with other multi-word terms in which the single word is used as a head noun. Each chain was constructed top down by linking the short term first, followed by longer terms containing the short term. The shorter terms represent the broader concepts at the higher level whereas the longer terms represent the narrower concepts at the lower level. The root node of each chain is a 1-word term representing the main concept and the leaf node is a full term representing the specific concept occurring in a particular document. The length of the chains can be different by linking different numbers of n-word terms but the maximum length is six nodes – the 1, 2, 3, 4, 5-word terms and the full term. A concept at the lower level can be a subclass concept or a facet concept of the parent concept at the higher level.

(3) Build cluster tree

All the chains sharing the same root node (1-word term) were combined to form a hierarchical cluster tree (see Figure 4-5). Each cluster tree uses the root node as its cluster label. The concepts in round boxes represent subclass concepts of their parent concepts whereas the concepts in rectangular boxes represent facet concepts. The specific concepts occurring in particular documents which are highlighted using shaded boxes are usually at the bottom of the cluster.

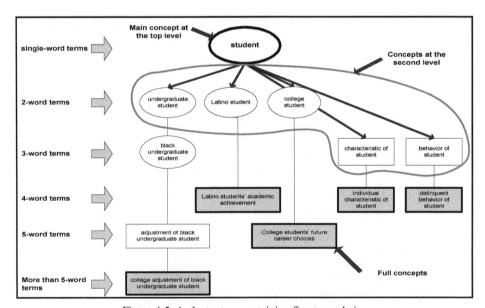

Figure 4-5. A cluster tree containing five term chains

90

In a hierarchical cluster tree, the similar concepts at the lower level can be generalized using a broader concept at a higher level. Then the selected broader concepts can be integrated into a new sentence. For example, all the concepts relating to *"student"* can be integrated in the following sentence by selecting the main concept at the top level and the concepts at the second level:

- *Student, including college student, undergraduate student, Latino student, and more ...*
  Its different aspects were investigated, including characteristics of student, behavior of student, and more ...

The concepts at the second level are divided into two groups – subclass concepts and facet concepts. Thus the sentence is divided into two parts – the first part giving the subclass concepts and the second part (*"its different aspects"*) giving the facet concepts.

For the full terms relating to *contextual relations*, the terms containing the same keyword represented the same type of contextual relations and were generalized and normalized using the keyword. For example, the three terms containing the keyword *"perception"* – *"Korean students' perception of being supported by parents"*, *"individual's perception of social support resources"* and *"adolescents' perception of parental caring"* – are generalized and normalized as *"perception"*. For the full terms relating *to research methods*, the synonymous terms represented the same type of research methods and were generalized and normalized using a uniform term. For example, the four synonymous terms – *"quantitative method"*, *"quantitative study"*, *"quantitative methodology"*, and *"quantitative finding"* – are generalized and normalized as *"quantitative research"*.

4.4.3 Relationship Integration and Regeneration

Relationship integration involves grouping the relationships about similar variables, normalizing different surface expressions for the same type of relationships using a standard expression, and conflating them together. The integrated relationships provide an overview of all the variables associated with a given variable.

I identified the types of the relationships from a manual analysis of the 300 sample dissertation abstracts, and found that these relationships generally belong to nine types. There are five first-order relationships:

(1) *Cause-effect relationship:* an independent variable (IV) causes a change or effect in a dependent variable (DV).

(2) *Correlation:* change in one variable (V1) is accompanied by a change in another (V2).

(3) *Interactive relationship:* one variable (V1) is interacted with another variable (V2).

(4) *Comparative relationship:* Differences between two or more variables (V1 and V2).

(5) *Predictive relationship:* One predictor variable (PV) predicts another criterion variable (CV).

A second-order relationship refers to the relationship between two or more variables influenced by a third variable. For example, a moderator variable influences the relationship between two variables; a mediator variable occurs between two other variables. Depending on which kind of relationships between two variables are moderated or mediated by a third variable, the second-order relationships can be:

(6) *Second-order cause-effect relationship*: A moderator/mediator (MV) variable influences the cause-effect relationship between independent and dependent variables (IV and DV).

(7) *Second-order correlation:* A moderator/mediator (MV) variable influences the correlation between two variables.

(8) *Second-order interactive relationship:* A moderator/mediator (MV) variable influences the interactive relationship between two variables.

(9) *Second-order comparative relationship*: A moderator/mediator (MV) variable influences the comparative relationship between two variables.

The 126 relationship patterns that were constructed based on the relationships found in the 300 sample dissertation abstracts were divided into nine groups. Each group corresponds to a type of relationship and contains various patterns representing different surface expressions for the same type of relationship.

Different surface expressions for the same type of relationship were normalized using a predefined standard form (see Table 4-14). If the variables contained in a relationship are differentiated by their roles, e.g. *independent* and *dependent* variables in a cause-effect relationship, more than one standard form was provided by regarding different variables as the main variable. For each standard form, there are three modalities – *positive, negative* or *hypothesized*. For example, for a cause-effect relationship regarding the independent variable as the main variable, the three modalities are:

- *Positive:* There was <u>an effect</u> on a dependent variable.
- *Negative:* There was <u>no effect</u> on a dependent variable.
- *Hypothesized:* There <u>may be an effect</u> on a dependent variable.

The relationship integration method includes the following steps:

(1) Identify the type of the relationship

Relationships that were extracted using the patterns in the same group were considered the same type.

Table 4-14. Predefined standard forms for nine types of relationship

Group ID	Relationship type	Main variable	Standard form (positive)
1	Cause-effect relationship	Independent variable	There was an effect on a *dependent variable.*
		Dependent variable	It was affected by an *independent variable.*
2	Correlation	One variable	There was a relation with *another variable.*
3	Interactive relationship	One variable	There was an interaction with *another variable.*
4	Comparative relationship	One variable	There was difference found with *another variable.*
5	Predictive relationship	Predictor variable	It was a predictor for a *criterion variable.*
		Criterion variable	It was predicted by a *predictor variable.*
6	Second-order cause-effect relationship	Moderator or mediator variable	There was an effect on the effect of the *independent variable* on the *dependent variable.*
		Independent variable	Its effect on *dependent variable* was affected by *moderator/mediator variable.*
		Dependent variable	The effect of *independent variable* was affected by *moderator/ mediator variable.*
7	Second-order correlation	Moderator or mediator variable	There was an effect on the relationship between *variable 1* and *variable 2.*
		One variable	Its relationship with *another variable* was affected by *moderator/mediator variable.*
8	Second-order interactive relationship	Moderator or mediator variable	There was an effect on the interaction between *variable 1* and *variable 2.*
		One variable	Its interaction with *another variable* was affected by *moderator/ mediator variable.*
9	Second-order comparative relationship	Moderator or mediator variable	There was an effect on the difference between *variable 1* and variable 2.
		One variable	Its difference with *another variable* was affected by *moderato/mediator variable.*

(2) Identify the modality of the relationship

Some relationship patterns are only for negative relations, e.g. *"[slot: V1] be unrelated with [slot: V2]"*, whereas some are only for hypothesized relations, e.g. *"effect of [slot: IV] on [slot: DV]"*. However, not every negative relation could be indicated in the patterns. In this work, if a relationship contained a negative indicator word (e.g. *no, not, negative*), it was considered a negative relation.

(3) Group the relationships about similar concepts

Similar concepts had been identified and clustered in the previous section. The relationships about similar concepts were grouped together. For example, the following relationships are associated with the main concept "*student*":

93

- *Expected economic returns affected the college students' future career choices.*
- *School socioeconomic composition has effect on Latino students' academic achievement.*
- *The study provides evidence that school discipline can have some effects on delinquent behavior of student. .*

(4) Normalize the same type of relationship using the standard form

In a group of relationships, the relationships which have the same type and modality were normalized using a standard form. For example, the above relationships associated with *"student"* are normalized as follows:

- *It was affected by expected economic returns.*
- *It was affected by school socioeconomic composition.*
- *It was affected by school discipline.*

(5) Conflate the same type of relationship

In each group of relationships, the normalized relationships having the same forms were conflated by combining the variables with the same roles together. For example, the above relationships associated with *"student"* are conflated in a simple sentence as follows:

- *It was affected by expected economic returns, school socioeconomic composition and school discipline.*

4.5 Information Presentation

This section first describes how a domain taxonomy was constructed using a semi-automatic method, and then the four kinds of information (i.e. *research concepts* and *their research relationships*, *contextual relations* and *research methods*) were organized based on the taxonomy, for presentation in a Web-based interface.

4.5.1 Taxonomy Construction

Taxonomy plays an important role in organization of information and knowledge. It has been used to facilitate information browsing and searching in many previous studies. For example, Wollersheim and Rahayu (2002) created a dynamic taxonomy to use in navigating medical text databases. Some studies also made use of a taxonomy to support summarization. Endres-Niggemeyer, Hertenstein, Villiger and Ziegert (2001) constructed an ontology for WWW summarization in Bone Marrow Transplantation. A lexical database WordNet was used to generalize concepts and identify topics of texts in a text summarization system SUMMARIST (Hovy & Lin, 1999).

In this work, the taxonomy played three important roles in the summarization process:

- To filter out non-concept terms;
- To specify the important concepts in the domain;
- To categorize concepts into different subjects.

Thus, the concept clusters presented in the summary are organized by subject using the taxonomy. This facilitates user browsing by giving them an initial overview of the covered subjects in the summary and helping them to locate the subjects of interest quickly. The taxonomy was constructed using a semi-automatic method.

In this work, a sample of 3214 dissertation abstracts indexed under *sociology, PhD degree* and *year of publication 2001* was retrieved from the Dissertation Abstracts International database and used as the source of concepts for constructing the taxonomy. The 1-word terms and multi-word terms (n=2, 3, 4 and 5) were extracted from the 3214 dissertation abstracts using the term extraction method described in Section 4.3.1. Then only the high frequency terms were retained – the 1-word terms must occur in at least 4 abstracts and the multi-word terms must occur in at least 2 abstracts. So the taxonomy construction involved term filtering and term classification in addition to term extraction. The 1-word terms and multi-word terms were refined manually by two domain experts to remove the non-concept terms (e.g. indicator phrases, common phrases etc.). These refined terms were considered important concepts in the sociology domain and used for constructing the taxonomy. Finally, the 1-word concepts were considered *main concepts* and categorized into different subjects (top-level subjects) and sub-subjects (second-level subjects) by the two domain experts.

To categorize the main concepts (1-word concepts), two existing thesauri in the sociology domain were consulted - *UNESCO Thesaurus, Humanities and Social Science Electronic Thesaurus* (HASSET). The UNESCO Thesaurus (http://www.ulcc.ac.uk/unesco/) is an online controlled vocabulary including subject terms, developed by the United Nations Educational, Scientific and Cultural Organization. HASSET (http://www.data-archive.ac.uk/search/hassetAbout.asp) is a subject thesaurus developed by the UK Data Archive initially based on the UNESCO thesaurus. Mainly based on the UNESCO Thesaurus, nine subjects and some sub-subjects under these subjects were defined in the taxonomy as follows.

1. Education
2. Science and Technology
    2.1 Medical sciences
    2.2 Science and technology (others)
3. Culture
    3.1 History, culture and language
    3.2 Religion
    3.3 Leisure
    3.4 Philosophy and ethics
4. Social and human sciences
    4.1 General social sciences
    4.2 Social problems
    4.3 Social welfare
    4.4 Social structure
    4.5 Social relations
    4.6 Social change and development
    4.7 Race and ethnicity
    4.8 Population
    4.9 Family and family planning
    4.10 Human settlements and land use
5. Information and communication
6. Politics and law
    6.1 Politics and government
    6.2 Law and human rights
7. Economics
    7.1 Economics
    7.2 Industry, agriculture and services
    7.3 Organizing and management
    7.4 Labor and personnel management
8. Psychology
    8.1 State of mind
    8.2 Higher mental processes
    8.3 Psychology
9. Geographic areas and countries

In addition, some concepts were found difficult to categorize into any of the above subjects. An additional category was created to contain general concepts. This category was further categorized into six sub-categories as follows (mainly according to the types of the concepts rather than subject areas):

10. General concepts

    10.1   Performance, quality and quantity

    10.2   Occurrence, risk and safety

    10.3   Circumstance and situation

    10.4   General scientific approach

    10.5   General persons

    10.6   General actions

4.5.2 Information Combination and Organization

In this step, the four kinds of information, i.e. *research concepts* and *their research relationships*, *contextual relations* and *research methods*, are combined and organized to generate the final summary. The summary is presented in an interactive Web-based interface rather than in traditional plain text so that it not only provides an overview of the topic but also allows users to zoom in and explore more details of interest. A compression rate in terms of the number of the words is specified to determine the length of the generated summary.

Based on the hierarchical structure of the variable-based framework, the four kinds of information are presented at three levels of generality:

- The top level – the summarized information;
- The second level – the specific information extracted from each dissertation abstract;
- The third level – the original dissertation abstracts.

The three levels are linked by hyperlinks. The user can click on the hyperlinks to access the more detailed information at the lower levels.

The summarized information at the top level is presented in the main window and viewed as the main summary. For the experimental evaluation (reported in Section 5.4), two presentation formats were used to present the summarized information: (1) *SYSTEM 1* summary was generated without the aid of the taxonomy; and (2) *SYSTEM 2* summary was generated with the aid of the taxonomy. At the second level, the specific information extracted from the original dissertation abstracts is presented in separate pop-up windows of the main window. At the third level, the original abstracts are presented in separate pop-up windows.

In the main window, a template is used to combine and present the four kinds of summarized information (see Figure 4-6). In the template, the number of dissertation abstracts being summarized is indicated first. The four kinds of information are organized separately – *contextual relations* and *research methods* are presented first followed by *research concepts* and *their research relationships*. Contextual relations are presented as a list of keywords (e.g. *perception*, *context*, and *hypothesis*). Research methods are presented as a list of uniform terms (e.g. *quantitative research*, *field work*, and *regression analysis*). Research concepts are presented as concept clusters labeled by main concepts. Only concept clusters with high document frequency are presented in the main summary. The others are truncated to satisfy the compression rate of the summary. The relationships associated with the main concept are presented as a list of simple sentences below the concept list in the cluster.

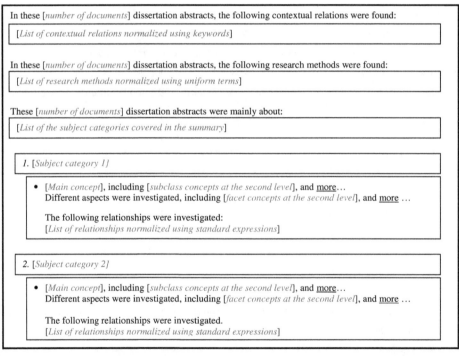

Figure 4-6. Template for combining and presenting the summarized information

In the SYSTEM 1 summary illustrated in Figure 4-7, the concept clusters are arranged in descending order of the document frequency of their labels (main concepts). The higher document frequency indicates the more important information that was repeated in many dissertation abstracts. In the SYSTEM 2 summary in Figure 4-8, the concept clusters are arranged by subject based on the taxonomy. Moreover, the non-concept terms not found in the taxonomy (e.g. *type*, *level*, and *rate*) are removed from the summary, and the important sociology concepts found in the taxonomy are highlighted in red. To control the number and size of the subjects, either the first-level subjects or the second-level subjects are used depending on the number of high frequency concept clusters appearing in the summary. If the number is more than 100, the categorization is based on the first-level subjects. Otherwise it is based on the second-level subjects.

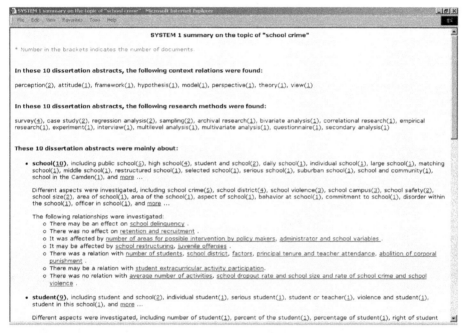

Figure 4-7. A SYSTEM 1 summary generated *without* the aid of the taxonomy on the topic of "school crime"

For each concept cluster, only the main concept and some of the second level concepts in the concept cluster (see Figure 4-5) are presented, rather than all the concepts. The main concept is displayed first followed by the second-level concepts occurring in at least two documents. The second-level concepts are divided into two subgroups – *subclass concepts* and *facet concepts*. For each subgroup, the 2-word, 3-word, 4-word and 5-word concepts whose document frequencies are above or equal to 2 are displayed in sequence. If the number of the concepts in each subgroup is more than 20, the longer concepts that represent more specific meaning are cut off. If the number of the concepts in each subgroup is less than 2, two concepts occurring in one document are displayed instead. Moreover, two separate pop-up windows are used to display all the subclass and facet concepts.

99

They are linked with the main window through two hyperlinks labeled "more" in the subclass concept subgroup and facet concept subgroup.

Figure 4-8. A SYSTEM 2 summary generated *with* the aid of the taxonomy on the topic of "school crime"

For each concept, the number of documents is given in parentheses. It is clickable and linked to a list of documents sharing a given concept in a separate pop-up window (see Figure 4-9). For each document, the title, research concepts, contextual relations and research methods are displayed.

After the concept list, the relationships associated with the main concept are presented as a list of sentences. Each sentence represents a type of relationship that is normalized, conflating different variable concepts found in the dissertation abstracts (reported in Section 4.4.3). When the mouse moves over a variable concept, the original expression of the relationship involving the concept is displayed in a pop-up box. The concept is also clickable and linked to the document describing it and its relationship in a separate pop-up window (see Figure 4-10). For the document, the title, the original sentence describing the relationship (highlighted in green), and adjacent sentences are displayed.

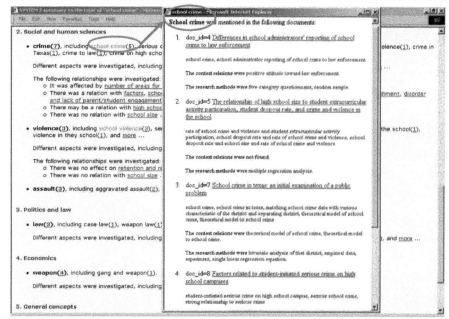

Figure 4-9. A list of summarized single documents sharing a given concept in a pop-up window

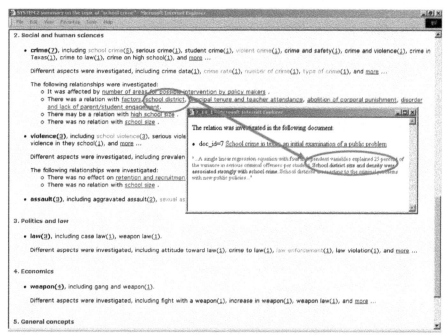

Figure 4-10. A summarized single document describing a relationship in a pop-up window

In Figure 4-9 and 4-10, the title of the document is also clickable and is linked to the original dissertation abstract in another separate pop-up window (see Figure 4-11).

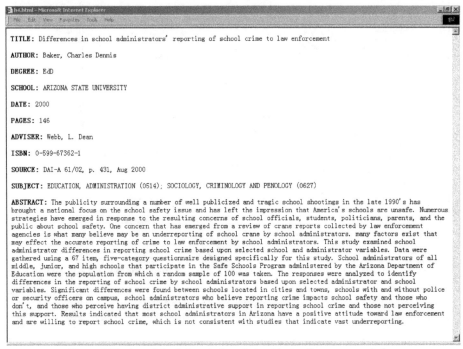

Figure 4-11. An original dissertation abstract in another pop-up window

4.6 Summary and Conclusion

This chapter has detailed the automatic method for summarizing a set of sociology dissertation abstracts. The summarization method involves several major processing steps, including:

(1) *Macro-level discourse parsing of each dissertation abstract*
An automatic macro-level discourse parsing method was developed using the C5.0 decision tree induction program and cue phrases found at the beginning of sentences to segment each dissertation abstract into five sections – *background, research objectives, research methods, research results* and *concluding remarks*.

(2) *Information extraction from the micro-level discourse structure of each dissertation abstract*

Four kinds of information – *research concepts* and *their research relationships, contextual relations* and *research methods* were extracted from the micro-level discourse structure of each dissertation abstract. An automatic information extraction method was developed to extract single-word and multi-word terms according to their syntactic patterns and extract research relationships between concepts using pattern-matching. Research concept terms were selected from the *research objectives* and *research results* sections. Research method terms and contextual relation terms were identified using indicator phrases.

(3) *Information Integration across different dissertation abstracts*

An automatic information integration method was developed involving concept clustering and generalization as well as relationship normalization and conflation. Similar concepts at different generality levels were identified and clustered based on their syntactic variations and generalized using the broader concepts. Then a cluster of generalized concepts was integrated together in a new sentence. Different surface expressions for the same types of relationships about similar concepts were normalized using a standard expression and conflated together. Similar research method terms and contextual relation terms were normalized using uniform terms.

(4) *Information presentation in a Web-based user interface*

A presentation method was developed to combine the four kinds of information using a template, organize them using a taxonomy and present them in a Web-based user interface. The Web-based interface had three hierarchies which were connected through hyperlinks: the summarized information was presented at the top level, specific information extracted from each dissertation abstract was presented at the second level, and the original dissertation abstract was at the third level.

Chapter 5

Evaluation and Results

5.1 Overview

This chapter reports the evaluation of the accuracy of the summarization method and the quality of the summaries generated. The quality of the final summaries depends on the accuracy and usefulness of each major step in the summarization process. Thus the summarization method was evaluated on two levels:

(1) accuracy and usefulness of each major summarization step;

(2) overall quality and usefulness of the final summaries.

There are two types of evaluation methods used in text summarization – intrinsic and extrinsic. In intrinsic evaluation, the summary's quality is assessed directly based on an analysis of the summary. In extrinsic evaluation, the summary's quality is assessed indirectly depending on its effect on the completion of some tasks (Jones & Galliers, 1996).

Intrinsic evaluation was carried out to assess each major step in this summarization method, since Mani (2001c) suggested using intrinsic evaluation at the early development stage of a summarization system. This was accomplished by comparing the system-generated output against the human codings. The evaluated summarization steps include macro-level discourse parsing, information extraction, and information integration.

The quality and usefulness of the final multi-document summaries in this work was also assessed intrinsically using a user evaluation. There is a lack of appropriate methods for evaluating multi-document summaries (Schlesinger et al., 2003). Existing tasks designed for extrinsic evaluations (e.g. relevance assessment task, categorization task) were mainly used for single-document summaries. It is difficult to design a reasonable task which reflects real-world users' goals to evaluate multi-document summaries.

In the intrinsic user evaluation, users were asked to assess the quality of the summaries and their usefulness for specific purposes, by comparing two types of the variable-based summaries generated using the summarization method – with and without the use of a taxonomy – against two types of sentence-based summaries – one generated by extracting only the research objective sentences from each dissertation abstract, and another generated by a state-of-the-art system, MEAD (Radev, Blitzer, Winkel, Allison & Topper, 2003), that uses a sentence extraction method. No human reference summaries were used in this evaluation, since it is time-consuming and mentally strenuous work for human abstractors to create multi-document summaries.

The evaluation was divided into three phases:

- Phase I aimed to address three specific questions based on a sample of 50 dissertation abstracts.
  - Q1: How accurate is the automatic macro-level discourse parsing?
  - Q2: Is the macro-level discourse parsing useful for identifying the more important concepts?
  - Q3: How accurate is the automatic extraction of research concepts, relationships between concepts, contextual relations and research methods?
- Phase II aimed to address a specific question based on 20 sets of dissertation abstracts.
  - Q4: How accurate is the automatic information integration method for integrating similar concepts?
- Phase III aimed to address two specific questions based on 20 real research topics provided by 20 sociology researchers.
  - Q5: Is the taxonomy useful for organizing the information?
  - Q6: Is the quality of the variable-based summary good?
  - Q7: Is the variable-based summary useful for users?

5.2 Phase I : Evaluation of Macro-level Discourse Parsing and Information Extraction

5.2.1 Evaluation Design

A set of dissertation abstracts (3214 records) indexed under *sociology*, *PhD* degree and *year of publication 2001* were retrieved from the Dissertation Abstracts International database, and the 300 abstracts for the system development were removed from them (see Section 3.2). Then 50 structured abstracts and 10 unstructured abstracts were selected using a random table from the set. Seven human coders, who were social science graduate students, as well as two experts – I and a faculty member in the School of Communication and Information, Nanyang Technological University, Singapore, carried out the following coding tasks:

- Coding of sentence categories by four human coders for evaluating the accuracy of the macro-level discourse parsing;

- Coding of concepts at three importance levels by three human coders for evaluating the usefulness of the macro-level discourse parsing;

- Coding of *contextual relations, research methods*, and *relationships between research variables* by the two experts for evaluating the accuracy of the information extraction.

To evaluate the accuracy of the *automatic macro-level discourse parsing*, four human coders were asked to manually assign each sentence in each structured abstract to one of the five predefined sections or categories – *background, research questions, research methods, research results*, and *concluding remarks*. To simplify the coding, each sentence was assigned to only one category, though some sentences could arguably be assigned to multiple categories or no category at all. For the 10 unstructured abstracts, the four human coders were asked to identify only the *research objective* sentences. The automatic macro-level discourse parsing was performed in two phases – (1) assign each sentence to a section or category using the decision tree classifier; and (2) improve the categorization using cue phrases found at the beginning of sentences. Although it is difficult to segment an unstructured abstract into the five standard sections, nevertheless the system will forcedly assign each sentence in the unstructured abstracts to a section or category. The categories assigned by the system were compared against the categories assigned by the four human coders.

To evaluate the accuracy of the *automatic extraction of research concepts*, three human coders were asked to extract all the *important concepts* from the whole text of each abstract (structured or unstructured), and from these to identify the *more important concepts* and then the *most important concepts*, according to the focus of the dissertation research. The human-extracted concepts at three importance levels were used to assess the accuracy of the automatic extraction of research concepts. A coding scheme for manual concept extraction is given to the human coders. For both the structured and unstructured abstracts that have been automatically parsed, the terms relating to research concepts were extracted by the system from three different combinations of sections:

- Extracting from the *research objectives* section (section 2) only;

- Extracting from the *research objectives + research results* sections (section 2 & 4);

- Extracting from all sections (the whole text).

The system-extracted concepts for the above three combinations were compared against the concepts extracted by the human coders at three importance levels.

The accuracy of the *automatic extraction of relationships between variables, contextual relations and research methods* was evaluated based on the 50 structured abstracts only. Since these three kinds of information are somewhat ambiguous and difficult for coders to identify in text consistently without extensive training, it was decided to use two experts to do the coding for this evaluation. From the two experts' codings, a "gold standard" was constructed by taking the agreements in the codings. The differences in the codings were resolved through discussion between the coders.

5.2.2 Evaluation Results for Macro-level Discourse Parsing

To evaluate the accuracy of the macro-level discourse parsing, two measures were used to calculate the inter-coder agreement between four codings – percentage agreement and Cohen's Kappa (Cohen, 1960). Cohen's Kappa is often used to measure inter-coder agreement for nominal categories. It is considered an improvement over percentage agreement since it takes chance agreement into account. Kappa has a range from 0 to 1.00 – 1.00 indicating prefect agreement, and 0 indicating purely chance agreement. The higher the value of Kappa, the stronger the agreement. Generally, a Kappa value of more than 0.7 is considered satisfactory (Bakeman & Gottman, 1986). The percentage agreement and Kappa values between every two coders and between the system and each coder were calculated using the SPSS statistical software and given in Table 5-1. Note that the percentage agreement between the system and the coder is also known as the accuracy of the system.

Table 5-1. Kappa values and percentage agreement between every two coders, and between the system and each coder for the 50 structured abstracts

	Coder 1	Coder 2	Coder 3	Coder 4	System
Coder 1	-	0.818(86.17%)	0.750(80.90%)	0.691(76.28%)	0.520(64.16%)
Coder 2	-	-	0.715(78.00%)	0.690(76.02%)	0.496(61.79%)
Coder 3	-	-	-	0.743(80.11%)	0.539(65.74%)
Coder 4	-	-	-	-	0.494(61.92%)
Average		**0.735(79.58%)**			**0.512(63.40%)**

- *Figures in bracket indicate percentage agreement.*

The average inter-coder agreement of Kappa=0.74 (79.6% agreement) is considered satisfactory as it is higher than the generally applied Kappa criterion of 0.70. However, the average agreement of

0.51 (63.4% accuracy) between the system and the human coder is lower. The automatic categorization method was not nearly as accurate as the human coders' manual categorization.

Since the summarization method focused on the *research objectives* and *research results* sections to extract more important research information, the identification of these two sections are more important. The accuracy of the system for identifying *research objectives* and *research results* sections from the 50 structured abstracts is reported in Table 5-2. The system obtained a high accuracy of 91.4% in identifying the *research results* section, but obtained a lower accuracy of 62.6% in identifying the *research objectives* section. It also worked well in identifying the *research objectives* and *research results* sections together with a high accuracy of 90.8%.

Although the unstructured abstracts are hard to segment into the five standard sections, the *research objective* section is still discernable in most of them. The accuracy of the system for identifying the *research objectives* section from the 10 unstructured abstracts is reported in Table 5-3. Although the system obtained a lower accuracy of 54.3% in identifying the *research objectives* section in the unstructured abstracts, compared with the accuracy of 62.6% for the structured abstracts, it would still be useful to perform discourse parsing to identify *research objectives* in the unstructured abstracts.

Table 5-2. Accuracy (percentage agreement) of the system in identifying the *research objectives* and *research results* sections in the 50 *structured* abstracts

Coder	*Research objectives* section (section 2)	*Research results* section (section 4)	*Research objectives + research results* sections (section 2 & 4) *
Coder 1	71.13%	90.61%	92.69%
Coder 2	62.39%	90.95%	89.97%
Coder 3	58.82%	92.28%	90.38%
Coder 4	58.21%	91.67%	90.11%
Average	**62.64%**	**91.38%**	**90.79%**

* *The research objectives and research results sections were combined together.*

Table 5-3. Accuracy (percentage agreement) of the system in identifying *research objectives* in the 10 *unstructured* abstracts

Coder	*Research objectives* section (section 2)
Coder 1	56.3%
Coder 2	54.5%
Coder 3	62.5%
Coder 4	43.8%
Average	**54.3%**

During the development of the decision tree classifier (described in Section 4.2.1), the selected decision tree model (Model 2) had obtained a high accuracy of 72%. So the accuracy obtained in this evaluation stage (63%) is worse than expected. This is possibly because the indicator words used as the attributes in the decision tree model were extracted both from the training set and test set used in the development stage. The evaluation documents contained new indicator words not found in the early training and test sets. In addition, during the development stage, both the training and test documents were coded by myself. Since the system was trained on my manual coding, it will be slightly less accurate in predicting other people's codings. In future, a big training set with more than one human codings will be used to improve the categorization accuracy of the system. Other machine learning techniques such as Support Vector Machine (SVM) and Naïve Bayes will also be investigated.

5.2.3 Evaluation Results for Extraction of Research Concepts

5.2.3.1 Evaluation Measures

To measure the accuracy of information extraction, measures of precision, recall and F-measure were used. Recall is a measure of completeness of extraction, whereas precision measures the correctness of the extracted information.

Precision is calculated for each document as the number of distinct system-extracted concepts matched to one or more human-extracted concepts divided by the total number of distinct system-extracted concepts in the document:

- Precision =

$$\frac{\textit{Number of distinct system-extracted concepts matched to one or more human-extracted concepts}}{\textit{Total number of distinct system-extracted concepts}}$$

Recall is calculated for each document as the number of distinct human-extracted concepts matched to one or more system-extracted concepts divided by the total number of distinct human-extracted concepts in the document.

- Recall =

$$\frac{\textit{Number of distinct human-extracted concepts matched to one or more system-extracted concepts}}{\textit{Total number of distinct human-extracted concepts}}$$

To obtain a single performance measure, the weighted harmonic mean of precision and recall is calculated as F-measure (Van Rijsbergen, 1979, p.174; Chinchor, 1995).

- F-measure = $\dfrac{2 * \textit{Precision} * \textit{Recall}}{\textit{Precision} + \textit{Recall}}$

In the above formula, precision and recall are assigned the same weight. The higher the F-measure, the better the effectiveness of the system in extracting important concepts.

The problem for calculating precision and recall is how to measure the degree of match between system-extracted concepts and human-extracted concepts. There are four possible types of matches between a system-extracted concept and a human-extracted concept:

(1) A system-extracted concept matches a human-extracted concept exactly.

(2) A system-extracted concept is covered by a human-extracted concept completely, for example, the system-extracted concept "*language ability*" and the human-extracted concept "*English language ability*". This can be considered an exact match for calculating precision.

(3) A human-extracted concept is covered by a system-extracted concept completely, for example, the system-extracted concept "*language ability*", and the human-extracted concept "*ability*". This can be considered an exact match for calculating recall.

(4) There are one or more (but not all) overlapping words between a system-extracted concept and a human-extracted concept, for example, the system-extracted concept "*Chinese language ability*", and the human-extracted concept "*English language ability*". This can be considered a partial match both for calculating precision and recall.

In this work, four levels of measures were used in calculating precision, recall and F-measure.

- *Level 1*, in which only exact match is considered a match. This gives a very strict estimate of precision and recall by counting the exact matches (type 1) only.

- *Level 2*, in which concept coverage is also considered a match. This is more lenient than *Level 1* by counting not only the exact matches (type 1) but also concept coverage (type 2 for precision and type 3 for recall).

- *Level 3*, in which partial matches are weighted. This gives more reasonable estimate of precision and recall by using weight to reflect the degree of match between a system-extracted concept and a human-extracted concept.

- *Level 4*, in which a partial match is considered a match. This gives a very lenient estimate of precision and recall by counting all four types of matches.

Among the four levels of measures, *Level 3* is in my opinion the most reasonable. Using it, the four types of matches were considered but assigned different weight values. To calculate the match weight, two key-based similarity functions were used as follows:

- Concept similarity value for calculating precision =

Number of common keywords between a system-extracted concept and a human-extracted concept
Number of keywords in a system-extracted concept

- Concept similarity value for calculating recall =

Number of common keywords between a system-extracted concept and a human-extracted concept
Number of keywords in a human-extracted concept

* Note that keywords are non-stop single words.

Using the above similarity function to calculate the match weight for precision, match type 1 and 2 both obtained the highest weight 1, and type 3 and 4 obtained weights from 0 to 1. If a system-extracted concept matches more than one human-extracted concept, the maximum concept similarity value is selected as the weight.

Using the above similarity function to calculate the match weight for recall, match type 1 and 3 both obtained the highest weight 1, and type 2 and 4 obtained weights from 0 to 1. If a human-extracted concept matches more than one system-extracted concept, the highest concept similarity value is selected as the weight.

5.2.3.2 Comparison Different Levels of Measures

Three coders identified the important concepts at three levels of importance (i.e. *important*, *more important* and *most important*). Precision, recall and F-measure were calculated using different levels of measures to compare the system's extraction of research concepts with the human's extraction of important concepts. The extraction was carried out in the whole text of each abstract. Table 5-4 shows the average precision, recall and F-measure for the system's extraction of research concepts from all sections of the 50 structured abstracts for the different levels of measures. Table 5-5 shows the average precision, recall and F-measure for the 10 unstructured abstracts.

Using different levels of measures in calculating precision, recall and F-measure, the values are quiet different. For extracting important concepts in the 50 structured abstracts, the precision ranged from 18% for *Level 1* to 64% for *Level 4* whereas the recall ranged from 48% for *Level 1* to 97% for *Level 4*. The recall (e.g. 48% for *Level 1*) was much higher than the precision (e.g. 18% for *Level 1*), indicating that the total number of system-extracted concepts was much more than human-extracted concepts and only a small percentage of system-extracted concepts (18%) exactly matched the human-extracted important concepts.

Table 5-4. Average precision, recall and F-measure for system concept extraction from all sections of the 50 *structured abstracts* for different levels of measures

Level of measure		For important concepts	For more important concepts	For most important concepts
Level 1	Precision (%)	18.00	8.81	4.03
(only counting exact	Recall (%)	48.33	48.45	47.91
match)	F-value (%)	25.80	14.78	7.39
Level 2	Precision (%)	28.38	16.28	8.76
(also counting concept	Recall (%)	82.26	83.07	84.42
coverage)	F-value (%)	40.99	26.57	15.58
Level 3	Precision (%)	46.18	31.02	20.36
(weighting partial	Recall (%)	89.93	90.93	92.26
match)	F-value (%)	60.44	45.94	33.15
Level 4	Precision (%)	63.55	48.13	35.84
(also counting partial	Recall (%)	96.81	97.74	99.18
match)	F-value (%)	76.54	64.41	52.56

Table 5-5. Average precision, recall and F-measure for system concept extraction from all sections of the 10 *unstructured abstracts* for different levels of measures

Level of measure		For important concepts	For more important concepts	For most important concepts
Level 1	Precision (%)	17.22	6.81	1.24
(only counting exact	Recall (%)	46.17	43.35	46.76
match)	F-value (%)	24.72	11.59	5.41
Level 2	Precision (%)	23.98	11.21	5.7
(also counting con-	Recall (%)	89.79	88.78	92.51
cept coverage)	F-value (%)	36.75	19.36	10.59
Level 3	Precision (%)	39.31	22.62	13.26
(weighting partial	Recall (%)	93.87	92.63	96.52
match)	F-value (%)	54.58	35.90	23.11
Level 4	Precision (%)	56.38	37.67	24.91
(also counting partial	Recall (%)	97.52	97.46	99.39
match)	F-value (%)	71.04	53.98	39.61

Using the more lenient measure *Level 2* that considers concept coverage, the precision increased a little to 28% but the recall increased substantially to 82%. This indicates that most of human-extracted concepts were completely covered by system-extracted concepts, but only a small number of system-extracted concepts were completely covered by human-extracted concepts. Using the weighted measure *Level 3*, the precision increased substantially to 46% but the recall increased a little to 90%, indicating that many system-extracted concepts matched human-extracted concepts partially to different degrees.

The precision of 64% and recall of 97% obtained for the lenient measure *Level 4* were quite good. This indicates that more than half of the system-extracted concepts (64%) had overlap with human-extracted concepts and almost all the human-extracted concepts (97%) had overlap with system-extracted concepts.

For the 10 unstructured abstracts, similar results were found. The difference is that the precision for unstructured abstracts was a little smaller than for structured abstracts, whereas the recall was about the same. This suggests that it is more difficult for the system to extract precise concepts at different levels of importance from unstructured abstracts than from structured abstracts.

In conclusion, the system seldom extracted exactly the same terms as the human coders. The system preferred to extract longer terms (i.e. full concepts) whereas the human coders preferred to extract shorter terms (i.e. main concepts). For each importance level, the system usually extracted more concepts than the human coders. That is to say, the system can extract most of the concepts at different levels of importance specified by the human coders and obtained a high recall, e.g. 90% for important concepts, 91% for the more important concepts and 92% for the most important concepts. But it also extracted some useless concepts which were ignored by the human coders and obtained a moderate level of precision, e.g. 46% for important concepts, 31% for the more important concepts, and 20% for the most important concepts.

5.2.3.3 Comparison for Different Types of Sections

To explore whether the macro-level discourse parsing can improve the accuracy of system concept extraction, the precision and recall for three combinations of the sections were compared, i.e. extracting from the *research objectives* section only, extracting from the *research objectives + research results* sections, and extracting from all five sections. Only the weighted measure *Level 3* was used because it reflects the degree of match between a human-extracted concept and a system-extracted concept. Table 5-6 shows the average precision, recall and F-measure for the system's extraction of research concepts from three types of sections of the dissertation abstracts for the 50 structured abstracts. Note that the set of *important* concepts includes the set of *more important* concept and *most important* concepts. Similarly, the set of *more important* concepts includes the set of *most important* concepts.

For the structured abstracts and considering all *important* concepts, the F-measures obtained for *all five sections* (60%) and for the *research objectives + research results* sections (59%) were similar, and both were better than that obtained for the *research objectives* section (52%). This suggests that important concepts were not focused only in the *research objectives* section, but scattered in all five sections. Therefore, the macro-level discourse parsing may not be helpful for identifying the *important* concepts.

Table 5-6. Average precision, recall and F-measure for system concept extraction from the three types of sections for the 50 *structured abstracts*

Importance level		All five sections	*Research objectives section (section 2)*	*Research objectives + research results sections (section 2 & 4)*
For most impor- tant concepts	Precision (%)	20.36	31.62	23.60
	Recall (%)	92.26	76.06	87.37
	F-measure (%)	33.15	**43.91**	36.80
For more impor- tant concepts	Precision (%)	31.02	44.51	34.28
	Recall (%)	90.93	59.31	78.81
	F-measure (%)	45.94	**50.27**	47.35
For important concepts	Precision (%)	46.18	59.05	49.76
	Recall (%)	89.93	46.65	75.64
	F-measure (%)	**60.44**	51.64	**59.40**

- *Precision, recall and F-measure are based on the weighted measure Level 3;*
- *Bold figures indicate the highest values at each importance level.*

For the *more important* concepts, the F-measure obtained for the *research objectives* section (50%) was a little higher than those for the *research objectives + research results* sections (47%) and for *all sections* (46%). This suggests that the *research objectives* section places a bit more emphasis on the *more important* concepts.

However, for the *most important* concepts, the F-measure (44%) obtained for the *research objectives* section was much higher than those for the *research objectives + research results* section (37%) and for *all sections* (33%). This suggests that the *research objective* section places more emphasis on the *most important* concepts.

A repeated measures analysis of variance (ANOVA) (Tabachnick & Fidell, 1996) was performed using the SPSS statistical software to investigate whether there were significant differences in the average F-measures for the three types of sections of the dissertation abstracts for the *more* and *most important* concepts. For each condition, there were three coders. So the within-documents effects were the different section types and the three coders. The results of the analysis of variance for the most important concept are given in Table 5-7. The results for the more important concept are given in Table 5-8. Because Mauchly's Test of Sphericity gave significant results, the Sphericity Assumption for repeated measures ANOVA was violated (Tabachnick & Fidell, 1996). So the Greenhouse-Geisser estimates (Tabachnick & Fidell, 1996) are reported in the two tables.

For the *most important* concepts (see Table 5-7), there was a significant difference in the average F-measure among the three types of sections (F=30.8, p=1.53E-7). Tukey's HSD test (Kirk, 1982) was performed to test for significant differences for every pair of section types (i.e. pairwise comparisons). The difference between *all sections* (33%) and the *research objectives + research results* sections (37%) was significant (p=5.82E-7). The difference between the *research objectives + research results* sections (37%) and the *research objectives* section (44%) was also significant (p=2.47E-5). On the other hand, there was no significant difference in the average F-measure among the three coders (p=0.32). However, there is significant interaction between the coders and the types of sections (p=1.96E-11).

Table 5-7. Repeated measures ANOVA to test for significant differences in the average F-measures among the three types of sections for the *most important* concepts for the 50 *structured* abstracts

Source of variation	Sum of squares	Degrees of freedom	Mean square	F-ratio	Significance (p)
SECTIONS	9176.475	1.195	7679.424	30.826	1.53E-7 *
Error (SECTIONS)	14586.827	58.552	249.125		
CODER	794.658	1.332	596.630	1.080	0.322
Error (CODER)	36068.397	65.264	552.657		
SECTIONS*CODER	6580.707	1.669	3943.910	39.241	1.96E-11 *
Error (SECTIONS*CODER)	8217.245	81.760	100.504		

- *SECTIONS variable has 3 levels: all sections, research objectives + research results sections, and only research objective section;*
- *CODER variable has 3 levels: coder 1, coder 2, and coder 3;*
- ** indicates significance at the 1% level;*
- *Figures given are Greenhouse-Geisser estimates.*
- *The number of degrees of freedom is equal to the number of observations minus the number of algebraically independent linear restrictions placed on them.*

For the *more important* concepts (see Table 5-8), there was no significant difference in the average F-measure among the three types of sections (p=0.06). But there was a significant difference in the average F-measure among the three coders (p=0.003). Table 5-9 shows the number of the *important*, *more important* and *most important* concepts identified by each coder. Table 5-10 shows the average F-measure for each coder for the *more important* concepts.

From the two tables, it can be seen that coder 1 and 3 were consistent but different from coder 2. As shown in Table 5-9, the number of the concepts at each importance level identified by coder 2 was much bigger than for the other two coders. As shown in Table 5-10, the average F-measures for coder 2 in all sections (52%) and the *research objectives + research results* sections (54%) were much bigger than those for the other two coders, whereas the average F-measure for the *research objective* section (47%) was smaller than for the other two coders.

116

Table 5-8. Repeated measures ANOVA to test for significant differences in the average F-measure among the three types of sections for the *more important* concepts for the 50 *structured* abstracts (with 3 coders)

Source of variation	Sum of squares	Degrees of freedom	Mean square	F-ratio	Significance (p)
SECTIONS	932.282	1.330	700.868	3.265	0.064
Error (SECTIONS)	13991.295	65.179	214.660		
CODER	2821.649	2	1410.824	6.339	0.003*
Error (CODER)	21812.068	93.249	233.912		
SECTIONS*CODER	4936.330	2.411	2047.420	21.840	6.99E-10*
Error(SECTIONS*CODER)	11074.906	118.139	93.745		

- *SECTIONS variable has 3 levels: all sections, research objectives + research results sections, and only research objective section;*
- *CODER variable has 3 levels: coder 1, coder 2, and coder 3;*
- ** indicates significance at the 1% level;*
- *Figures given are Greenhouse-Geisser estimates.*

Table 5-9. Number of the concepts at three importance level identified by each coder

Coder	Important concepts	More important concepts	Most important concepts
Coder 1	656	335	148
Coder 2	`1170	551	266
Coder 3	642	322	140

Table 5-10. Average F-measure for each coder for the *more important* concepts for the 50 *structured* abstracts

Coder	All sections	Research objectives section (Section 2)	Research objectives + research results sections (Section 2 & 4)
Coder 1	41.56	53.89	45.18
Coder 2	**52.44**	**47.49**	**53.94**
Coder 3	43.81	49.44	42.94
Average	45.94	50.27	47.35

To reduce the effect of the inter-coder differences, coder 2 was removed from the coders, and the ANOVA test for the *more important* concepts was performed again and given in Table 5-11. Because Mauchly's Test of Sphericity gave significant results, Greenhouse-Geisser estimates are reported in the table.

For the *more important* concepts (see Table 5-11), there was now a significant difference in the average F-measures among the three types of sections (p=1.13E-4). Tukey's HSD test (Kirk, 1982) was performed to test for significant differences for every pair of section types. The difference between all sections (46%) and the *research objectives + research results* sections (47%) was not significant. But the difference between the *research objectives + research results* sections (47%) and the *research objectives* section (50%) was significant at the 5% level.

117

Table 5-11. Repeated measures ANOVA to test for significant differences in the average F-measure among the three types of sections for the *more important* concepts for the 50 *structured* abstracts (with 2 coders)

Source of variation	Sum of squares	Degree of freedom	Mean square	F-ratio	Significance (p)
SECTIONS	3829.454	1.328	2884.695	13.812	1.13E-4 *
Error (SECTIONS)	13585.284	65.048	208.851		
CODER	165.140	1.000	165.140	0.901	0.347
Error (CODER)	8980.322	49.000	183.272		
SECTIONS * CODER	582.946	1.143	510.033	4.918	0.026 *
Error (SECTIONS* CODER)	5808.108	56.005	103.707		

- *SECTIONS variable has 3 levels: all sections, research objectives + research results sections, and only research objective section;*
- *CODER variable has 2 levels: coder 1 and coder 3;*
- ** indicates significance at the 5% level;*
- *Figures given are Greenhouse-Geisser estimates.*

In addition, the usefulness of the macro-level discourse parsing in unstructured abstracts was also investigated. Table 5-12 shows the average precision, recall and F-measure for the system's extraction of research concepts from the three types of sections of the dissertation abstracts for the 10 unstructured abstracts.

Table 5-12. Average precision, recall and F-measure for system concept extraction from the three types of sections for the 10 *unstructured* abstracts

Importance level		All sections	Research objectives (Section 2)	Research objectives and research results (Section 2 & 4)
For most important concepts	Precision (%)	13.26	20.67	13.99
	Recall (%)	96.52	72.2	91.4
	F-value (%)	23.11	**30.87**	23.95
For more important concepts	Precision (%)	22.62	28.09	22.54
	Recall (%)	92.63	44.98	76.49
	F-value (%)	**35.90**	33.17	34.18
For important concepts	Precision (%)	39.31	43.95	39.84
	Recall (%)	93.87	27.74	71.96
	F-value (%)	**54.58**	33.36	50.51

- *Precision, recall and F-measure are based on the weighted measure Level 3;*
- *Bold figures indicate the highest values at each importance level.*

For the unstructured abstracts and considering all *important* concepts, the F-measure obtained from *all sections* (55%) was a little better than that from the *research objectives + research results* sections (51%) and much better than that from the *research objectives* section (33%). For the *more important* concepts, the highest F-measure obtained from *all sections* (36%) was a little better than those from the *research objectives* section (33%) and from the *research objectives + research results* sections (34%). This suggests that the macro-level discourse parsing is not helpful for identifying the *important concept* and *more important* concepts. For the *most important* concepts, the F-measure obtained from the *research objectives* section (31%) was much better than those from the *research objectives + research results* section (24%) and from *all sections* (23%). This suggests that the *research objectives* section also focuses on the *most important* concepts in unstructured abstracts.

In conclusion, the macro-level discourse parsing was helpful in identifying the *more important* and *most important* concepts in structured abstracts. Although the discourse structure of unstructured abstracts is ambiguous, they also contain a clear *research objectives* section. Discourse parsing for identifying the *research objectives* section should be helpful in identifying the *most important* concepts in unstructured abstracts. Since research concepts are generally found in the *research objectives* section compared to other kinds of concepts in other sections, this suggests that research concepts are more likely to be considered the *most important* concepts.

5.2.3.4 Inter-coder Precision

The inter-coder precision for extracting concepts at three importance levels from all sections of the dissertation abstracts was calculated using the weighted measure *Level 3* that considers the degree of match between two concepts. The inter-coder precision between coder i and coder j is calculated using the following formula:

- $\text{Precision}(\text{coder}_{ij}) =$

$$\frac{\textit{Number of distinct concepts extracted by coder i that match one or more concepts extracted by coder j}}{\textit{Total number of distinct concepts extracted by coder i}}$$

Table 5-13 shows the average inter-coder precision among the three coders for the 50 structured abstracts. Table 5-14 shows the average inter-coder precision among the three coders for the 10 unstructured abstracts. Note that the average precision between the system and each coder is considered the precision of the system (reported earlier in Table 5-6 for the structured abstracts and Table 5-12 for the unstructured abstracts).

For the structured abstracts, the average inter-coder precision for all *important* concepts (70%) was quite good and better than for the *more important* concepts (56%) and for the *most important* concepts (57%). This indicates good agreement on the *important* concepts among the three coders. But for the *more important* concepts and the most important concepts, the agreement decreases. The system's precision for the concepts at each level of importance, i.e. 46% for *important* concepts, 31% for the *more important* concepts, and 20% for the *most important* concepts, was much lower than the average inter-coder precision.

119

Table 5-13. Inter-coder precision among the three coders for the 50 *structured* abstracts

Importance level	Precision	Coder 1	Coder 2	Coder 3	Average
For most important concepts	Coder 1	-	58.95	88.12	
	Coder 2	33.50	-	37.50	56.5
	Coder 3	67.91	52.98	-	
	System	16.86	24.87	19.35	**20.36**
For more important concepts	Coder 1	-	68.85	67.90	
	Coder 2	42.76	-	44.05	56.24
	Coder 3	54.02	59.81	-	
	System	26.99	37.95	28.13	**31.02**
For important concepts	Coder 1	-	84.57	72.55	
	Coder 2	54.60	-	58.13	69.66
	Coder 3	64.79	83.38	-	
	System	39.84	58.08	40.44	**46.18**

Table 5-14. Inter-coder precision among the three coders for the 10 *unstructured* abstracts

Importance level	Precision	Coder 1	Coder 2	Coder 3	Average
For most important concepts	Coder 1	-	43.27	72.42	
	Coder 2	11.04	-	8.67	44.11
	Coder 3	87.06	42.18	-	
	System	11.38	18.12	10.28	**13.26**
For more important concepts	Coder 1	-	58.61	51.76	
	Coder 2	28.57	-	23.84	48.57
	Coder 3	64.39	64.20	-	
	System	20.11	31.49	16.26	**22.62**
For important concepts	Coder 1	-	83.62	55.50	
	Coder 2	50.42	-	44.21	63.71
	Coder 3	62.39	86.09	-	
	System	34.31	54.28	29.33	**39.31**

For the unstructured abstracts, the average inter-coder precision values were 64% for *important* concepts, 49% for the *more important* concepts, and 44% for the *most important* concepts. These were lower than those for the structured abstracts. The system's precision for the concepts at each level of importance, i.e. 39% for *important* concepts, 23% for the *more important* concepts, and 13% for the *most important* concepts, also became worse. This suggests that it is more difficult to identify the important concepts from the unstructured abstracts even for human coders.

Both for the structured and unstructured abstracts, coder 2 is quite different from the other two coders - coder 1 and coder 3. For each importance level, coder 2 obtained much lower inter-coder precisions with the other two coders. This is because coder 2 preferred to extract more concepts at each importance level (see Table 5-9).

For each importance level, the system obtained higher precision for coder 2 than for the other two coders. For example, for the *most important* concepts in the structured abstracts, the system obtained a higher precision of 25% for coder 2 than 17% for coder 1 and 19% for coder 3. This is because coder 2 preferred to extract longer terms than the other two coders and the system also preferred to extract longer terms.

5.2.4   Evaluation Results for Extraction of Contextual Relations and Research Methods

I and a faculty member identified research methods and contextual relations manually in the 50 structured abstracts and discussed differences in the coding to obtain an agreement on the "gold standard". The summarization system identified the terms relating to contextual relations and research methods automatically in the text using indicator phrases. The system-extracted contextual relations and research methods were manually compared against the "gold standard". Binary weighting was used to indicate whether a contextual relation or research method identified by the system was correct or not. The precision and recall were calculated as follows:

- Precision =

$$\frac{\textit{Total number of the "gold standard" terms correctly extracted by the system}}{\textit{Total number of the contextual relations or research methods terms extracted by the system}}$$

  - Result for research methods: 139/143=97.20%
  - Result for contextual relations: 72/84=85.71%

- Recall =

$$\frac{\textit{Total number of the "gold standard" terms correctly extracted by the system}}{\textit{Total number of the "gold standard" terms extracted by the two coders}}$$

  - Result for research methods: 139/194 = 71.65%
  - Result for contextual relations: 72/80 = 90.00%

The system obtained a very high precision of 97% for extracting *research methods* and a smaller one of 86% for extracting *contextual relations*. This indicates that it is effective to use indicator phrases to identify contextual relations and research methods. The precision for extracting *contextual relations* (86%) is lower than that for extracting *research methods* (97%). This is because all the contextual relations were identified using *indicator words* whereas most of research methods were identified using more specific *indicator phrases*. Single words are more likely to have different meanings in different contexts than multi-word terms.

The obtained recall of 72% for extracting *research methods* is not very high. One reason is that the list of indicator phrases used in the work was derived only from the sample of 300 dissertation abstracts was not complete. However, the indicator words for extracting *contextual relations* are a short list containing 13 words (e.g. *context, perception, insight* etc.). It is easy to derive them exhaustively from the sample dissertation abstracts. Thus the recall of 90% for extracting *contextual relations* is much better than that for extracting *research methods* (72%). Another reason for the lower recall is that the system only extracted nouns or noun phrases relating to contextual relations and research methods. The contextual relations and research methods expressed in other grammatical forms were not identified by the system, for example,

(1) Verb

 – *Each participant was __interviewed__ twice.*

 – *A major finding was that both groups __perceived__ the new communication technologies will help Sub-Saharan African development.*

(2) One or more sentences

 – *Eighty adolescents 14-17 years of age, whose parents had divorced within the previous one to four years. Forty subjects had not been hospitalized for psychiatric treatment since the divorce; forty subjects had been hospitalized for psychiatric treatment.*

(3) Adverb

 – *Primary data was obtained from 197 __randomly__ selected households from three representative data.*

 – *Data for this study were gathered __qualitatively__.*

(4) Others

 – *We find a critical __case to study__ the mechanics of these rural experiences.*

5.2.5 Evaluation Results for Extraction of Relationships between Variables

Two experts, I and a faculty member, identified the relationships between research variables manually in the text and negotiated to obtain an agreement on the "gold standard". The system extracted the relationships automatically using 126 pre-constructed relationship patterns. It included two steps: (1) detecting a relationship pattern (i.e. indicator words) in the text using pattern matching and; (2) combining the indicator words with the terms filling the slots to form a complete relationship. The system-extracted relationships were manually compared against the "gold standard". A 3-level weighting was used to indicate whether a relationship extracted by the system was completely correct, partially correct, or not correct at all.

(1) If the system-extracted relationship was not in the "gold standard", it was considered wrong and assigned the weight 0.

(2) If the system-extracted relationship was in the "gold standard" but its variables were not extracted correctly, it was considered partially correct and assigned the weight 0.5;

(3) If the system-extracted relationship was in the "gold standard" and its variables were also extracted correctly, it was considered completely correct and assigned the weight 1.

For the 50 structured dissertation abstracts, the precision and recall were calculated as follows:

- Precision =

Total number of the "gold standard" relationships correctly extracted by the system
Total number of the relationships extracted by the system

= 175/216=81.02%

- Recall =

Total number of the "gold standard" relationships correctly extracted by the system
Total number of the "gold standard" extracted by the coders

=175/319= 54.86%

The system obtained a high precision of 81% for extracting relationships between variables. This indicates that the constructed relationship patterns are specific enough to extract most of relationships correctly. However, the recall of 55% was low. The first reason was that the constructed relationship patterns were too specific and missed many correct relationships. For example, the pattern "<IV> play <DET> (<ADJ>) role in <DV>" cannot recognize the relationship "*local setters and local institutions played as important a role in Indian/white relations as did a weak and limited national state*". The second reason was that the set of the constructed relationship patterns was not complete since it was derived only from the sample of 300 dissertation abstracts. The third reason was that the system only can identify the relationships that were located within sentences and with clear indicator words. For example, the following relationships cannot be extracted by the system:

(1) Relationships across sentences

- *Divorce rates in the United States are high. Extensive research reports the negative effects on the children involved.* (The cross-sentence relationship is "*divorce rates in the United States have negative effects on the children involved.*")

(2) Implied relationships that do not contain clear indicator words and need inferring

- *As a country moves from one stage of the demographic transition to another, the estimated domestic food demand changes.*
- *As income increase, the population growth rate rises due to a falling death rate.*

123

5.3   Phase II : Evaluation of Information Integration

5.3.1 Evaluation Design

In Phase II of the evaluation, 15 research topics on sociology were haphazardly selected from the titles of dissertations. The topics are listed in Table 5-15. For each topic, a set of PhD sociology dissertation abstracts were retrieved from the Dissertation Abstracts International database by using the topic as the search query, and five abstracts were selected to form a document set. Moreover, for five of the topics (i.e. Document set ID 11 to 15), additional five abstracts were selected for each of them and combined with the previously chosen five abstracts to form a second bigger document set. These bigger document sets were used to examine the difference in information integration between small (5-document) and bigger (10-document) sets. For each abstract, the important concepts were extracted from the *research objectives* and *research results* automatically by the system.

Table 5-15. Topics used in Phase II evaluation

Document set ID	Topic	Number of retrieved documents	Number of selected documents
1	attachment and marriage	483	5
2	racial socialization	12	5
3	adolescent suicide	13	5
4	demographic transition	16	5
5	school success	21	5
6	intermarriage	25	5
7	unemployment	129	5
8	health policy	36	5
9	family planning	45	5
10	mass media	49	5
11	rural development	64	5
12	juvenile delinquency	71	5
13	welfare reform	89	5
14	substance abuse	106	5
15	childhood sexual abuse	57	5
16	rural development	64	5 + 5 (from set 11)
17	juvenile delinquency	71	5 + 5 (from set 12)
18	welfare reform	89	5 + 5 (from set 13)
19	substance abuse	106	5 + 5 (from set 14)
20	childhood sexual abuse	57	5 + 5 (from set 15)

Human coders were asked to examine the list of concepts extracted by the system and identify similar concepts in each document set. The similar concepts were clustered and generalized by assigning a category label to each cluster. A coding scheme for the manual integration of similar concepts is given to the human coders. The human coders were also social science graduate students at Nanyang Technological University, Singapore. Each document set was coded by two human coders, and each human coder coded three 5-document sets and one 10-document set on different topics.

5.3.2 Evaluation Results for Concept Integration

5.3.2.1 Number and Size of Concept Clusters

Table 5-16 shows the number and average size of clusters created by each coder and the system for each of the 20 document sets.

Table 5-16. Number and average size of clusters created by each coder and the system for each of the 20 document sets

Document set ID	Coder 1		Coder 2		Average of two coders		System	
	Number	Size	Number	Size	Number	Size	Number	Size
1	8	10.4	1	25	4.5	17.7	17	5.5
2	3	17	1	14	2	15.5	18	4.7
3	5	12.6	2	13.5	3.5	13.1	16	6.3
4	5	12.8	5	10.2	5	11.5	24	5.9
5	7	11.4	5	13.8	6	12.6	16	9.2
6	5	11.6	7	8.7	6	10.2	15	4.9
7	4	12	5	9.8	4.5	10.9	12	5.1
8	3	12.3	4	7.5	3.5	9.9	23	4.5
9	5	11	7	8.9	6	10.0	22	5.6
10	4	13	8	14	6	13.5	25	6.9
11	4	8.5	5	12.2	4.5	10.4	16	6.3
12	3	11	2	13.5	2.5	12.3	12	7
13	3	10	5	9.8	4	9.9	18	6.7
14	6	6.7	2	17.5	4	12.1	12	6.3
15	3	10.3	2	8	2.5	9.2	8	6.1
Average	**4.5**	**11.4**	**4.1**	**12.4**	**4.3**	**11.9**	**16.9**	**6.1**
16	6	11.8	5	12.2	5.5	12	32	7.3
17	4	20.8	6	18	5	19.4	28	7
18	7	15.3	12	12.1	9.5	13.7	35	8.2
19	6	18.7	5	18.6	5.5	18.7	30	8.1
20	9	11.8	6	6.2	7.5	9.0	36	6.1
Average	**6.4**	**15.7**	**6.8**	**13.4**	**6.6**	**14.6**	**32.2**	**7.3**

On average, the coders created 4 clusters for the 5-document sets and 7 clusters for the 10-document sets, whereas the system created 17 clusters for the 5-document sets and 32 clusters for the 10-document sets. This indicates that the system created many more clusters than the human coders. The average size of the clusters created by the coders was 12 concepts for the 5-document sets and 15 concepts for the 10-document sets, whereas the average size created by the system was 6 concepts for the 5-document sets and 7 concepts for the 10-document sets. The average size of the system-created clusters was almost half of that of human-created clusters. The system created much smaller clusters than the human coders.

The total number of concepts clustered by the coders and the system in each of the 20 document sets is given in Table 5-17.

Table 5-17. Total number of the concepts clustered by each coder and the system for each of the 20 document sets

Document set ID	Total number of concepts clustered by coder 1	Total number of concepts clustered by coder 2	Total number of concepts clustered by the system
1	78	25	71
2	51	14	63
3	58	27	70
4	57	48	92
5	79	67	84
6	53	65	60
7	45	48	45
8	33	32	66
9	47	62	83
10	52	95	114
11	33	45	60
12	32	34	58
13	30	44	78
14	39	33	42
15	30	15	34
Average	45.7		68
16	61	52	155
17	84	94	134
18	96	135	180
19	105	85	139
20	100	38	135
Average	85		148.6

As shown in Table 5-17, for a 5-document set, on average, the system clustered 68 concepts in total whereas the coders clustered 46 concepts in total. For a 10-document set, on average, the system clustered 149 concepts in total whereas the coders clustered 85 concepts in total on average. This indicates that the system was capable of clustering a bigger number of concepts than the human coders. Especially, when the size of the document set increases, the capability of the system becomes stronger.

5.3.2.2   Overall Inter-coder Similarity

For each document set, two sets of clusters were created by two human coders and one set of clusters was created by the system. The similarity measure, which was employed by Macskassy, Banerjee, Davison and Hirsh (1998) and Khoo, Ng and Ou (2002), was used to calculate the overall inter-coder similarity between *coding 1* and *coding 2*. The measure is based on the frequency with which the two coders assigned common pairs of concepts to the same cluster. First, for each coding, all possible pairs of concepts in each cluster were identified to obtain the set of same-cluster-pairs of concepts. Next, the number of common same-cluster-pairs between coding 1 and coding 2 was determined. The total number of unique same-cluster-pairs from coding 1 and coding 2 was also determined, which equals the number of same-cluster-pairs for coding 1 plus the number of same-cluster-pairs for coding 2 minus the number of common same-cluster-pairs between coding 1 and coding 2. The overall similarity between coding 1 and coding 2 was calculated using the following formula:

- Overall similarity =

  Number of common same-cluster-pairs between coding 1 and coding 2
  Total number of unique pairs obtained from coding 1 and coding 2

The overall similarity between two coders and between the system and each coder for each of the 20 document sets is given in Table 5-18.

If the two human coders created the same clusters, the pairs of terms obtained for both codings will be the same, and the similarity value obtained will be 1. The similarity value ranges from 0.04 to 0.44 across the 20 document sets. The average similarity obtained for the 20 document sets was a low 0.19. This means that clustering is a very subjective operation. The average inter-coder similarity obtained for the 10-document sets (0.15) was lower than that for the 5-document sets (0.20). This indicates that human clustering becomes more difficult when the size of the document sets increases. However, there is no difference between the system-coder similarity for the 10-document sets (0.24) and that for the 5-document sets (0.25). This indicates that the system's clustering does not become worse when the size of the document sets increases.

Among the 20 document sets, the average similarity between the system and the coder (0.25) was surprising higher than the average inter-coder similarity (0.19). A Paired-Samples T-test procedure was carried out to compare the system-coder similarity and the inter-coder similarity. The system-coder similarity was found to be significantly better than the inter-coder similarity (p=0.04).

In conclusion, the system identified more clusters than humans. Human-generated clusters are bigger but maybe there is more noise or inconsistency, whereas system-generated clusters are smaller but have a fair amount of overlap with the human-generated clusters in terms of the number of common pairs of terms occurring in the same clusters. Using this measure, the system-generated clusters obtained a higher similarity with the human-generated clusters than the similarity between two human-generated clusters. When the size of the document set increases, the human clustering became a little worse, but the system's clustering was still as good.

Table 5-18. Overall similarity between two coders and between the system and each coder for each of the 20 document sets

Document set ID	Similarity between two coders	Similarity between the system and coder 1	Similarity between the system and coder 2	Average similarity between the system and the coder
1	0.111	0.149	0.533	0.341
2	0.092	0.093	0.137	0.115
3	0.144	0.106	0.137	0.122
4	0.196	0.236	0.274	0.255
5	0.170	0.259	0.085	0.172
6	0.092	0.199	0.123	0.161
7	0.438	0.085	0.171	0.128
8	0.274	0.182	0.131	0.157
9	0.147	0.080	0.123	0.102
10	0.172	0.321	0.452	0.387
11	0.394	0.374	0.602	0.488
12	0.258	0.227	0.550	0.389
13	0.035	0.040	0.403	0.222
14	0.216	0.244	0.698	0.471
15	0.234	0.172	0.433	0.303
Average for the 5-document sets	**0.198**			**0.254**
16	0.136	0.154	0.205	0.180
17	0.258	0.236	0.588	0.412
18	0.163	0.205	0.274	0.240
19	0.173	0.235	0.300	0.268
20	0.038	0.081	0.083	0.082
Average for the 10-document sets	**0.154**			**0.236**
Average for all the document sets	**0.187**			**0.249**
Std. Deviation	0.103			0.127
Significance (p)	**0.042 ***			

- *Note: * indicates significance at the 5% level.*

5.4   Phase III : User Evaluation

5.4.1 Evaluation Design

In Phase III of the evaluation, a user evaluation was carried out to evaluate the overall quality and the usefulness of the final summaries. 20 research topics were obtained from 20 researchers in the field of sociology, who were Master's or PhD research students and faculty members at Nanyang

Technological University, Singapore and the National University of Singapore. Each subject was asked to submit one research topic that he/she was working on or had worked on.

For each topic, a set of PhD sociology dissertation abstracts, including both structured and unstructured abstracts, was retrieved from the Dissertation Abstracts International database using the topic as the search query. The set of dissertation abstracts retrieved for each topic was condensed into a summary. Although the summarization method can in theory condense any number of dissertation abstracts into a summary, a big number of abstracts results in a long summary that is hard for humans to read and evaluate. Moreover, in life, few literature surveys (a kind of multi-document summary) cover more than 200 documents or references. Thus, for the user evaluation, at most 200 abstracts were retained for each topic for summarization.

For each topic, four types of summaries were provided with two kinds of structures – variable-based structure and sentence-based structure. The four types of summaries were:

- **A variable-based summary generated without the aid of a taxonomy:** It focuses on research concepts and their research relationships, as well as research methods and contextual relations. This type of summary was labeled *SYSTEM 1* (see Figure 4-4).

- **A variable-based summary generated with the aid of a taxonomy:** It also focuses on research concepts and their research relationships. Furthermore, based on the taxonomy, non-concept terms were filtered out, important sociology concepts were highlighted in red, and concepts were categorized into different subjects. This type of summary was labeled *SYSTEM 2* (see Figure 4-5).

- **A sentence-based summary generated by extracting the research objective sentences only from each abstract:** It consists of the sentences that were extracted from the *research objective* section of each dissertation abstract. The type of summary was labeled *OBJECTIVES* (see Figure 5-1).

- **A sentence-based summary generated by a state-of-the-art system MEAD:** It consists of the sentences that were ranked as important, according to certain sentence features, in the set of dissertation abstracts. It was created by a state-of-the-art multi-document summarization system MEAD 3.08 (Radev et al., 2003), built by the University of Michigan using a centroid-based cross-document sentence extraction method (Radev et al., 2000). This type of summary was labeled *MEAD* (see Figure 5-2).

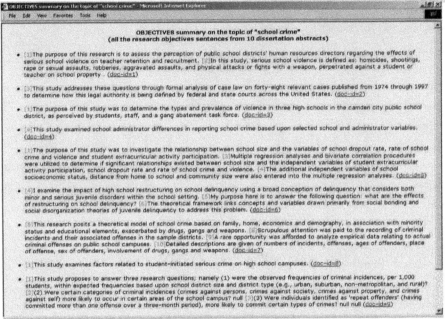

Figure 5-1. An OBJECTIVES summary on the topic of "school crime"

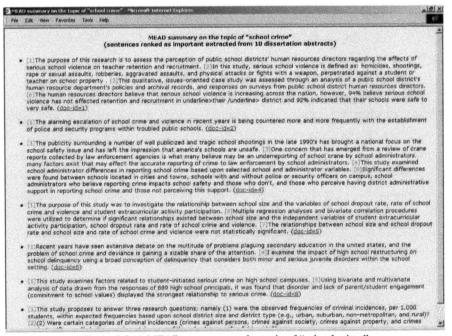

Figure 5-2. A MEAD summary on the topic of "school crime"

The four types of summaries were constructed using the same compression rate of 20%, i.e. the number of words in the summary is approximately 20% of the total number of words in the set of dissertation abstracts. However, it is hard to limit the summaries to a specific length, since the minimum text unit in each summary is not a word. For the two variable-based summaries (SYS-TEM 1 & 2), the minimum text unit is a concept cluster and their length is controlled by filtering out the low document frequency concept clusters. For the sentence-based MEAD, the minimum text unit is a sentence and its length is controlled by filtering out the low ranked sentences. For the sentence-based OBJECTIVES, its length is fixed, including all the sentences belonging to the *research objectives* section. Thus the compression rate of each summary is only approximately 20%. An example of the three types of summaries for the topic of "school crime" (SYSTEM 2, OBJECTIVES, and MEAD) is given in Appendix I.

The 20 research topics used in the user evaluation are listed in Table 5-19.

Table 5-19. Research topics used in Phase III user evaluation

Topic ID	Topic	Number of documents	Number of words	Compression rate (%) (in terms of the number of words)			
				SYSTEM 1	SYSTEM 2	OBJEC-TIVES	MEAD
1	social support	200	62,432	20	19.8	20	19.6
2	inter-cultural communication	64	20,391	20	20	18.8	19.6
3	internet use	20	6,435	19.8	19.6	18.1	20.2
4	inter-cultural adaptation	15	4,467	20.0	19.3	22	19.7
5	rural poverty	41	13,221	20	19.9	18.8	19.7
6	computer-mediated communication	34	10,316	20.0	20	17.1	19.5
7	legal system and China	167	55,370	20.0	19.9	12.4	19.8
8	media system	16	5,549	20.0	20.0	26.0	19.7
9	democracy and China	35	11,826	20.0	19.9	21.3	19.8
10	women and Korea	79	27,155	19.8	19.7	21.0	19.7
11	media and migration	33	11,463	19.7	19.8	27.0	19.9
12	ethnicity	200	62,022	19.9	19.9	25.2	19.6
13	European integration	20	7,021	20	19.9	19.4	19.8
14	Globalization	95	31,112	20.0	20.0	23.1	19.8
15	(HIV or AIDS) and politics	29	9,371	19.5	19.9	25.2	19.6
16	knowledge sharing	12	3,810	19.6	19.4	20.6	19.7
17	(social capital or cultural capital or economic capital) and education	165	56,634	20	19.3	21.6%	19.8
18	homosexual or homosexuals	42	10,852	20.0	19.7	18.1	19.6
19	public health care	18	6,050	19.8	19.7	21.3	20
20	ICT or (information communication technology)	18	5,717	20.0	20.0	20.7	19.7
	Average			**19.9**	**19.8**	**20.9**	**19.7**

For each topic, the four types of summaries were compared and evaluated by human subjects (both researchers and general users). Two aspects of the summaries were evaluated:

(1) quality of the summaries, including readability and comprehensibility;

(2) usefulness of the summaries for research-related purposes or general understanding of the topic.

Both quality and usefulness were assessed subjectively by the human subjects. They were asked to score and rank the summaries on different criteria (e.g. readability, comprehensibility and usefulness) and answer some open-ended questions. A questionnaire was used to record the subjects' evaluation. Follow-up interviews were carried out to clarify the subjects' answers in their questionnaire responses.

The design of the questionnaire was based on evaluation criteria used in previous studies (e.g. Mani, 2001c; Minel et al., 1997; Saggion et al., 2002). It is divided into five parts as follows. The complete questionnaire is shown in Appendix II.

- *Part A* evaluates the readability of the four summaries according to six criteria – presence of vacuous or general information, presence of duplicate information, presence of dangling anaphor, fluent, concise and coherent;
- *Part B* evaluates the comprehensibility of the four types of summaries according to two criteria – understandability and indication of the main ideas of the topic.
- *Part C* evaluates the usefulness of the four types of summaries for a specific purpose.
- *Part D* examines the user's ranking and preference for the four types of summaries to obtain an overall evaluation.
- *Part E* examines the user's preference for the structure of the summaries, usefulness of the taxonomy, and preference between the two sentence-based summaries, using in-depth questions.

Since the four types of summaries were generated from the same source documents and the subjects had to read each of the summaries, there may be carry-over effects from the summaries read earlier. After the subject has read the first summary, familiarity with the first summary and its content may influence the subject's reading and assessment of the subsequent summaries. Also the subject may not read the subsequent summaries as thoroughly. To compensate for this, four presentation orders were used in the user evaluation to present the four types of summaries:

(1) SYSTEM 1 → SYSTEM 2 → OBJECTIVES → MEAD

(2) SYSTEM 1 → SYSTEM 2 → MEAD → OBJECTIVES

(3) OBJECTIVES → MEAD → SYSTEM 1 → SYSTEM 2

(4) MEAD → OBJECTIVES → SYSTEM 1 → SYSTEM 2

For a particular topic, the four types of summaries were presented in only one order. The presentation order varies from topic to topic. The 20 research topics were divided into four groups. Each group included five topics and was assigned one presentation order.

The first group of subjects was 20 researchers, who were Master's or PhD research students or faculty members at Nanyang Technological University, Singapore, and National University of Singapore. They submitted their research topics for generating the summaries for evaluation and used the summaries for their research-related purposes, e.g. Master's or PhD projects, course works, and teaching purposes. Each researcher read a set of summaries generated for his/her topic, evaluated them and filled in the questionnaire at his/her own time.

A second group of subjects was 40 general users, who were graduate students in the MSc (Information Studies and Knowledge Management) programs taking a research methods course at Nanyang Technological University, Singapore. They were not familiar with the research topics and read the summaries to obtain an overview or general information on the topic. Each general user read a set of summaries for a topic that was assigned to him/her randomly, evaluated them and filled in the questionnaire in one hour. Each of the 20 topics contributed earlier by the researchers was evaluated by two general users.

Each human subject only assessed one set of summaries for one topic. However, whether the assessor was a researcher or a general user, the same presentation order was used to present the four types of summaries for the same topic.

5.4.2 Evaluation Results for Researchers

This section reports the evaluation by 20 researchers in the field of sociology. The data from the questionnaires for the 20 researchers is given in Appendix III.

(1) Readability

The overall readability was scored on a 7-point scale, from 1 indicating unreadable to 7 indicating very fluent. The average scores for the four types of summaries from the 20 researchers are shown in Table 5-20.

SYSTEM 2 obtained the second highest readability score (5.2) among the four types of summaries. It was worse than OBJECTIVES (5.7) but better than MEAD (5.0). This indicates that with the use of a taxonomy for information filtering and organization, the readability of the variable-based summary can be substantially improved, and was better than the set of important sentences generated by MEAD, but still worse than the research objective sentences in OBJECTIVES.

Table 5-20. Average readability scores for the four types of summaries from the 20 researchers

	SYSTEM 1	SYSTEM 2	OBJECTIVES	MEAD
Average score	4.40	**5.20**	**5.70**	5.00
Std. Deviation	1.818	1.576	1.342	1.556

A repeated measures analysis of variance (ANOVA) was performed using the SPSS statistical software to investigate whether there were significant differences in the average readability scores of the four types of summaries. The results are shown in Table 5-21.

Table 5-21. Repeated measures ANOVA to test for significant differences in the average readability scores among the four types of summaries from the 20 researchers

Source of variation	Sum of squares	Degrees of freedom	Mean square	F-ratio	Significance (p)
SUMMARY	17.873	3	5.958	4.036	0.012*
SUMMARY * ORDER	39.796	9	4.422	2.996	0.006*
Error (SUMMARY)	70.854	48	1.476		

- *SUMMARY variable has four levels: SYSTEM1, SYSTEM2, OBJECTIVES, and MEAD;*
- *ORDER variable has four levels: S1→S2→O→M, S1→S2→M→O, O→M→S1→S2, M→O→S1→S2;*
- ** indicates significance at the 5% level;*
- *Figures given are Sphericity Assumed estimates.*

The concept "degrees of freedom" refers to the number of observations with values that can be assigned arbitrarily (Kirk, 1982). In Table 5-21, the number of degrees of freedom is equal to the number of observations minus the number of algebraically independent linear restrictions placed on them (Roscoe, 1975). There are four types of summaries and four presentation orders. Thus, the numbers of degrees of freedom for SUMMARY and ORDER are both equal to 3 (i.e. 4-1=3). The number of degrees of freedom for SUMMARY * ORDER is equal to 9 (i.e. 3*3=9).

There was a significant difference in the average readability scores among the four types of summaries (p=0.012). Turkey's HSD test (Kirk, 1982) was performed to compare the readability of every pair of summary (pairwise comparisons). It was found that only the difference between SYSTEM 2 (5.2) and SYSTEM 1 (4.4) was significant (p=0.008). The differences between SYSTEM 2 (5.2) and OBJECTIVES (5.7), and between SYSTEM 2 and MEAD (5.0), were not significant.

Considering the presentation order of the four types of summaries, there was a significant difference in the average readability scores for the four presentation orders (p=0.006). As shown in Table 5-22, when SYSTEM 2 was presented earlier than MEAD (order 1 & 2), SYSTEM 2 obtained a lower readability score (4.3) than MEAD (5.6). However, when SYSTEM 2 was presented later than MEAD (order 3 & 4), SYSTEM 2 obtained a higher readability score (5.9) than MEAD (4.5). It appears that the summary that was read earlier obtained a lower readability score. However, the readability scores of OBJECTIVES did not change too much among the four presentation orders. This may be because research objectives sentences were easy to read.

Table 5-22. Average readability scores for the four types of summaries for the four presentation orders from the 20 researchers

Order	SYSTEM 1	SYSTEM 2	OBJECTIVES	MEAD
1. S1→S2→O→M	4.00	4.67	5.67	5.67
2. S1→S2→M→O	2.75	4.00	5.00	5.50
Average for 1 and 2	3.38	**4.34**	5.34	**5.59**
3. O→M→S1→S2	4.75	5.25	5.75	5.25
4. M→O→S1→S2	5.67	6.50	6.17	3.83
Average for 3 and 4	5.21	**5.88**	5.96	**4.54**

More detailed questions on different aspects of readability were asked:

Q1: Does the summary contain vacuous or very general information?

Figure 5-3 shows the percentage of researchers who indicated *none*, *a little*, *some*, and *a lot* of "vacuous or very general information" for each of the four summaries.

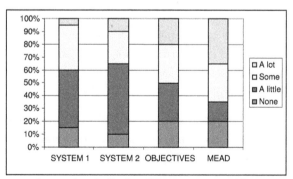

Figure 5-3. Percentage of researchers indicating different amounts of "vacuous or general information" for the four types of summaries

In this aspect, SYSTEM 1 and 2 were better than OBJECTIVES and MEAD. For SYSTEM 1 and 2, 60% and 65% of the researchers ticked *none* or *a little* vacuous information. For OBJECTIVES and MEAD, 50% and 35% of researchers ticked *none* or *a little*.

Q2: Does the summary contain duplicate information?
Figure 5-4 shows the percentage of researchers who indicated *none*, *a little*, *some*, and *a lot* of "duplicate information" for each of the four summaries.

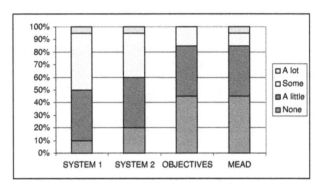

Figure 5-4. Percentage of researchers indicating different amounts of "duplicate information" for the four types of summaries

In this aspect, OBJECTIVES and MEAD were better than SYSTEM 1 and 2. For SYSTEM 1 and 2, 50% and 60% of the researchers ticked *none* or *a little* duplicate information. For OBJECTIVES and MEAD, 85% of the researchers ticked *none* or *a little*.

Q3: Does the summary contain dangling anaphor (e.g. unresolved pronouns)?
Figure 5-5 shows the percentage of researchers who indicated *none*, *a little*, *some*, and *a lot* of "dangling anaphor" for each of the four summaries.

In this aspect, OBJECTIVES and MEAD were better than SYSTEM 1 and 2. For SYSTEM 1 and 2, 55% and 60% of the researchers ticked *none* or *a little* dangling anaphor. For OBJECTIVES and MEAD, 85% of the researchers ticked *none* or *a little*.

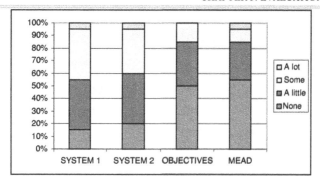

Figure 5-5. Percentage of researchers indicating different amounts of "dangling anaphor" for the four types of summaries

Q4: Is the summary fluent?

Figure 5-6 shows the percentage of researchers who indicated *very fluent, quite fluent, a little,* and *not at all* for each of the four summaries.

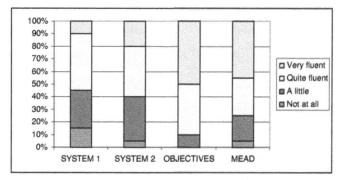

Figure 5-6. Percentage of researchers indicating different degrees of "fluent" for the four types of summaries

In this aspect, OBJECTIVES and MEAD were more fluent than SYSTEM 1 and 2. For SYSTEM 1 and 2, 55% and 60% of the researchers ticked *quite* or *very* fluent. For OBJECTIVES and MEAD, 75% and 90% of the researchers ticked *quite* or *very* fluent.

Q5: Is the summary concise?

Figure 5-7 shows the percentage of researchers who indicated *very concise, quite concise, a little,* and *not at all* for each of the four summaries.

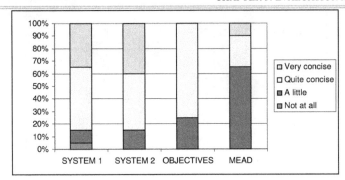

Figure 5-7. Percentage of researchers indicating different degrees of "concise" for the four types of summaries

In this aspect, SYSTEM 1 and 2 were more concise than OBJECTIVES, which was more concise than MEAD. For SYSTEM 1 and 2, 85% of the researchers ticked *quite* or *very* concise. For OB-JECTIVES, 75% of the researchers ticked *quite* concise. For MEAD, 35% of researchers ticked *quite or very* concise.

Q6: Is the summary coherent?

Figure 5-8 shows the percentage of researchers who indicated *very coherent*, *quite coherent*, *a little*, and *not at all* for each of the four summaries.

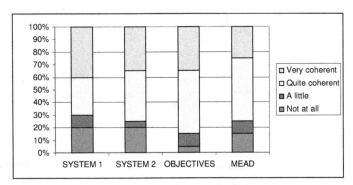

Figure 5-8. Percentage of researchers indicating different degrees of "coherent" for the four types of summaries

In this aspect, there was no much difference among the four summaries. OBJECTIVES was a little more coherent than SYSTEM 2 and MEAD, which were a little more coherent than SYSTEM 1. For OBJECTIVES, 85% of the researchers ticked *quite* or *very* coherent. For SYSTEM 2 and

MEAD, 75% of the researchers ticked *quite* or *very* coherent. For SYSTEM 1, 70% of the researchers ticked *quite* or *very* coherent.

In conclusion, the researchers indicated that SYSTEM 1 and 2 were more concise and contained less vacuous or general information than OBJECTIVES and MEAD. This is because SYSTEM 1 and 2 present important concepts and simple relationship sentences whereas OBJECTIVES and MEAD present complete sentences. On the other hand, the researchers indicated that SYSTEM 1 and 2 contained more duplicate information and dangling anaphor and were less fluent than OBJECTIVES and MEAD. This is because a concept may be assigned to multiple clusters from different perspectives. Moreover, separate concepts are less fluent than complete sentences. Although OBJECTIVES and MEAD both contained important sentences, the researchers indicated that the research objective sentences in OBJECTIVES were more concise and easier to read than the set of important sentences generated by MEAD.

(2) Comprehensibility

The overall comprehensibility was scored on a 7-point scale, from 1 indicating incomprehensible to 7 indicating very comprehensible. The average scores for the four types of summaries from the 20 researchers are shown in Table 5-23.

Table 5-23. Average comprehensibility scores for the four types of summaries from the 20 researchers

	SYSTEM 1	SYSTEM 2	OBJECTIVES	MEAD
Average score	4.75	**5.10**	**5.60**	4.95
Std. Deviation	1.832	1.774	1.095	1.572

SYSTEM 2 obtained the second highest comprehensibility score (5.1) among the four types of summaries. It was worse than OBJECTIVES (5.6) but better than MEAD (5.0). This indicates that with the use of a taxonomy for information filtering and organization, the comprehensibility of the variable-based summary can be improved, and was better than the set of important sentences generated by MEAD, but still worse than the research objective sentences in OBJECTIVES.

A repeated measures analysis of variance (ANOVA) was performed using the SPSS statistical software to investigate whether there were significant differences in the average comprehensibility scores among the four types of summaries. The results are shown in Table 5-24. Because Mauchly's Test of Sphericity gave significant results ($p=0.02$), the Sphericity assumption for repeated measures ANOVA was violated (Tabachnick & Fidell, 1996). Greenhouse-Geisser estimates are reported instead in the table.

Table 5-24. Repeated measures ANOVA to test for significant differences in the average comprehensibility scores among the four types of summaries from the 20 researchers

Source of variation	Sum of squares	Degrees of freedom	Mean square	F-ratio	Significance (p)
SUMMARY	8.540	1.985	4.301	1.748	0.191
SUMMARY * ORDER	36.412	5.956	6.114	2.484	0.044*
Error (SUMMARY)	78.188	31.764	2.461		

- *SUMMARY variable has four levels: SYSTEM1, SYSTEM2, OBJECTIVES, and MEAD;*
- *ORDER variable has four levels: S1→S2→O→M, S1→S2→M→O, O→M→S1→S2, M→O→S1→S2;*
- ** indicates significance at the 5% level;*
- *Figures given are Green-Geisser estimates.*
- *The number of degrees of freedom is equal to the number of observations minus the number of algebraically independent linear restrictions placed on them*

There was no significant difference in the average comprehensibility scores among the four types of summaries (p=0.19). Considering the presentation order of the four summaries, there was a marginally significant difference in the average comprehensibility scores for the four presentation orders (p=0.04). As shown in Table 5-25, when SYSTEM 2 was presented earlier than MEAD (order 1 & 2), SYSTEM 2 obtained a lower comprehensibility score (4.4) than MEAD (5.7). When SYSTEM 2 was presented later than MEAD (order 3 & 4), SYSTEM 2 obtained a higher comprehensibility score (5.6) than MEAD (4.3). It appears that the summary that was read earlier obtained a lower comprehensibility score. However, the comprehensibility scores of OBJECTIVES did not change too much for the four presentation orders. This may be because the research objectives sentences were easy to comprehend.

Table 5-25. Average comprehensibility scores for the four types of summaries for the four presentation orders from the 20 researchers

Order	SYSTEM 1	SYSTEM 2	OBJECTIVES	MEAD
1. S1→S2→O→M	4.67	5.00	5.83	5.67
2. S1→S2→M→O	3.25	3.75	5.25	5.75
Average for 1 and 2	3.96	**4.38**	5.54	**5.71**
3. O→M→S1→S2	4.50	5.25	5.25	4.75
4. M→O→S1→S2	6.00	6.00	5.83	3.83
Average for 3 and 4	5.25	**5.63**	5.54	**4.29**

More detailed questions on different aspects of readability were asked:

Q8: Is the summary easy or hard to understand?

Figure 5-9 shows the percentage of researchers who indicated *very easy*, *quite easy*, *quite hard*, and *very hard* for each of the four summaries.

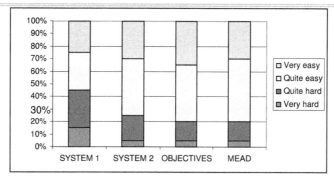

Figure 5-9. Percentage of researchers indicating different degrees of "understandability" for the four types of summaries

In this aspect, OBJECTIVES and MEAD were a little easier to understand than SYSTEM 2, which was much easier to understand than SYSTEM 1. For OBJECTIVES and MEAD, 80% of the researchers ticked *quite* or *very easy* to understand. For SYSTEM 2, 75% of the researchers ticked *quite* or *very easy*. For SYSTEM 1, 55% researchers ticked *quite* or *very easy*.

Q9: Does the summary give a clear indication of the main ideas of the topic?
Figure 5-10 shows the percentage of researchers who indicated *a lot, some, a little*, and *not at all* "indication of the main ideas of the topic" for each of the four summaries.

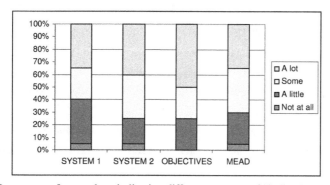

Figure 5-10. Percentage of researchers indicating different amounts of "indication of the main ideas of the topic" for the four types of summaries

In this aspect, there was not much difference among the four types of summaries. SYSTEM 2 and OBJECTIVES were a little better than MEAD, which was a little better than SYSTEM 1. For SYSTEM 2 and OBJECTIVES, 75% of the researchers ticked *some* or *a lot* of indication of the main ideas of the topic. For MEAD, 70% of the researchers ticked *some* or *a lot*. For SYSTEM 1, 60% of researchers ticked *some* or *a lot*.

In conclusion, the researchers indicated that OBJECTVIES and MEAD were a little easier to understand than SYSTEM 1 and 2. This is because complete sentences are easier to understand than separate concepts. Furthermore, the researchers indicated that the research objective sentences in OBJECTIVES can indicate the main ideas of the topic to a greater extent than the set of important sentences generated by MEAD. With the use of the taxonomy for information filtering and organization, SYSTEM 2 was easier to understand and can indicate the main ideas of the topic to a greater extent than SYSTEM 1.

(3) Usefulness

The overall usefulness was scored on a 7-point scale, from 1 indicating useless to 7 indicating very useful. The average scores for the four types of summaries from the 20 researchers are shown in Table 5-26.

Table 5-26. Average usefulness scores for the four types of summaries from the 20 researchers

	SYSTEM 1	SYSTEM 2	OBJECTIVES	MEAD
Average score	5.0	**5.70**	**5.65**	4.9
Std. Deviation	1.864	1.418	1.137	1.714

For research-related work, SYSTEM 2 and OBJECTIVES were more useful than SYSTEM 1 and MEAD. SYSTEM 2 and OBJECTIVES obtained similar usefulness scores (5.7 and 5.65) whereas SYSTEM 1 and MEAD obtained similar scores (5.0 and 4.9). This indicates that with the use of the taxonomy for information organization, the usefulness of the variable-based summary can be improved, and was as useful as the research objective sentences in OBJECTIVES and much more useful than the set of important sentences generated by MEAD. In addition, this indicates that the researchers were more concerned about research objectives than other kinds of information in a dissertation.

A repeated measures analysis of variance (ANOVA) was performed using the SPSS statistical software to test whether there were significant differences in the average usefulness scores among the four types of summaries. The results are shown in Table 5-27.

Table 5-27. Repeated measures ANOVA to test for significant differences in the average usefulness scores among the four types of summaries from the 20 researchers

Source of variation	Sum of squares	Degree of freedom	Mean square	F-ratio	Significance (p)
SUMMARY	8.290	3	2.763	1.271	0.295
SUMMARY * ORDER	26.800	9	2.978	1.370	0.228
Error (SUMMARY)	104.313	48	2.173		

- *SUMMARY variable has four levels: SYSTEM1, SYSTEM2, OBJECTIVES, and MEAD;*
- *ORDER variable has four levels: S1→S2→O→M, S1→S2→M→O, O→M→S1→S2, M→O→S1→S2;*
- *Figures given are Sphericity Assumed estimates.*

There was no significant difference in the average usefulness scores for the four types of summaries (p=0.30). Considering the presentation order of the four types of summaries, there was also no significant difference in the average usefulness scores for the four presentation orders (p=0.23).

The researchers were also asked in what ways each summary was useful for their purpose. Nine aspects of usefulness were listed for the researchers to select. The scores for the different aspects of usefulness are given in Table 5-28.

Table 5-28. Frequency (percentage) of researchers selecting the different aspects of usefulness for the four types of summaries

Usefulness criteria	SYSTEM 1	SYSTEM 2	OBJEC-TIVES	MEAD
1. Gives you an overview of the research area	11 (55%)	**14 (75%)**	11 (55%)	10 (50%)
2. Helps you identify research gaps in the area easily	5 (25%)	6 (30%)	4 (20%)	3 (15%)
3. Helps you identify the documents of interest easily	10 (50%)	10 (50%)	**13 (65%)**	**13 (65%)**
4. Indicates research trends in the area	10 (50%)	9 (45%)	8 (40%)	8 (40%)
5. Indicates similarities among previous studies	**10 (50%)**	**12 (60%)**	3 (15%)	2 (10%)
6. Indicates differences among previous studies	3 (15%)	5 (25%)	5 (25%)	2 (10%)
7. Indicates important concepts in the area	**14 (70%)**	**15 (75%)**	9 (45%)	8 (40%)
8. Indicates important theories, views, or ideas in the area	5 (25%)	7 (35%)	**10 (50%)**	**10 (50%)**
9. Indicates important research methods used in the area	**14 (70%)**	**11 (55%)**	6 (30%)	5 (25%)

- *Bold figures are the higher frequency (percentage) of the summaries for each criterion.*

SYSTEM 1 and 2 were selected by more researchers than OBJECTIVES and MEAD on the following three aspects of usefulness:

- 5. Indicates similarities among previous studies;

- 7. Indicates important concepts in the area;
- 9. Indicates important research methods used in the area.

OBJECTIVES and MEAD were also found to be useful to a lesser extent in the aspect "7. *Indicates important concepts in the area*". However, OBJECTIVES and MEAD were found to be almost useless in the aspect "5. *Indicates similarities among previous studies*" and "9. *Indicates important research methods used in the area*".

OBJECTIVES and MEAD were selected by more researchers than SYSTEM 1 and 2 on the following two aspects of usefulness:

- 3. Helps you identify the documents of interest easily;
- 8. Indicates important theories, views, or ideas in the area.

SYSTEM 1 and 2 were also found to be useful to a lesser extent in the aspect "3. *Helps you identify the documents of interest easily*". However, SYSTEM 1 and 2 were found to be almost useless in the aspect "8. *Indicates important theories, views, or ideas in the area*".

The four summaries were selected by similar numbers of researchers on the following three aspects of usefulness:

- 2. Helps you identify research gaps in the area easily;
- 4. Indicates research trends in the area;
- 6. Indicates differences among previous studies.

All the four summaries were found to be useful in the aspect "6. *Indicates differences among previous studies*", but almost useless in the aspect "2. *Helps you identify research gaps in the area easily*".

SYSTEM 2 was selected by the majority of researchers (70%) among the four summaries on the following aspect:

- 1. Gives you an overview of the research area.

However, the remaining three types of summaries were also found to be useful to a lesser extent in this aspect.

(4) Overall Evaluation

The 20 researchers were asked to rank the four types of summaries. A weighted rank score was calculated for each summary. A weight value of 4 was assigned to the first rank, 3 to the second rank, 2 to the third rank, and 1 to the fourth rank. The researchers were also asked to select one or more summaries that they preferred to use for their research-related work. The ranks and the researchers' preferences are shown in Table 5-29.

Table 5-29. Ranks and preferences for the four types of summaries from the 20 researchers

Rank	SYSTEM 1	SYSTEM 2	OBJECTIVES	MEAD
No.1 (weight=4)	3 (15%)	11 (55%)	6 (30%)	0
No.2 (weight=3)	5 (25%)	2 (10%)	7 (35%)	6 (30%)
No.3 (weight=2)	5 (25%)	6 (30%)	5 (25%)	4 (20%)
No.4 (weight=1)	7 (35%)	1 (5%)	2 (10%)	10 50%)
Weighted rank score	2.15	**3.15**	2.85	1.8
Preference	6 (30%)	**14 (70%)**	11 (55%)	5 (25%)

- *Bold figures indicate the highest weighted rank score and the highest percentage of researchers indicating preference among the four summaries.*

The overall ranking for the four types of summaries based on the weighted rank scores was:

1. SYSTEM 2
2. OBJECTIVES
3. SYSTEM 1
4. MEAD

70% of the researchers indicated preference for SYSTEM 2 for their research-related work. 55% of the researchers indicated preference for OBJECTIVES. Only 25% indicated preference for MEAD.

SYSTEM 1 and 2 used the variable-based structure whereas OBJECTIVES and MEAD used a sentence-based structure. The comments given by the researchers for the two kinds of summary structures (variable-based and sentence-based) are listed in Table 5-30.

In SYSTEM 2, a taxonomy was used to filter out non-concepts terms, highlight important concepts in the domain, and categorize main concepts into different subjects. 70% of the researchers indicated "concept categorization" *quite* or *very useful*, and 75% of the researchers indicated "important concept highlighting" *quite* or very useful. The comments given by the researchers for the usefulness of the taxonomy are listed in Table 5-31.

For the two sentence-based summaries (research objectives sentences in OBJECTIVES and set of important sentences generated by MEAD), the comments given by the researchers for OBJECTIVES and MEAD are listed in Table 5-32.

Table 5-30. Comments by the researchers on the variable-based and sentence-based summary structures

Researchers' comments	Variable-based structure	Sentence-based structure
Positive points	• It is more efficient to give an overview of a topic. • It can help researchers find what has been done easily; • It is well-organized and concise. • It makes easier for researchers to find similar information. • It is useful for information scanning • For quantitative studies which focus on relationships between variables, it is more useful.	• It provides more direct information and is easy to understand; • It is useful to provide more specific and detailed information; • It is useful for understanding research questions and key findings;
Negative points	• It is too brief to provide accurate information on the topic. • The simple terms in the variable-based structure are easy to make users confused and lost.	• Researchers have to read all the sentences in the summary to know what it is about; • Only parts of sentences are presented in the summary, which can not cover all important aspects of a topic; • It is not very well-organized and sometimes confusing; • It is time-consuming to read the complete sentences; • It is too broad to find out the right information.

Table 5-31. Comments by the researchers on the usefulness of the taxonomy

Researchers' comments	Concept categorization	Important concept highlighting
Positive points	• It can make the summary clearer and well-organized; • It give researchers more hints on what the summary is talking about; • It can help researchers to locate information in the categories of interest; • It can make reading easier and browsing quicker and more efficient to save researchers lots of time and efforts; • It can help researchers understand the contents of the summary more quickly; • It makes easier to find similar information.	• It is more helpful to give an indication of important concepts for researchers who are in the preliminary stage of the research. • It can draw researcher's attention to certain concepts; • It can help researchers find something beyond their expectation; • It can help researchers save time and effort by focusing important concepts directly;
Negative points	• The categorization is not accurate and sometimes even misleading. • The categories may be too general to provide effective support for researchers' reading and understanding.	• It seems not very helpful for researchers in in-depth stage, since they have their own opinions on which concepts are important.

Table 5-32. Comments by the researchers for the two types of sentence-based summaries

Researchers' comments	OBJECTIVES	MEAD
Positive points	• It is more concise than MEAD; • It is much more comprehensible and coherent than MEAD; • It often indicates the most important concepts in the dissertation; • It can give a better indication of research gaps in the subject area and which studies have been done to fill that area; • It can indicate research focus of each dissertation more clearly; • It can help users to identify relevant documents more easily; • The researchers are more interested in the central problems of the research; • It can give a more straight indication of the main points of the dissertation. • It can provide an introduction to the previous studies. For a new topic, it is more useful.	• It can provide more detailed information about the research. • For in-depth studies, important sentences provided by MEAD are more useful. • It can provide a more complete overview of a topic rather than just research questions.
Negative points	• Only research questions are vague and indistinct.	• It is too complicated and hard to read since MEAD contains too many sentences; • Researchers often have their own opinions to determine important sentences, so that those in MEAD can not cater for each person. • MEAD seems more mixed up and confusing • In most of cases, researchers are not interested in looking for "facts" that MEAD can provide.

For the five biggest topics (containing 200, 200, 167, 165, 95 abstracts), the researchers who evaluated them indicated that the summaries were too long and hard to read, though I had restricted the maximum number of the dissertation abstracts to be summarized to 200. They suggested summarizing at most 50 dissertation abstracts in a summary. In addition, the researchers suggested combining the variable-based summary with the OBJECTIVE summary. They pointed out that the variable-based summary can give an overview of a topic whereas the research objective sentences can provide more detailed and direct information on the focus of the research.

5.4.3 Evaluation Results for General Users

This section reports the evaluation by 40 general users to see how casual users perceive the system. The data from the questionnaires for the 40 general users is given in Appendix IV.

(1) Readability, Comprehensibility and Usefulness

The overall readability, comprehensibility, and usefulness were scored on a 7-point scale. The average scores for the four types of summaries from the 40 general users are shown in Table 5-33.

Table 5-33. Average readability, comprehensibility, and usefulness scores for the four types of summaries from the 40 general users

	SYSTEM 1	SYSTEM 2	OBJECTIVES	MEAD
Readability	3.90	**5.00**	3.78	3.80
Comprehensibility	3.88	**4.58**	3.85	3.73
Usefulness	3.73	**4.57**	3.73	3.76

- *Bold figures are the highest scores for each aspect.*

SYSTEM 2 obtained the highest readability score (5.0), the highest comprehensibility score (4.6), and the highest usefulness score (4.6) among the four summaries.

There was a significant difference in the average readability scores among the four types of summaries ($p=0.012$). Moreover, Tukey's HSD test (Kirk, 1982) for pairwise comparisons found significant differences between SYSTEM 2 and SYSTEM 1 ($p=2.21E-7$), between SYSTEM 2 and OBJECTIVES ($p=0.01$), and between SYSTEM 2 and MEAD ($p=0.01$). Considering the presentation order of the four types of summaries, there was no significant difference in the average readability scores for the four presentation orders ($p=0.24$). This indicates that the presentation order had no significant influence on the readability scores from the general users.

There was no significant difference in the average comprehensibility scores among the four types of summaries ($p=0.10$). Considering the presentation order of the four types of summaries, there was a significant difference in the average comprehensibility scores for the four presentation orders ($p=0.03$). However, only the difference between SYSTEM 2 and MEAD was significant ($p=0.04$). As shown in Table 5-34, When MEAD was presented later than SYSTEM 2, it obtained a lower score of 4.1 than SYSTEM 2 (4.4). However, when MEAD was presented earlier than SYSTEM 2, its comprehensibility score (3.6) became worse. It appears that the summary that was read earlier obtained a lower comprehensibility score.

Table 5-34. Average comprehensibility scores for the four types of summaries for the four presentation orders from the 40 general users

Ordering	SYSTEM 1	SYSTEM 2	OBJECTIVES	MEAD
1. S1→S2→O→M	3.21	4.21	3.79	3.71
2. S1→S2→M→O	3.50	4.50	4.50	4.38
Average for 1 and 2	3.36	**4.36**	4.15	**4.05**
3. O→M→S1→S2	4.14	4.00	3.71	4.29
4. M→O→S1→S2	4.82	5.45	3.55	2.91
Average for 3 and 4	4.48	**4.73**	3.63	**3.6**

There was no significant difference in the average usefulness scores among the four types of summaries (p=0.13). Considering the presentation order of the four types of summaries, there was also no significant difference for the four presentation orders (p=0.3).

(2) Overall Evaluation

The 40 general users were asked to rank the four types of summaries. A weighted rank score was calculated for each summary using the same method for the 20 researchers. The general users were also asked to select one or more summaries that they preferred to use for obtaining the general information on a topic. The ranks and the general users' preferences are shown in Table 5-35.

Table 5-35. Rank and preference for the four types of summaries from the 40 general users

Rank	SYSTEM 1	SYSTEM 2	OBJECTIVES	MEAD
No.1 (weight=4)	4(10%)	22(55.0%)	6(15.0%)	8(20.0%)
No.2 (weight=3)	19(47.5%)	6(15.0%)	10(25.0%)	5(12.5%)
No.3 (weight=2)	9(22.5%)	4(10.0%)	15(37.5%)	12(30.0%)
No.4 (weight=1)	8(20.0%)	8(20.0%)	9(22.5%)	15(37.5%)
Weighted rank score	2.475	**3.05**	2.325	2.15
Preference	7(17.9%)	**25(64.1%)**	12(30.8%)	13(33.3%)

- Bold figures are the highest weighted rank score and the highest percentage of general users for preference among the four summaries.

The overall ranking for the four types of summaries based on the weighted rank scores was:

1- SYSTEM 2

2- SYSTEM 1

3- OBJECTIVES

4- MEAD

64% of the general users indicated preference for SYSTEM 2 for obtaining general information on the topic. But only 31% of the general users indicated preference for OBJECTIVES. 72% of the general users indicated "concept categorization" *quite* or *very useful*, and 62% of the general users indicated "important concept highlighting" *quite* or very useful.

5.4.4 Comparison between Researchers and General Users

Both researchers and general users ranked SYSTEM 2 first and MEAD last among the four types of summaries. 70% of the researchers indicated their preference to use SYSTEM 2 for their research-related work, whereas 64% of the general users indicated their preference for it for obtaining general information on a topic. In addition, 30% of the researchers and 18% of the general users indicated preference for SYSTEM 1, another variable-based summary that did not use the taxonomy for organizing the extracted information. A higher percentage of researchers appear to prefer the variable-based summaries than general users.

The researchers ranked the OBJECTIVES summary second whereas the general users ranked it third. Moreover, more researchers (55%) preferred to use OBJECTIVES than the general users (31%). For the general users, approximately the same percentage indicated preference for using MEAD (33%) as for OBJECTIVES (31%). However, for the researchers, only 25% indicated preference for using MEAD. This suggests that the researchers found the research objectives sentences more useful than the general important sentences extracted by MEAD, whereas the general users did not find the research objective sentences more useful.

70% of the researchers indicated "concept categorization" quite or very useful. The percentage was similar to that for the general users (72%). However, more researchers (75%) indicated "important concept highlighting" quite or very useful than the general users (62%). This may be because the researchers were more familiar with the important concepts in sociology and were better able to appreciate the usefulness of highlighting them in the summary.

5.5 Summary and Conclusion

The summarization method was evaluated on two levels: (1) accuracy and usefulness of each major summarization step; and (2) overall quality and usefulness of the final summaries. Each major summarization step was evaluated by comparing the system-generated output against human codings. Two types of the variable-based summaries were evaluated by researchers and general users who compared them against two types of sentence-based summaries generated using a sentence extraction method used in MEAD and a method that extracts research objective sentences only.

The automatic macro-level discourse parsing obtained a lower accuracy rate than expected, having an agreement of 63% with human coding. Still, it was useful in helping to identify the more important and the most important concepts from the dissertation abstracts. For extracting the *more impor-tant* concepts, the F-measure obtained using terms from the *research objectives* section (50%) was significantly higher than that using terms from the whole text (46%). For extracting the *most impor-tant* concepts, the F-measure obtained for *the research objectives + research results* sections (37%) was significantly higher than that for the whole text (33%).

The automatic information extraction was of acceptable quality: 46% precision and 90% recall for research concepts, 81% precision and 55% recall for research relationships between variables, 86% precision and 90% recall for contextual relations, and 97% precision and 72% recall for research methods.

The automatic information integration can generate reasonably good clusters compared to human clustering. It obtained a significantly better system-coder similarity (0.25) than the inter-coder simi-larity (0.19). Accurate and reliable clustering can integrate similarities across documents effectively so that the main ideas of the topic can be indicated clearly in the final summaries.

The use of a simple taxonomy for concept filtering and information organization can substantially improve the quality and usefulness of the variable-based summaries. Using the taxonomy, the non-concept terms were filtered out, the important concepts in the domain were highlighted, and the concepts were categorized into different subjects. The majority of the researchers and general users indicated that "concept categorization" (70% and 72%) and "important concept highlighting" (75% and 62%) were useful. The use of the taxonomy improved the ranking of the variable-based sum-mary in the user evaluation. Moreover, the researchers indicated that the use of the taxonomy can make the summary more useful to give an overview of the research area, easier to understand, and indicate the main ideas of the topic to a greater extent.

In the user evaluation, the variable-based summaries obtained a higher overall rank than the sum-maries generated by the sentence extraction methods, from both the researchers and general users who participated in the user study. The majority of the researchers (70%) and general users (64%) preferred to use the variable-based summaries for their research-related work or for obtaining gen-eral information on a topic. In addition, the researchers (55%) showed a greater interest in the re-search objective summary than the general users (31%), whereas the general users (33%) showed a greater interest in the MEAD summary than the researchers (25%).

Interestingly, the presentation order of the different summaries has influenced the users' assessments. The summaries presented later were more likely to be assessed favorably and be given a better score. This is possibly because after the user had read the previous summaries, familiarity with the content helped the user to understand the subsequent summaries more easily.

In the user evaluation, the researchers, who evaluated the five biggest topics, suggested summarizing at most 50 dissertation abstracts in a summary, though the summarization method can condense any number of dissertation abstracts into a summary.

Chapter 6

Conclusion and Discussion

6.1 The Overall Summarization Method

This work developed a method for automatic construction of multi-document summaries of sociology dissertation abstracts, focusing on research concepts and their research relationships. A discourse analysis of 300 sample dissertation abstracts found that much of sociology research adopts the traditional quantitative research paradigm of looking for relationships between concepts operationalized as variables. Although some studies adopt a qualitative research paradigm, many of them also seek to identify relationships between concepts that represent events, behaviors, attributes, and situations. Thus, research concepts and their research relationships are the focus of sociology research and researchers' interest. A variable-based framework was proposed for integrating and organizing four kinds of information extracted from each dissertation abstract. The framework focused on *research concepts* and *their research relationships*, as well as *contextual relations* and *research methods* used. It has a hierarchical structure in which the summarized information is presented at the top level and the more detailed information given at the lower levels.

Based on the variable-based framework, a summarization method was developed. It extracts *research concepts* and *their research relationships* as well as *contextual relations* and *research methods* from different dissertation abstracts, integrates them across dissertation abstracts using concept generalization and relationship normalization and conflation, combines and organizes the four kinds of information, and presents them in a Web-based interface. The summarization method developed in this work is just one way of operationalizing the variable-based framework. Different presentation formats can be used to present the summarized information. Two presentation formats were investigated in this work. One presentation format made use of a taxonomy to filter out non-concept terms, highlight important concepts in the domain, and categorize concepts into different subjects, whereas the other presentation format did not use a taxonomy for information filtering, highlighting and categorization. A user evaluation was carried out to compare the two types of variable-based summaries against two types of sentence-based summaries – one generated by displaying research objective sentences only and another generated by the MEAD system which extracted important sentences using various features (e.g. centroid words, sentence position and first-sentence overlap).

In the user evaluation, 70% of the researchers and 64% of the general users indicated their preference for the variable-based summaries to the summaries generated by the sentence extraction methods. They indicated that the variable-based summaries were efficient in giving an overview of the topic and useful for information scanning. More researchers (70%) preferred the variable-based summaries than the general users (64%), possibly because the general users lack domain knowledge and find it a little difficult to understand the concepts displayed in the summary. Nevertheless, the conclusion that can be derived from the user evaluation was that the variable-based summaries were preferred by the majority of researchers (70%) and general users (64%) to the sentence-based summaries.

Comparing the two types of variable-based summaries, the summary generated with the aid of a taxonomy obtained the highest rank score from the researchers and general users, whereas the one that did not make use of a taxonomy obtained lower scores. 70% of the researchers and 72% of the general users indicated that the concept categorization was useful to give a general idea of the content of the summary and help users to locate relevant information in the summary quickly. 75% of the researchers and 62% of the general users indicated that the important concept highlighting was useful to give users an indication of important concepts in the subject area. A higher percentage of researchers (75%) than general users (62%) found the important concept highlighting useful, possibly because the highlighted concepts made better sense to the researchers with their domain knowledge. In conclusion, using a taxonomy for filtering out non-concept terms, highlighting important concepts in the domain and categorizing concepts into different subjects can substantially improve the quality and usefulness of the variable-based summaries.

On the other hand, 55% of the researchers and 31% of the general users indicated preference for the research objective sentences, and 25% of the researchers and 33% of the general users indicated preference for the set of important sentences extracted by the MEAD system. They indicated that the sentence-based summaries could provide more direct information and were easy to understand. A higher percentage of researchers (55%) than general users (31%) preferred the research objective summary, indicating that researchers had a greater interest in the research objectives.

Interestingly, in the user evaluation, I found that the presentation order of the different types of summaries can influence the assessment of the users. The summaries presented later were more likely to be assessed favorably and be given a better score. This is because of the carry-over effect from the summaries read earlier. After a user had read the previous summaries, familiarity with the content may make the subsequent summaries easier to understand.

This work did not present summaries as fluent sentences. Instead, it adopted a simple presentation design orienting concepts extracted from dissertation abstracts. Although the majority of users (70% of researchers and 64% of general users) preferred the variable-based summaries, some users also indicated that the variable-based summaries (i.e. concept-oriented presentation) are too brief to provide accurate information on the topic and also has potential to confuse users. In the future, sophisticated presentation designs for operationalizing the variable-based framework can be investigated. Some suggestions are given as follows.

(1) In the current variable-based summaries, *contextual relations* and *research methods* were displayed separately from the *research concepts* and *their relationships*. However, contextual relations and research methods complement the information on research concepts and relationships, giving more details of how they are studied. Future presentation methods should integrate the research concepts and relationships with the contextual relations and research methods used, to provide more complete information.

(2) The researchers also showed an interest in the research objective sentences. Thus, the research objective sentences can be added to the variable-based summaries to provide alternative information presentation. The users can select to browse research concepts or the sentences that contain the research concepts and relationships. Moreover, the research objective sentences can be ranked according to the criteria used in MEAD and only the highly ranked research objective sentences need to be displayed. Furthermore, the research concepts can be extracted only from the research objective sentences rather than from the research objectives + research results sections as used in this work.

(3) Visual presentation methods will also be investigated in future work. The variable-based framework not only provides an overview of a research area but also allows users to zoom in to more details of interest. A graphical interface can help users to interact with the summary so that users can select what they want more quickly than using the text-based interactive interface developed in this work.

155

The summarization method was developed to summarize a set of related dissertation abstracts retrieved from the database using a topic as the search query. However, it can also handle a small number of abstracts that are non-relevant to the query topic in the document set retrieved. The research concepts extracted from these non-relevant abstracts have lower document frequency and are often cut off automatically from the summary with a threshold value. In this way, the summarization system can be used as a filtering system for information retrieval to filter out documents non-relevant to a search query. On the other hand, if the threshold value is set low enough, information extracted from the non-relevant abstracts can also be included in the summary. Human authors write literature surveys only for the documents that are relevant to the topic and ignore non-relevant documents. Summarizing a set of documents is like writing a literature survey. Thus the variable-based summarization system can be said to be more powerful than human summarization in that it can locate similar and related information in non-relevant documents as well. In this work, I did not analyze what happened to non-relevant documents in the summarization. This can be investigated in the future.

Though this summarization method focuses on quantitative research presented in the standard report structure, it can also handle the qualitative research abstracts to some extent. Many qualitative research studies also seek to identify relationships between concepts. Others seek to describe one or more aspects of the main concept of interest. Different from the concepts operationalized as variables in quantitative research, the concepts in qualitative research usually represent events, phenomena, behaviors, attributes, and situations. These important concepts and their relationships can be identified from the qualitative research abstracts in the same way as for quantitative research abstracts. But the identification of important concepts for qualitative research is not as easy as for quantitative research. Firstly, many related concepts and mediating and moderating factors are mentioned together with the main concepts. These related concepts represent noises that interfere with the identification of the important concepts. Secondly, some qualitative research abstracts do not have a clear structure. Many unstructured abstracts found in this work were for qualitative research. Although the *research objectives* section is still discernable in some unstructured abstracts and contains the *most important* concepts, many important concepts are scattered throughout the whole abstract. In the future, the unstructured abstracts should be identified and processed separately from the structured abstracts. Other methods to identify the important information in unstructured abstracts need to be investigated. For example, using sentence extraction to identify the important sentences and then extracting concepts from them, or identifying important concepts based on their term frequency.

156

Although the summarization method was developed to handle dissertation abstracts in the field of sociology, it can be applied to dissertation abstracts in other domains, such as psychology, education, medicine, crop agriculture and chemistry, which adopt the same research paradigm of seeking to investigate concepts and their relationships and use a similar research report structure. In the summarization process, three processing steps – macro-level discourse parsing, information extraction and information integration – are mostly based on the research report structure and linguistic features of dissertation abstracts and are, to a large extent, not domain-specific. These three steps can be applied to dissertation abstracts in other domains with little modification. One exception is research method terms because different research methods are used in different domains. For domains related to social science (e.g. education), only a small sample of dissertation abstracts will be needed to test the existing indicator phrases extracted in the sociology domain. In the information presentation step, a taxonomy was constructed for the sociology domain and cannot be applied to other domains. For a different domain, a new taxonomy should be constructed for categorizing concepts by subject and for indicating the important concepts in this domain.

The summarization method can also be extended to handle full research papers. Research papers are much longer than abstracts. They have the same general sections as abstracts (e.g. *introduction, research methods, research findings*, etc.) but have more detailed structure in each section. Thus, the summarization method needs to be improved to handle more detailed and deeper discourse structure. The macro-level discourse structure of full research papers needs to be analyzed to identify which parts contain more important research information. Secondly, the language used in the full papers is probably more complex. Thus more indicator phrases for contextual relations and research methods need to be identified, as well as more relationship patterns. However, the taxonomy constructed for sociology dissertation abstracts still can be used for the full research papers in the same domain. But more concepts should be extracted from the full papers and added into the taxonomy.

The summarization method developed in this work focused more on extraction and integration of semantic content and semantic relations expressed in the text. This idea can also be applied to other corpora. For example, in news stories, the semantic content should be news events, and the information can be organized according to events and different aspects of events (e.g. *background, central occurrences, consequences, commentary* and *follow-up*) (Ou et al., 2005); in medical articles, the semantic content should be diseases, and the information can be organized based on diseases and different aspects of a disease (e.g. *pathology, symptom, therapy* and *medicine*).

6.2   The Summarization Steps

The summarization method developed in this work included several major summarization steps. Each of the major steps was evaluated by comparing the system-generated output against human codings.

An automatic macro-level discourse parsing method was developed by treating discourse parsing as a sentence categorization problem. It included two phases: (1) assigning each sentence to a category using a decision tree classifier which used sentence position in the document and presence of indicator words in the sentences as attributes; and (2) improving the categorization using cue phrases found at the beginning of sentences. The automatic discourse parsing had an agreement of 63% (Kappa=0.51) with human coding. The accuracy was rather lower than the inter-coder agreement of 80% (Kappa=0.74). This was probably because only 200 dissertation abstracts were used as the training set to develop the decision tree classifier and the training was based on one human coding. The accuracy of the macro-level discourse parsing should be improved to at least 75% (Kappa=0.7) which is generally considered satisfactory (Bakeman & Gottman, 1986). In future, a bigger training set with more than one human codings should be used. Other machine learning techniques such as Support Vector Machine (SVM) and Naïve Bayes should also be investigated.

An automatic information extraction method was developed including term extraction and relationship extraction. All the terms were extracted from the whole text using a list of syntactic rules for specifying the possible sequences of part-of-speech tags in a noun phrase. Research concept terms were selected from the *research objectives* and *research results* sections. For extracting the more important concepts from these two sections, the system obtained a high recall of 79% but the precision of 34% was low. Some of the recall failures were due to errors in part-of-speech tagging by the Conexor parser. Incorrect part-of-speech tags will cause errors in the identification of terms from the sequence of words using the syntactic rules. There are two main reasons for precision failures. Firstly, identifying terms based on syntactic rules is not an accurate method – many non-term word sequences were misidentified as terms. In the future, statistical association between component words of a noun phrase can be used to improve the accuracy of term identification. Moreover, this work made use of the macro-level discourse structure to identify the more important concepts, which were more likely to represent research concepts, from the extracted terms. This is different from using traditional statistical measures (e.g. term frequency, TF*IDF, and likelihood ratio). The evaluation results indicated that macro-level discourse parsing was useful in identifying the more important concepts. The F-measure obtained using terms from the *research objectives* section (50%) was significantly higher than that using terms from the whole text (46%). However, there is much room for improvement. Important concepts do occur outside the *research objectives* and *research results* sections, especially for unstructured abstracts. For unstructured abstracts, macro-level discourse parsing did not work so well, though the *research objective* section could still be identified. Thus, other methods for identifying important concepts should be investigated in the future, for example, using term frequency in the document and using sentence extraction methods to identify the more important sentences and then extracting concepts from them.

Contextual relations and research methods were identified from the extracted terms throughout the whole text using indicator phrases. The accuracy obtained was good – 86% precision and 90% recall for contextual relations, and 97% precision and 72% recall for research methods. This indicates that using indicator phrases to identify specific information can give accurate results. A higher precision was obtained for identifying research methods (90%) than for contextual relations (86%). This is because all the contextual relations were identified using *indicator words* (e.g. *perception*, *context* and *model*), whereas most of research methods were identified using more specific *indicator phrases* (e.g. *qualitative research, field work* and *telephone interview*). Single words are more likely to have different meanings in different contexts than multi-word terms. A higher recall was obtained for identifying contextual relations (90%) than for research methods (72%). This is because there is a great variety of research methods used in sociology and it is hard to exhaustively derive a list of indicator phrases from just 300 sample dissertation abstracts. Some of the recall failures both for extracting contextual relations and research methods were because the contextual relations and research methods expressed in other grammatical forms, such as adverb, verb and infinitive, cannot be identified using indicator phrases. Moreover, some contextual relations and research methods were not explicitly stated but had to be inferred from the text.

Relationship extraction was based on a set of pre-constructed relationship patterns. It obtained a high precision of 81% but the recall of 55% was low. The first reason for the low recall was that the relationship patterns were not exhaustive, being derived from just 300 sample dissertation abstracts. The second reason was that the constructed patterns were too specific and missed some correct relationships. To make the patterns more general and thus improve the recall, the slots in the patterns cam be programmed to match with the research concepts extracted in an earlier processing step rather than the text strings. However, this may worsen the precision because some times the concepts associated with the relationships were not extracted correctly and completely. The third reason was that the system only could identify the relationships within sentences. Relationships across sentences and implied relationships without clear indicator phrases could not be identified.

An automatic information integration method was developed including concept integration and relationship integration. Since relationship integration was implemented as simple text replacement for normalizing and conflating different surface expressions for the same type of relationship, only concept integration was evaluated in the work. The concept integration method identified and clustered similar concepts based on their syntactic variations. It generated relatively good clusters compared to human clustering, according to the similarity measure used. The system-generated clusters obtained a significantly higher similarity with the human-generated clusters (0.25) than the similarity between two human-generated clusters (0.19). However, this clustering did not take into account the semantic meanings of concepts and thus cannot handle similar concepts having quite different syntactic forms, e.g. *"computer"*, *"desktop"* and *"workstation"*. Moreover, all the clusters were labeled using single-word terms. A single-word term often has multiple meanings in different contexts. Thus, the clustered concepts are sometimes not semantically similar enough. For example, *"computer network"* and *"social network"* were assigned into the same cluster labeled *"network"*, though they are quite different in meaning. Inaccurate clustering can result in inappropriate subject categorization for some concepts in the cluster. For example, *"social network"* in the *"network"* cluster was wrongly categorized under the *"information and communication"* subject. In the future, concept integration at the semantic level should be implemented to improve the clustering accuracy of similar concepts.

Semantic integration requires a meaningful concept hierarchy provided by a thesaurus or taxonomy. However, the taxonomy constructed in this work only contained lists of 1, 2, 3, 4, and 5-word terms extracted from 3214 sociology dissertation abstracts for a complete year (2001) and further filtered by two domain experts to remove non-concept terms. In the future, the taxonomy should be improved by domain experts to provide hierarchical concept categorization based on semantic relations among the concepts of different lengths. Although existing thesauri such as the UNESCO[9] and HASSET[10] (Humanities and Social Science Electronic Thesaurus) cover only some of the sociology concepts, they can be used as a reference by domain experts for manual construction of the taxonomy. With the improved taxonomy, the extent of the syntactic integration can be controlled at appropriate levels to reduce some clustering errors, for example, *"computer network"* and *"social network"* should not be further integrated into the *"network"* cluster. Semantic integration can also be

---

[9] http://www.ulcc.ac.uk/unesco/
[10] http://www.data-archive.ac.uk/search/hassetAbout.asp

applied to cluster related concepts that do not have any word in common. For example, *"PC"*, *"workstation" "desktop"* can be integrated into the *"computer"* cluster according to their semantic meanings.

6.3   Contributions of the Work

This work proposed a variable-based framework for integrating and organizing different kinds of information extracted from different dissertation abstracts using a hierarchical structure. This framework provides a way to summarize a set of dissertation abstracts that is different from the traditional sentence extraction methods. It not only gives an overview of a research area by presenting the summarized information at the top level but also allows users to zoom in to more details of interest by exploring the specific information at the lower levels.

This work developed a new method for automatic construction of multi-document summaries of sociology dissertation abstracts. The summarization method is a hybrid method involving both extraction and abstraction techniques. It focuses on extracting research concepts and their research relationships from different dissertation abstracts, integrating them across dissertation abstracts, and presenting the integrated information in Web-based interactive interface. The summarization method differs from the traditional extractive approaches used in previous studies in the following five ways:

(1) It extracts separate terms and text fragments from sentences, instead of complete sentences, to create a more concise summary;

(2) It identifies similarities and differences across documents at a more semantic level by focusing on research concepts and their research relationships, rather than words, phrases, sentences and their rhetorical relationships;

(3) It makes use of the macro-level discourse structure of documents to identify the more important terms that are more likely to represent research concepts, rather than purely statistical criteria;

(4) It performs some amount of concept generalization, i.e. generalizing similar concepts extracted from different documents using a broader concept.

(5) It performs some shallow text generation, i.e. integrating a cluster of similar concepts in a new sentence, normalizing different surface expressions for the same type of relationships using a standard expression and conflating them in one sentence, combining all kinds of information using a template.

This work has developed lexical resources useful in multi-document summarization of research abstracts:

- *Decision tree rulesets* for categorizing sentences into different sections or categories;
- *A list of cue phrases found at the beginning of sentences* for identifying research objectives and research results sentences from dissertation abstracts.
- *A list of indicator words* for identifying contextual relations from dissertation abstracts;
- *A list of indicator phrases* for identifying research methods from dissertation abstracts;
- *A list of attributes* representing a kind of special facets of concepts that can be measured quantitatively, e.g. *size, degree, level, rate* etc. (Attributes were expected to be used in future work for identifying more accurate information, though they were not used in this work.)
- *A list of syntactic rules* for identifying multi-word terms;
- *A set of relationship patterns* for extracting research relationships between concepts from dissertation abstracts;
- *A list of standard relationship forms* for representing different types of relationships;
- *A taxonomy* for specifying important concepts in the sociology domain and providing subject categorization for single-word main concepts.

These resources were stored in a knowledge base and used to support the summarization process. They can be applied to other domains to different extents. The d*ecision tree rulesets* and c*ue phrases found at the beginning of sentences* can be applied to dissertation abstracts in other domains. Moreover, they also can be applied to other informative research abstracts in other domains to a smaller extent. *Indicator phrases for contextual relations and research methods, attributes, relationship patterns* and *standard relationship forms* can be applied to other documents in sociology domain.

This work also developed some useful text processing techniques as follows:

- *A discourse parsing method* using the decision tree induction and cue phrases found at the beginning of sentences ;
- *A term extraction method* using syntactic rules for multi-word terms;
- *A relationship extraction method* using a pattern matching algorithm;
- *A concept integration method* by linking term variants of different lengths according to specific syntactic variations among them to form a hierarchical chain and generalizing the terms at the lower level using the broader terms at the higher level;

- *A relationship integration method* by normalizing different surface expressions for the same type of relationships and conflating them in one sentence;

In addition, this work also developed evaluation methods for evaluating different components of the summarization systems and the final summaries, including:

- *An evaluation method for evaluating each major summarization step* by comparing the system-generated output against more than one human codings;

- *A user evaluation method for evaluating the quality and usefulness of the final summaries* by comparing the system-generated summaries against other summaries generated using sentence-extraction methods.

The user evaluation method with the designed questionnaire can be applied to evaluate other multi-document summarization systems.

6.4   Future Work

The multi-document summarization method developed in this work includes four major steps: discourse parsing, information extraction, information integration and summary presentation. Actually, each step is a research area in which researchers in natural language processing can investigate in depth.

Precious studies have used surface cues, supervised learning and unsupervised learning for automatic discourse parsing. In this work, I used only decision tree induction to categorize sentences into five predefined sections. Other supervised learning techniques such as SVM and Naive Bayes can be investigated in the future. However, supervised learning requires manual assignment of pre-defined category labels to the training data. It is time consuming to code a big training set manually. In the future, unsupervised learning will be investigated for discourse parsing of research abstracts and research articles. Since unsupervised learning can automatically derive sentence categories form a un-coded sample, a very big training set can be used for developing the classifier.

Previous studies have used mainly rule-based methods and statistics-based methods to extract terms. In this work, I used only rule-based method, i.e. syntactic rules, to extract multi-word terms. The evaluation results indicated that the precision (46%) is not high. Statistics-based methods can be investigated by examining the statistical association among the component words in multi-word terms to refine the extracted terms. Moreover, it is hard to extract implied relationships that don not contain clear indicator phrases using the current pattern matching method. Other methods such as association rules can be investigated to extract such relationships.

Information integration is an important method to create abstracts imitating human's abstracting behavior. Lin (1995) and Hovy and Lin (1997) created summaries by replacing a collection of similar concepts with a higher-level unifying concept. Concept generalization or fusion can be performed at the semantic level and syntactic level. In this work, only syntactic-level generalization was performed since it is easy to realize without the need of an ontology, taxonomy or thesaurus. However, such generalization is not very accurate without considering the semantic meanings of concepts. In the future, semantic-level generalization will be investigated. A taxonomy or ontology needs to be used to support the semantic-level generalization.

In this work, only a simple concept-oriented design was adopted to present the generated summaries. However, a well-designed presentation is important for end-users. Other presentation designs will be investigated for operationalizing the variable-based framework. Graphical presentation has been done for single-document summaries in many previous studies. But there is no many such studies found for multi-document summaries. Actually, multi-document summaries need a more sophisticated user interface. A multi-document summary is required to provide a domain-overview of a topic and also allow users to zoom in for more details on aspects of interest. A graphical interface can help users to interact with the summary to locate what they want more rapidly and effectively.

The current summarization method focuses on the quantitative research paradigm (i.e. seeking to investigate relationships between research concepts) and standard research report structure with five sections. Most of the unstructured abstracts are for qualitative research and do not follow such a report structure. Thus, the summarization method is not ideal for unstructured abstracts. Unstructured abstracts need to be identified and handled separately from structured abstracts. Some unstructured abstracts adopt a different structure to report information, e.g. summarizing the contents of each chapter. Some have no discernable structure – just describing the qualitative research findings. How to identify and extract important research information from unstructured abstracts is a research issue.

The current summarization method was developed to process research abstracts rather than full-text research articles. Full-text research articles contain much more information than research abstracts and have a more complex research report structure. Furthermore, the language used is more complex. In the future, the summarization method will be extended to process full-text research articles. A possible approach is to preprocess long research articles by extracting the most important sentences from each section to generate a set of single-document summaries and then summarize the set of single-document summaries using the current variable-based summarization system.

Finally, the current summarization method focuses on research concepts and seeks to organize different kinds of information extracted from dissertation abstracts according to research concepts. Different types of semantic content are important in different corpora. For example, types of information related to events may be important in news articles, whereas diseases may be central concepts in medical articles. So, for medical articles, different types of information such as pathology, *symptom*, *therapy* and *medicine* can be organized based on diseases to summarize a set of related medical articles.

Multi-document summaries are more useful than single-document summaries in digital libraries and Web search engines. It can help users to grasp the recent trends and new achievements in a specific research area. However, in multi-document summarization, more challenges need to be overcome in the issues of compression rate, repeated information, cohesion, coherence, etc. Although there is a large body of literature on how to write good single-document summaries or abstracts, not much is found on how to write good multi-document summaries and literature surveys (summarizing a set of documents is like writing a literature survey). More studies are needed to find out how good literature surveys are written and structured in different situations (e.g. for different purpose and users). More intelligent and useful summarization system can be developed by following human cognitive process in summarizing a set of documents and writing a literature survey.

Chapter 7

Future Trends

This chapter outlines the principal trends of the area of automatic text summarization in the context of digital libraries. Single-document summarization has been employed in most of digital library systems for helping users to identify documents of interest. With the growth of similar information across different information sources, single-document summarization cannot remove redundant information from a variety of related documents and thus often result in a set of similar summaries for individual documents. In recent years, more attention has been paid to multi-document summarization in digital library systems (e.g. Mckeown et al., 2001b). Initially, multi-document summarization focused on the most important topics that are often repeated in many documents of a document set to create generic summaries. Recently, there is a trend towards developing advanced multi-document summaries that go beyond the classical, generic summaries to user-focused summaries, answer-focused summaries, and update summaries.

(1) User-focused Summaries

In the real world, different users have different information needs to the same search query and even the same user may have different information needs at different points in time for the same topic. Based on this fact, some intelligent search systems (e.g. MyYahoo and Google Web History) return personalized results to users according to their behavior models and profiles. This idea leads to the development of user-focused summarization systems, e.g. WebInEssence (Radev, Fan & Zhang, 2001), which select documents based on users' personal profiles and produce user-focused summaries with the selected documents. A user-focused summary focuses on the content that matches the user's specific requirement and discards others to reduce information overload. Since the DUC 2005, user-focused summaries have been extensively evaluated. These summaries were produced based on the pre-defined context that was modeled as a set of open-ended questions. The ability to generate user-focused summaries is an important step towards a personalized digital library environment.

(2) Answer-focused Summaries

In the DUC 2003 and 2004, a task was designed to produce a summary of a document set which aimed to answer a given question like *"Who is X?"* (X is a person name).This indicates a recent trend towards answer-focused summaries which are related to but still different from user-focused summaries. User-focused summaries aim to provide an indication of the main contents of a document or a set of documents according to a specific user' preference and help the user to locate documents of interest quickly. However, users often want to express their information needs in the form of natural language questions, e.g. *"What is text summarization?"*, instead of several key words, and require specific answers to a question rather than whole documents. Many questions cannot be answered in one or two words but require a number of relevant facts which may be distributed across multiple documents returned by a search engine. The answer is thus a multi-document summary of these facts extracted from different documents. Some answer-focused summarization systems have been developed in previous studies. Mori, Nozawa and Asada (2005) calculated sentence importance with the scores from a question answering system and then integrated the calculation to a generic multi-document summarization system for answering multiple questions. Wu, Radev and Fan (2004) identified question types and integrated them into a proximity-based summary extraction system for question answering, and they furthermore proposed a set of criteria and performance metrics for evaluating answer-focused summarization systems.

(3) Update Summaries

In the DUC 2007, an update task was defined to produce short multi-document summaries of news articles under the assumption that the user has already read a set of earlier articles and is only interested in new information which has not been covered before. An update summary is used to inform the reader of new information about a particular topic. It can be traced back to the temporal summaries produced by Alan, Gupta and Khandelwal (2001) and Jatowt and Ishizuka (2004). Since the web sites of news are built dynamically to show different information content evolving over time in the same URL, it is expected that update summaries will be very useful in a digital library of Web news to provide a trace of a news event.

Bibliography

Afantenos, S., Doura, I., Kapellou, E., & Karkaletsis, V. (2004). Exploiting cross-document relations for multi-document evolving summarization. In G. A. Vouros, & T. Panayiotopoulos (Eds.), *Methods and Applications of Artificial Intelligence in Volume 3025 of Lecture Notes in Computer Science: Proceedings of the 3rd Helenic Conference on Artificial Intelligence* (pp.410-419). Berlin: Springer-Verlag.

Afantenos, S., Karkaletsis, V., & Stamatopoulos, P. (2005a). Summarization from medical documents: A survey. *Journal of Artificial Intelligence in Medicine*, in press.

Afantenos, S., Liontou, K., Salapata, M., & Karkaletsis, V. (2005b). An introduction to the summarization of evolving events: Linear and non-linear evolution. In *Proceedings of Natural Language Understanding and Cognitive Science Conference* (pp.91-99). Retrieved 10 April 2005 from http://arxiv.org/abs/cs.CL/0503033

Alonso, L. (2005). Representing discourse for automatic text summarization via shallow NLP techniques. *PhD Thesis*. Department de Lingüística General, Universitat de Barcelona. Retrieved 10 April 2005 from http://lalonso.sdf-eu.org/tesi.pdf

Allan, J. Gupta, R., & Khandelwal, V. (2001). Temporal summaries of new topics. In *Proceedings of the 24th Annual International ACM SIGIR Conference on Research and Development in Information Retrieval* (pp.10-18). New York, NY: ACM. Retrieved 15 July 2009 from http://maroo.cs.umass.edu/pub/web/getpdf.php?id=226

Amigo, E., Gonzalo, J., Peinado, V., Penas, A., & Verdejo. (2000). Using syntactic information to extract relevant terms for multi-document summarization. In *Proceedings of the 36th Annual Conference on Computational Linguistics*. Morristown, NJ: ACL. Retrieved 10 April 2005 from http://nlp.uned.es/pergamus/pubs/eamigoColing04.pdf

Andernach, T. (1996). A machine learning approach to the classification of dialogue utterances. In *Proceedings of NeMLaP-2*. Retrieved 10 April 2005 from http://arxiv.org/abs/cmp-lg/9607022

Andernach, T., Poel, M., & Salomons, E. (1997). Finding classes of dialogue utterances with Kohonen networks. In W. Daelemans, A. Van den Bosch, & A. Weijters (Eds.): *Workshop Notes of the ECML/MLnet Workshop on Empirical Learning of Natural Language Processing Tasks* (pp. 85–94). Retrieved 10 April 2005 from http://www.cnts.ua.ac.be/ecml97/ecml97-notes.html

Ando, R., Boguraev, B., Byrd, R., & Neff, M. (2000). Multi-document summarization by visualizing topic content. In *Proceedings of ANLP/NAACL 2000 Workshop on Automatic Summarization*. Retrieved 10 January 2006 from http://acl.ldc.upenn.edu/W/W00/W00-0409.pdf

Angheluta, R., Mitra, R., Jing, X., & Moens, M. (2004). K.U. Leuven summarization system at DUC 2004. In *Proceedings of the Document Understanding Conference 2004*. Retrieved 10 April 2005 from http://www-nlpir.nist.gov/projects/duc/pubs.html

Aone, Chinatsu, Okurowski, M. E., & Gorlinsky, J. (1998). Trainable, scalable summarization using robust NLP and machine learning. In *Proceedings of the 17th International Conference on Computational Linguistics and 36th Annual Meeting of Association for Computational Linguistics* (vol. 1, pp. 62-66). Morristown, NJ: ACL. Retrieved 10 April 2005 from http://protal.acm.org/citation.cfm?id=980856

Aone, C., Okurowski, M., Gorlinsky, J., & Larsen, B. (1999). A trainable summarizer with knowledge acquired from robust NLP techniques. In I. Mani, & M.T. Maybury (Eds.), *Advances in automatic text summarization* (pp. 71-80). Cambridge, MA: The MIT Press.

Azzam, S., Humphreys, K., & Gaizauskas, R. (1999). Using coreference chains for text summarization. In *ACL-99 Workshop on Coreference and its Applications* (pp.77-84). Retrieved 10 April 2005 from http://acl.ldc.upenn.edu/W/W99/W99-0211.pdf

Bakeman, R. & Gottman, J. (1986). *Observing interaction: An introduction to sequential analysis.* London: Cambridge University Press.

Baron, R. M., & Kenny, D. A. (1986). The moderator-mediator variable distinction in social psychological research: Conceptual, strategic, and statistical considerations. *Journal of Personality and Social Psychology*, *51*, 1173-1182.

Barzilay, R., & Elhadad, M. (1997). Using lexical chains for text summarization. In *Proceedings of the ACL Workshop on Intelligent Scalable Text Summarization* (pp.10-17). Retrieved 10 April 2005 from http://acl.ldc.upenn.edu/W/W97/W97-0703.pdf

Barzilay, R., & Elhadad, M. (1998). Using lexical chains for text summarization. In *Proceedings of the ACL-97/EACL-97 Workshop on Intelligent Scalable Text Summarization* (pp.10-17). Retrieved 10 April 2005 from http://www.cs.bgu.ac.il/~elhadad/lexical-chains.pdf

Barzilay, R. McKeown, K. R., & Elhadad, M. (1999). Information fusion in the context of multi-document summarization. In *Proceedings of the 37ᵗʰ Annual Meeting of the Association of Computational Linguistics* (pp.550-557). Morristown, NJ: ACL. Retrieved 15 July 2009 from http://www.cs.bgu.ac.il/~elhadad/papers/fusion.pdf

Baxendale, P. B. (1958). Man-made index for technical literature – An experiment. *IBM Journal of Research & Development*, 2(4), 354-361.

Boguraev, B., & Neff, M. (2000). Discourse segmentation in aid of document summarization. In *Proceedings of the 33ʳᵈ Hawaii International Conference on System Sciences* (vol. 3, pp.3004). Washington, DC: IEEE Computer Society. Retrieved 10 April 2005 from http://portal.acm.org/citation.cfm?id=820269

Bergler, S., Witte, R., Li, Z., Khalife, M., Chen, Y., Doandes, M., & Andreevskaia, A. (2004). Multi-ERSS and ERSS 2004. In *Proceedings of the Document Understanding Conference 2004*. Retrieved 10 April 2005 from http://www-nlpir.nist.gov/projects/duc/pubs.html

Blair-Goldenshohn, S., Evans, D., Hatzivassiloglou, V., McKeown, K., Nenkova, A., Passonneau, R., Schiffman, B., Schlaikjer, A., Siddharthan, A., & Siegelman, S. (2004). Columbia University at DUC 2004. In *Proceedings of the Document Understanding Conference 2004*. Retrieved 10 April 2005 from http://www-nlpir.nist.gov/projects/duc/pubs.html

Borgigault, D., & Jacquemin, C. (1999). Term extraction + term clustering: An integrated platform for computer-aided terminology. In *Proceedings of the 9ᵗʰ Conference on European Chapter of the Association for Computational Linguistics* (pp. 15-22). Morristown, NJ: ACL. Retrieved 10 April 2005 from http://portal.acm.org/citation.cfm?id=977039

Brandow, R., Mitze, K., & Rau, L. F. (1995). Automatic condensation of electronic publications by sentence selection. *Information Processing and Management*, 31(5), 675-685.

Brunn, M., Chali, Y., & Dufour, B. (2002). The University of Lethbridge text summarizer at DUC 2002. In *Proceedings of the Document Understanding Conference 2002*. Retrieved 10 April 2005 from http://www-nlpir.nist.gov/projects/duc/pubs.html

Buyukkokten, O., Garcia-Molina, H., & Paepcke, A. (1999). Seeing the whole in parts: Text summarization for web browsing on handheld devices. In *Proceedings of the 10ᵗʰ International WWW Conference* (pp.652-662). New York: ACM. Retrieved 10 April 2005 from http://www10.org/cdrom/papers/594/

Carbonell, J. G., & Goldstein, J. (1998). The use of MMR, diversity-based reranking for reordering documents and producing summaries. In *Proceedings of the 21st Annual International ACM SIGIR Conference on Research and Development in Information Retrieval* (pp. 335-336). New York: ACM. Retrieved 10 April 2005 from http://portal.acm.org/citation.cfm?id=291025

Chali, Y., & Kolla, M. (2004). Summarization techniques in DUC 2004. In *Proceedings of the Document Understanding Conference 2004*. Retrieved 10 July 2005 from http://www-nlpir.nist.gov/projects/duc/pubs.html

Chinchor, N. (1995). Four scores and seven years ago: The scoring method for MUC-6. In *Proceedings of the 6th Conference on Message Understanding* (pp.33-38). Morristown, NJ: ACL. Retrieved 10 April 2005 from http://portal.acm.org/citation.cfm?id=1072399.1072403

Clark, A. (2003). Machine learning approaches to shallow discourse parsing: A literature review. *Technical Report in Interactive Multimodal Information Management / Multimodal Dialogue Management (IM2.MDM-03)*. Retrieved 10 April 2005 from http://www.issco.unige.ch/staff/clark/sdp_lr.pdf

Cohen, J. (1960). A coefficient of agreement for nominal scales. *Educational and Psychological Measurement, 20, 37–46.*

DeJong, G. (1982). An overview of the FRUMP system. In W.G. Lehnert, & M.H. Ringle (Eds), *Strategies for natural language processing* (pp. 149-176). Hillsdale, NJ: Lawrence Erlbaum Associates.

Edmundson, H. P. (1969). New methods in automatic extracting. *Journal of the ACM*, 16(2), 264-285.

Elhadad, Noemie, & McKeown, K. (2001). Towards generating patient specific summaries of medical articles. In *Proceedings of NAACL Automatic Summarization Workshop*. Retrieved 10 April 2005 from http://www.isi.edu/~cyl/was-naacl2001/papers/elhadad-p1.pdf

Elhadad, Michael. (1993). Using argumentation to control lexical choice: A functional unification implementation. *PhD Thesis*, Department of Computer Science, Columbia University. Retrieved 10 April 2005 from http://www1.cs.columbia.edu/nlp/theses/michael_elhadad.pdf

Endres-Niggemeyer B., Hertenstein B., Villiger C., & Ziegert C. (2001). Constructing an ontology for WWW summarization in Bone Marrow Transplantation (BMT).In *Proceedings of the 12th Annual Classification Research Workshop of the ASIS Conference*. Retrieved 10 April 2005 from http://summit-bmt.fh-hannover.de/papers/pdf/WashingtonOcto11.pdf.

Erkan, G., & Radev, D.R. (2004). The University of Michigan in DUC 2004. In *Proceedings of the Document Understanding Conference 2004*. Retrieved 10 July 2005 from http://www-nlpir.nist.gov/projects/duc/pubs.html

Farzindar, A. & Lapalme G. (2004a). The use of thematic structure and concept identification for legal text summarization. In *Proceedings of Computational Linguistics in the North-East (CLiNE-04)*. Retrieved 10 January 2006 from http://www.iro.umontreal.ca/~farzinda/FarzindarCLINE04.pdf

Farzindar, A., & Lapalme, G. (2004b). LetSum, an automatic legal text summarizing system. In T.F. Gordon (Eds.), *Volume 120 of Frontiers in Artificial Intelligence and Applications: Proceedings of the 17ᵗʰ Annual Conference on Legal Knowledge and Information Systems*. Amsterdam: IOS Press.

Fatma, J. K., Maher, J., Lamia, B. H., & Abdelmajid, B. H. (2004). Summarization at LARIS Laboratory. (2004). In *Proceedings of the Document Understanding Conference 2004*. Retrieved 10 July 2005 from http://www-nlpir.nist.gov/projects/duc/pubs.html

Firmin, T., & Chrzanowski, M. J. (1999). An evaluation of automatic text summarization systems. In I. Mani & M.T. Maybury (Eds.): *Advances in automatic text summarization* (pp.325-336). Cambridge, MA: The MIT Press.

Fukumoro, J., & Sugimura, T. (2004). Multi-document summarization using document set type classification. In N. Kando, & H. Ishikawa (Eds.), *Proceedings of the 4ᵗʰ NTCIR Workshop on Research in Information Access Technologies Information Retrieval, Question Answering and Summarization*. Tokyo: National Institute of Informatics. Retrieved 10 April 2005 from http://research.nii.ac.jp/ntcir-ws4/NTCIR4-WN/TSC3/NTCIR4WN-TSC-FukumotoJ.pdf

Goldstein, J., Kantrowitz, M., Mittal, V., & Carbonell, J. (1999). Summarizing text documents: sentence selection and evaluation metrics. In *Proceedings of the 22ⁿᵈ ACM SIGIR International Conference on Research and Development in Information Retrieval* (pp. 121-128). New York: ACM.

Goldstein, J., Mittal, V., Carbonell, J., & Kantrowitz, M. (2000). Multi-document summarization by sentence extraction. In *Proceedings of ANLP/NAACL 2000 Workshop on Automatic Summarization* (pp.40-48). Morristown, NJ: ACL. Retrieved 30 April 2005 from http://acl.ldc.upenn.edu/W/W00/W00-0405.pdf

Hahn, U., & Reimer, U. (1999). Knowledge-based text summarization: salience and generalization operators for knowledge base abstraction. In In I. Mani & M.T. Maybury (Eds.): *Advances in automatic text summarization* (pp.215-232). Cambridge, CA: The MIT Press.

Hahn, U., & Mani, I. (2000). The challenges of automatic summarization. *IEEE Computer*, 33 (11), 29-36.

Hand, T. F. (1997). A proposal for task-based evaluation of text summarization systems. In *Proceedings of ACL/EACL-97 Summarization Workshop* (pp.31-36).

Harabagiu, M. S. & Lacatusu, F. (2002). Generating single and multi-document summaries with GISTEXER. In *Proceedings of the Document Understanding Conference 2002*. Retrieved 20 April 2005 from http://www-nlpir.nist.gov/projects/duc/pubs.html

Hardy, H., Shimizu, N., Strzalkowski, T., Ting, L., Wise, G., & Zhang, X. (2002). Cross-document summarization by concept classification. In *Proceedings of the 25th Annual International ACM SIGIR Conference on Research and Development in Information Retrieval* (pp.121-128). New York: ACM. Retrieved 15 April 2005 from http://portal.acm.org/citation.cfm?id=564376.564399

Hearst, M. (1994). Multi-paragraph segmentation of expository text. In *Proceedings of the 32nd Annual Meeting of the Association for Computational Linguistics* (pp.9-16). Morristown, NJ: ACL. Retrieved 20 April 2005 from http://portal.acm.org/citation.cfm?id=981734

Herther, N. K. (2000). Searching dissertation abstracts: Moving into the digital age. *Information Technology Newsletter*, 5. Retrieved 20 April 2005 from http://www1.umn.edu/oit/newsletter/0400-itn/disseration.html

Hirao, T. Suzuki, J. Isozaki, H., & Maeda, E. (2004). NTT's multiple document summarization system in DUC 2004. In *Proceedings of the Document Understanding Conference 2004*. Retrieved 10 July 2005 from http://www-nlpir.nist.gov/projects/duc/pubs.html

Hobbs, J. (1993). Summaries from structure. In B. Endres-Niggemeyer, J. Hobbs, & K. Sparck Jones (Eds.), *Proceedings of Workshop on Summarizing Text for Intelligent Communication*. Retrieved 20 April 2005 from http://transfer.ik.fh-hannover.de/ik/projekte/Dagstuhl/Abstract/Abstracts/Hobbs/Hobbs.html

Holiday, M., & Hasan, R. (1976). *Cohesion in English*. London: Longman.

Hovy, E. H., & Lin, C.-Y. (1998). Automated text summarization and the SUMMARIST system. In *Proceedings of a Workshop in TIPSTER Text Program Phrase III* (pp. 197-214). Retrieved 20 April 2005 from http://www.isi.edu/~cyl/papers/TIPSTER-proc-Hovy-Lin-final.pdf

Hovy, E. H., & Lin, C.-Y. (1999). Automated text summarization in SUMMARIST. In I. Mani & M.T. Maybury (Eds.): *Advances in automatic text summarization* (pp.81-94). Cambridge, MA: The MIT Press.

Ibekwe-SanJuan, F., & SanJuan, E. (2004a). Mining textual data through term variant clustering: the Term-Watch system. In *Proceedings of RIAO 2004* (pp. 487-503). Retrieved 5 May 2005 from http://archivesic.ccsd.cnrs.fr/sic_00001405.en.html

Ibekwe-SanJuan, F., & SanJuan, E. (2004b). Mining for knowledge chunks in a terminology network. In I.C. McIlwaine (Eds.), *Volume 9 of Advances in Knowledge Organization*: *Proceedings of the 8th International Society for Knowledge Organization Conference* (pp. 41-46). Verkehrs-Nr: Ergon-Verlag.

Jacobs, P., & Rau, L. (1990). SCISOR: Extracting information from on-line news source. *Communications of the ACM*, 33(11), 88-97.

Jansen, B. J., Spink, A., & Saracevic, T. (2000). Real life, real users and real needs: A study and analysis of user queries on the Web. *Information Processing and Management*, 36(2), 207-227.

Jatowt, A. & Ishizuka, M. (2004). Change summarization in web collections. In *Proceedings of the 5th International Conference on Web Information Systems Engineering* (pp.303-312). Berlin: Springer-Verlag.

Jing, H., Barzilay, R., McKeown, K., & Elhadad, M. (1998). Summarization evaluation methods: Experiment and analysis. In *Working Notes of the AAAI Spring Symposium on Intelligent Text Summarization* (pp.60-68). Retrieved 15 April 2005 from http://www.cs.cornell.edu/~regina/my_papers/evaluation.ps.gz

Johnson, F.C., Paice, C. D., Black, W. J., & Neal, A. P. (1993). The application of linguistic processing to automatic abstract generation. *Journal of Documentation and Text Management*, 1(3), 215-241.

Jones, K.S., & Galliers, J.R. (1996). *Evaluating natural language processing systems: An analysis and review*. In J.G. Carbonell, & J. Siekmann (Eds.), *Volume 1083 of Lecturer Notes in Artificial Intelligence*. Berlin: Springer-Verlag.

Jones, S., Lundy, S., & Paynter, G. W. (2002). Interactive document summarization using automatically extracted keyphrases. In *Proceedings of the 35th Hawaii International Conference on System Sciences* (vol.4, pp. 101.3). Washington, DC: IEEE Computer Society.

Kan, M.-Y., McKeown, K. R., & Klavans, J. L. (2001). Domain-specific informative and indicative summarization for information retrieval. In *Proceedings of the Document Understanding Conference 2001*. Retrieved April 15, 2005, from http://www-nlpir.nist.gov/projects/duc/pubs.html

Kirk, R. E. (1982). *Experimental design: Procedures for the behavioral sciences*. Pacific Grove, CA: Brooks/Cole Publishing Company.

Khoo, C., Ou, S., & Goh, D. (2002). A hierarchical framework for multi-document summarization of dissertation abstracts. In E.-P. Lim, S. Foo, C. Khoo, H. Chen, E. Fox, S. Urs, & T. Costantino (Eds.), *Volume 2555 of Lecturer Notes in Computer Science: Proceedings of the 5ᵗʰ International Conference on Asian Digital Libraries* (pp. 99-110). Berlin: Springer-Verlag.

Khoo, C., Ng, K., & Ou, S. (2002). An exploratory study of human clustering of Web pages. In Lopez-Huertas, Maria J. (Eds.), *Volume 8 of Advances in Knowledge Organization: Proceedings of the 7ᵗʰ International Society for Knowledge Organization Conference* (pp. 351-357). Verkehrs-Nr: Ergon-Verlag.

Knight K., & Marcu, D. (2000). Statistics based summarization – step one: Sentence compression. In *Proceedings of the 17ᵗʰ National Conference on Artificial Intelligence and 12ᵗʰ Conference on Innovative Application of Artificial Intelligence* (pp.703-710). Menlo Park, CA: AAAI. Retrieved 19 April 2005 from http://portal.acm.org/citation.cfm?id=647288.721086

Kraaij, W., Spitters, M., & Hulth, A. (2002). Headline extraction based on a combination of uni- and multi-document summarization techniques. In *Proceedings of the Document Understanding Conference 2002*. Retrieved 20 April 2005 from http://www-nlpir.nist.gov/projects/duc/pubs.html

Kupiec, J., Pedersen, J., & Chen, F. (1995). A trainable document summarizer. In EA Fox, P. Ingwersen, & R. Fidel (Eds.), SIGIR-95: *Proceedings of the 18ᵗʰ Annual International ACM SIGIR Conference on Research and Development in Information Retrieval* (pp. 68-73). New York: ACM Press. Retrieved 22 April 2005 from http://portal.acm.org/citation.cfm?id=215333

Kurohashi, S. & Nagan, M. (1994). Automatic detection of discourse structure by checking surface information in sentences. In *Proceedings of the 15ᵗʰ International Conference on Computational Linguistics* (vol. 2, pp.1123-1127). Morristown, NJ: Association for Computational Linguistics. Retrieved 20 April 2005 from http://portal.acm.org/citation.cfm?id=991334

Lacatusu, F., Hickl, A., Harabagiu, S., & Nezda, L. (2004). Lite-GISTexter at DUC2004. In *Proceedings of the Document Understanding Conference 2004*. Retrieved 16 April 2005 from http://www-nlpir.nist.gov/projects/duc/pubs.html

Le, H. T. & Abeysinghe, G. (2003). A study to improve the efficiency of a discourse parsing system. In A. F. Gelbukh (Eds.), *Volume 2588 of Lecture Notes in Computer Science: Proceedings of the 4ᵗʰ International*

Conference on Intelligent Text Processing and Computational Linguistics (pp. 101-114). Berlin: Springer-Verlag.

Leskovec, J., Milic-Frayling, N., & Grobelnik, M. (2005). Extracting summary sentence based on the document semantic graph. *Microsoft Technical Report TR-2005-07*. Redmond, WA: Microsoft Corporation. Retrieved 16 April 2005 from
http://research.microsoft.com/research/pubs/view.aspx?type=Technical%20Report&id=854

Leuski, A, Lin, C. –Y., & Stubblebine, S. (2003). iNEATS: interactive multidocument summarization. In *Proceedings of the 41ˢᵗ Annual Meeting of the Association of Computational Linguistics*. Morristown, NJ: Association for Computational Linguistics. Retrieved April 22, 2005, from
http://www.ict.usc.edu/~leuski/publications/papers/iNeATS-acl.pdf

Liddy, E. D. (1991). Discourse-level structure of empirical abstracts: An exploratory study. *Information Processing and Management*, 27(1), 55-81.

Lin, C.-Y. (1995). Topic identification by concept generalization. In *Proceedings of the 33ʳᵈ Annual Meeting of the Association for Computation Linguistics* (pp. 308-310). Morristown, NJ: ACL.

Lin, C. -Y. (2004). ROUGE: A package for automatic evaluation of summaries. In *Proceedings of the Workshop on Text Summarization Branches Out* (pp. 74-81). Morristown, NJ: ACL. Retrieved 17 April 2005 from
http://www.isi.edu/~cy/ROUGE/papers/WAS2004.pdf

Lin, C. -Y. , & Hovy, E. H. (1997). Identifying topics by position. In *Proceedings of the 5ᵗʰ Conference on Applied Natural Language Processing* (pp. 283-290). San Francisco, CA: Morgan Kaufmann Publishers Inc. Retrieved 18 April 2005 from http://portal.acm.org/citation.cfm?id=974599

Lin, C.-Y, & Hovy, E. H. (2001). NEATS: A multidocument summarizer. In *Proceedings of the Document Understanding Conference 2001*. Retrieved 20 April 2005 from http://www-nlpir.nist.gov/projects/duc/pubs.html

Lin, C.-Y., & Hovy, E. H. (2000). The automated acquisition of topic signatures for text summarization. In *Proceedings of the 18ᵗʰ International Conference on Computational Linguistics* (vol. 1, pp.495-501). Morristown, NJ: ACL. Retrieved 21 April 2005 from http://portal.acm.org/citation.cfm?id=990892

Lin, C.-Y., & Hovy, E. H. (2002). From single to multi-document summarization: A prototype system and its evaluation. In *Proceedings of the 40ᵗʰ Annual Meeting of the Association for Computational Linguistics* (pp.457-464). Morristown, NJ: ACL.

Lin, C.-Y., & Hovy, E. H. (2003). Automatic evaluation of summaries using N-gram co-occurrence statistics. In *Proceedings of the 2003 Conference of the North American Chapter of the Association for Computational Linguistics on Human Language Technology* (vol.1, 71-78). Morristown, NJ: ACL. Retrieved 21 April 2005 from http://portal.acm.org/citation.cfm?id=1073445.1073465

Litkowski, K. C. (2004). Summarization experiments in DUC 2004. In *Proceedings of the Document Understanding Conference 2004*. Retrieved 10 July 2005 from http://www-nlpir.nist.gov/projects/duc/pubs.html

Luhn, H. P. (1958). The automatic creation of literature abstracts. *IBM Journal of Research and Development*, 2(2), 159-165.

Macionis, John, J. (2000). Sociology (8th ed.). Prentice Hall.

Macskassy, S.A., Banerjee, A., Davison, B.D., & Hirsh, H. (1998). Human performance on clustering Web pages: A preliminary study. In *Proceedings of the 4th International Conference on Knowledge Discovery and Data Mining* (pp.264-268). Menlo Park, CA: AAAI. Retrieved 22 April 2005 from http://www.research.rutgers.edu/~sofmac/paper/kdd1998/macskassy-kdd1998.pdf

Mani, I. (2001a). *Automatic summarization*. Amsterdam: John Benjamins Publishing Company.

Mani, I. (2001b). Recent developments in text summarization. In H. Paques, L. Liu, & D. Grossman (Eds.), CIKM-01: *Proceedings of the 10th International Conference on Information and Knowledge Management* (pp.529-531). New York: ACM. Retrieved 23 April 2005 from http://portal.acm.org/citation.cfm?id=502677

Mani, I. (2001c). Summarization evaluation: an overview. In *Proceedings of the 2nd NTCIR Workshop on Research in Chinese and Japanese Text Retrieval and Text Summarization*. Tokyo: National Institute of Informatics.

Mani, I., & Bloedorn, E. (1999). Summarizing similarities and differences among related documents. *Information Retrieval*, 1(1-2), 35-67. Reprinted in I. Mani & M.T. Maybury (Eds.): *Advances in automatic text summarization* (pp.357-389). Cambridge, MA: The MIT Press.

Mani, I., Bloedorn, E., & Gates, Barbara. (1998). Using cohesion and coherence models for text summarization. In *Working Notes of the AAAI-98 Spring Symposium on Intelligent Text Summarization* (pp.69-76). Retrieved 10 May 2005 from http://complingone.georgetown.edu/~linguist/papers/Spring98Symp.pdf

Mani, I., Firmin, T., House, D., Chrzanowski, M., Klein, G., Hirschman, L., Sundheim, B., & Obrst, L. (1998). The TIPSTER SUMMAC text summarization evaluation: Final report. *MITRE Technical Report MTR 98W0000138*. McLean, VA: MITRE Corporation.

Mani, I. & Maybury, M. T. (Eds.). (1999). *Advances in automatic text summarization*. Cambridge, MA: The MIT Press.

Mann, W., & Thompson, S. (1988). Rhetorical structure theory: Toward a functional theory of text organization. *Text*, 8(3), 243-281.

Marcu, D. (1997a). The rhetorical parsing of natural language texts. *In Proceedings of the 35th Annual Meeting of the Association for Computational Linguistics* (pp.96-103). Morristown, NJ: ACL. Retrieved 11 May 2005 from http://portal.acm.org/citation.cfm?id=979630

Marcu, D. (1997b). From discourse structure to text summaries. In I. Mani, & M. Maybury (Eds.): *Proceedings of the ACL/EACL-97 Workshop on Intelligent Scalable Text Summarization* (pp.82-88). Retrieved 12 May 2005 from http://www1.cs.columbia.edu/~gmw/candidacy/Marcu97.pdf

Marcu, D. (1999a). Discourse trees are good indicators of important in text. In I. Mani & M.T. Maybury (Eds.): *Advances in automatic text summarization* (pp.123-136). Cambridge, MA: The MIT Press.

Marcu, D. (1999b). A decision-based approach to rhetorical parsing. In *Proceedings of the 37th Annual Meeting of the Association for Computational Linguistics* (pp. 365-372). Morristown, NJ: ACL. Retrieved 8 May 2005 from http://acl.ldc.upenn.edu/P/P99/P99-1047.pdf

Marcu, D., & Echihabi, A. (2002). An unsupervised approach to recognizing discourse relations. In *Proceedings of the 40th Annual Meeting of the Association for Computational Linguistics* (pp.368-375). Morristown, NJ: ACL. Retrieve 8 May 2005 from http://acl.ldc.upenn.edu/P/P02/P02-1047.pdf

Matthiessen, C., & Thompson, S. (1988).The structure of discourse and 'subordination'. In Haiman, J., & Thompson, S. (Eds.), *Clause Combining in Grammar and Discourse, Volume 18 of Typological Studies in Language* (pp.275-329). Amsterdam: John Benjamins Publishing.

Maybury, M. T. (1995). Generating summaries from event data. *Information Processing and Management*, 31 (5), 735-751.

McKeown, K., & Radev, D. (1995). Generating summaries of multiple news articles. In *Proceedings of the 18th Annual International ACM SIGIR Conference on Research and Development in Information Retrieval* (pp.74-82). New York: ACM. Retrieved 11 May 2005 from http://portal.acm.org/citation.cfm?id=215334

McKeown, K., Klavans, J. L., Hatzivassiloglou, V., Barzilay, R, & Eskin, E. (1999). Towards multidocument summarization by reformulation: Progress and prospects. In *Proceedings of the 16th National Conference on Artificial Intelligence* (pp. 453-460). Retrieved 10 May 2005 from http://www1.cs.columbia.edu/nlp/newsblaster/papers/stim2.pdf

McKeown, K., Barzilay, R., Evans, D., Hatzivassiloglou, V., Kan M. Y., Schiffman, B. & Teufel, S. (2001a). Columbia multi-document summarization: Approach and evaluation. In *Proceedings of the Document Understanding Conference 2001*. Retrieved from 10 May 2005 from http://www-nlpir.nist.gov/projects/duc/pubs.org.html

McKeown, K., Chang, S., Cimino, J., Feiner, K., Friedman, C., Gravano, L., Hatzivassiloglou, V., Johnson, S., Jordan, A., Klavans, L., Kushniruk, A., Patel, V. & Teufel, S. (2001b). PERSIVAL, a system for personalized search and summarization over multimedia healthcare information. In *Proceedings of the 1st ACM/IEEE-CS Joint Conference on Digital Libraries* (pp.331-340). New York, NY: ACM. Retrieved from 15 July 2009 from http://www.eric.ed.gov/ERICDocs/data/ericdocs2sql/content_storage_01/0000019b/80/19/94/05.pdf

McKeown, K., Barzilay, R., Evans, D., Hatzivassiloglou, V., Klavans, J., Nenkova, A., Sable, C., Schiffman, B., & Sigelman, S. (2002). Tracking and summarizing news on a daily basis with Columbia's Newsblaster. In *Proceedings of the Human Language Technology Conference 2002*. Retrieved 12 May 2005 from http://www1.cs.columbia.edu/nlp/newsblaster/papers/hlt-blaster.pdf

Message Understanding Conference (MUC). (1992). In *Proceedings of the 4th Conference on Message Understanding*. DARPA Software and Intelligent Systems Technology Office.

Minel, J. -L., Nugier, S., & Piat, G. (1997). How to appreciate the quality of automatic text summarization. In I. Mani, & M. T. Maybury (Eds.): *Proceedings of the ACL/EACL-97 Workshop on Intelligent Scalable Text Summarization* (pp.25-33). Retrieved 12 May 2005 from http://www.lalic.paris4.sorbonne.fr/~minel/fichiers/EACL.pdf

Mitra, M., Singhal, A., & Buckley, C. (1997). Automatic text summarization by paragraph extraction. In I. Mani, & M. Maybury (Eds.): *Proceedings of the 14th National Conference on Artificial Intelligence* (pp. 31-36). Menlo Park, CA: AAAI. Retrieved 16 May 2005 from http://acl.ldc.upenn.edu/W/W97/W97-0707.pdf

Moller, J.-U. (1997). CLASSITALL: Incremental and unsupervised learning in the DIA-MOLE framework. In Daelemans, W., Van den Bosch, A., & Weijters, A. (Eds.), *Workshop Notes of the ECML/MLnet Workshop on Empirical Learning of Natural Language Processing Tasks* (pp. 95–104). Retrieved 10 April 2005 from http://www.cnts.ua.ac.be/ecml97/ecml97-notes.html

Moller, J.-U. (1998). Using unsupervised learning for engineering of spoken dialogues. In *AAAI 1998 Spring Symposium on Applying Machine Learning to Discourse Processing* (pp.75-81). Menlo Park, CA: AAAI. Retrieved 10 April 2005 from http://www.issco.unige.ch/staff/clark/papers/moeller-aaai98ss-ml+dp.ps

Mori, T., Nozawa, M. & Asada, Y. (2005). Multi-answer-focused multi-document summarization using a question-answering engine. *ACM Transactions on Asian Language*, 4(3), 305-320.

Morris, J., & Hirst, G. (1991). Lexical cohesion computed by thesaural relations as an indicator of the structure of the text. *Computational Linguistics*, 17(1), 21-45.

Morris, A., Kasper, G., & Adams, D. (1992). The effects and limitations of automatic text condensing on reading comprehension performance. *Information Systems Research*, 3(1), 17-35.

Moxley, Joseph M. (2001). Universities should require electronic theses and dissertations. *Educause Quarterly*, 3, 61-63. Retrieved 16 May 2005 from http://www.educause.edu/ir/library/pdf/eqm0139.pdf

Myaeng, S. H., & Jang, D. H. (1999). Development and evaluation of statisitcally-based document summarization system. In I. Mani & M.T. Maybury (Eds.): *Advances in automatic text summarization* (pp.61-70). Cambridge, MA: The MIT Press.

Nakagawa, H., & Mori, T. (2002). A simple but powerful automatic term extraction method. In *Proceedings of the 2nd International Workshop on Computational Terminology* (pp.29-35). Retrieved 10 May 2005 from http://acl.ldc.upenn.edu/W/W02/W02-1407.pdf

Nakagawa, H. (2000). Automatic term recognition based on statistics of compound nouns. *Terminology* 6(2), 195–210.

National Information Standard Organization (NISO). (2003). Guidelines for the construction, format, and management of monolingual thesauri. *ANSI/NISO-2003*. Retrieved 10 May 2005 from http://download.www.techstreet.com/cgi-bin/pdf/free/403963/Z39-19_2003.pdf

National Institute of Standards and Technology (NIST). (2002). In *Proceedings of the Document Understanding Conferences 2002*. Retrieved 24 April 2005 from http://www-nlpir.nist.gov/projects/duc/index.html

Neff, M.S., & Cooper, J. W. (1999). ASHRAM: Active summarization and markup. In *Proceedings of the 32nd Annual Hawaii International Conference on System Sciences* (Vol. 2, pp. 2037). Washington, DC: IEEE Computer Society. Retrieved 10 May 2005 from http://portal.acm.org/citation.cfm?id=876017

Nobata, C., & Sekine, S. CRL/NYU Summarization System at DUC-2004. (2004). In *Proceedings of the Document Understanding Conference 2004.* Retrieved 10 July 2005 from http://www-nlpir.nist.gov/projects/duc/pubs.html

Nomoto, T. & Matsumoto, Y. (1998). Discourse parsing: A decision tree approach. In *Proceedings of the 6th Workshop on Very Large Corpora* (pp. 216-224). Retrieved 11 May 2005 from http://acl.ldc.upenn.edu/W/W98/W98-1125.pdf

Ono, K., Sumita, K., & Miike, S. (1994). Abstract generation based on rhetorical structure extraction. In *Proceedings of the 15th International Conference on Computational Linguistics* (vol. 1, pp. 344-348). Morristown, NJ: ACL. Retrieved 25 May 2005 from http://portal.acm.org/citation.cfm?id=991946

Paice, C. D. (1990). Constructing literature abstracts by computer: techniques and prospects. *Information Processing and Management*, 26(1), 171-186.

Paice, C. D., & Jones, A. P. (1993). The identification of important concepts in highly structured technical papers. In *Proceedings of the 16th Annual International ACM SIGIR Conference on Research and Development in Information Retrieval* (pp.69-78). New York: ACM. Retrieved 26 May 2005 from http://portal.acm.org/citation.cfm?id=160688.160696

Pasi, T., & Timo, J. (1997). A non-projective dependency parser. In *Proceedings of the 5th Conference on Applied Natural Language Processing* (pp.64-71). San Francisco, CA: Morgan Kaufmann Publishers Inc. Retrieved 26 May 2005 from http://portal.acm.org/citation.cfm?id=974568

Polanyi L., (1993). Linguistic dimensions of text summarization. In B. Endres-Niggemeyer, J. Hobbs, & K. Sparck Jones (Eds.), *Proceedings of Workshop on Summarizing Text for Intelligent Communication.* Retrieved May 10, 2005, from http://transfer.ik.fh-hannover.de/ik/projekte/Dagstuhl/Abstract/Abstracts/Polanyi/Polanyi.html

Pollock, J. J., & Zamora, A. (1975). Automatic abstracting research at the Chemical Abstracts service. *Journal of Chemical Information & Computer Science*, 15(4), 226-232. Reprinted in I. Mani & M.T. Maybury (Eds.): *Advances in automatic text summarization* (pp.43-49). Cambridge, MA: The MIT Press.

Quanlan, R. (1998). C5.0: An informal tutorial. Retrieved March 20, 2005, from http://www.rulequest.com/see5-unix.html

Radev, D. (2000). A common theory of information fusion from multiple text sources step one: Cross-document structure. In *Proceedings of the 1ˢᵗ SIGdial Workshop on Discourse and Dialogue*. Retrieved 24 May 2005 from http://www.sigidal.org/sigdialworkshop/proceedings/radev.pdf

Radev, D., Jing, H., & Budzikowska, M. (2000). Centroid-based summarization of multiple documents: Sentence extraction, utility-based evaluation and user studies. In *ANLP/NAACL 2000 Workshop on Automatic Summarization* (pp.21-29). Retrieved 30 May 2005 from http://tangra.si.umich.edu/~radev/papers/centroid.pdf

Radev, D., Fan, W. & Zhang, Z. (2001). WebInEssence: A personalized web-Based multi-document summarization and recommendation system. In *Proceedings of the Automatic Summarization Workshop of the 2ⁿᵈ Meeting of the North American Chapter of the Association for Computational Linguistics*. Morristown, NJ: ACL. Retrieved 15 July 2009 from http://tangra.si.umich.edu/~radev/papers/naacl-summ01.ps

Radev, D., Blair-Goldensohn, S., Zhang, Z., & Raghavan, R.S. (2001). Newsinessence: A system for domain-independent, real-time news clustering and multi-document summarization. In *Proceedings of the 1ˢᵗ International Conference on Human Language Technology Research*. Retrieved 24 May 2005 from http://acl.ldc.upenn.edu/H/H01/H01-1056.pdf

Radev, D., Blitzer, J., Winkel, A., Allison, T., & Topper, M. (2003). MEAD Documentation, Version 3.08. Retrieved May 24, 2005, from http:// www.summarization.com/mead/

Radev, D., Jing, H., Stys, M., & Tam, D. (2004). Centroid-based summarization of multiple documents. *Information Processing and Management*, 40, 919-938.

Rath, G.J., Resnick, A., & Savage, T.R. (1961). The formation of abstracts by the selection of sentences. *American Documentation*, 12 (2), 139-141.

Robin, J. (1994). Revision-Based generation of natural language summaries providing historical background: Corpus-based analysis, design, implementation, and evaluation. *PhD Thesis*, Department of Computer Science, Columbia University.

Roscoe, J. T. (1975). *Fundamental research statistics for the behavioral sciences* (2ⁿᵈ version). Fort worth: Holt, Rinehart and Winston, Inc.

Rush, J., Salvador, R., & Zamora, A. (1971). Automatic abstracting and indexing production of indicative abstracts by application of contextual inference and syntactic coherence criteria. *Journal of American Society for Information Sciences*, 22 (4), 260-274.

Salton, G., Singhal, A., Mitra, M., & Buckley, C. (1997). Automatic text structuring and summarization. *Information Processing and Management*, 33(2), 193-207.

Saggion, H., Radev, D., Teufel, S., Lam, W., & Strassel, S. M. (2002). Developing infrastructure for the evaluation of single and multi-document summarization systems in a cross-lingual environment. In *Proceedings of Language Resources and Evaluation Conference 2002* (pp. 29-31). Retrieved 5 June 2005 from http://www.cl.cam.ac.uk/users/sht25/papers/jhu_workshop_lrec2002.pdf

Saggion, H., & Caizauskas, R. (2004). Multi-document summarization by cluster/profile relevance and redundancy removal. In *Proceedings of the Document Understanding Conference 2004*. Retrieved 10 July 2005 from http://www-nlpir.nist.gov/projects/duc/pubs.html

Schiffman, B., Nenkova, A., & McKeown, K. (2002). Experiments in multi-document summarization. In *Proceedings of the Human Language Technology Conference 2002*.

Schlesinger, J. D. & Conroy, J. M. Okurowski, M. E. & O'Leary, D. P. (2003). Machine and human performance for single and multidocument summarization. *IEEE Intelligent Systems*, 18(1), 46-54.

Summary Evaluation Environment. (2001). http://www.isi.edu/~cyl/SEE/

Spink, Amanda, & Xu, Jack L. (2000). Selected results from a large study of Web searching: The Excite study [electronic version]. *Information Research*, 6(1). Retrieved 6 June 2005 from http://informationr.net/ir/6-1/paper90.html

Stein, G. C., Strzalkowski, T., & Wise, G. B. (2000). Interactive, text-based summarization of multiple documents. *Computational Intelligence*, 16(4), 606-613.

Sparck Jones, K. (1993). What might be in a Summary? In G. Knorz, J. Krause, & C. Womser-Hacker (Eds.), *Information Retrieval, 1993*, 9-26.

Song S. K., Jang D. H. & Myaeng S. H. (2005). Text summarization based on sentence clustering with rhetorical structure information. *International Journal of Computer Processing of Oriental Languages*, 18(2), 153-170.

Sowa, J. F. (1984). *Conceptual structures: Information processing in mind and machine.* Reading, MA: Addison-Wesley Publishing Company.

Sui, Z., Chen, Y., Hu, J., Wu, Y., & Yu, S. (2002). The research on the automatic term extraction in the domain of information science and technology. In *Proceedings of the 5th East Asia Forum of the Terminology.* Retrieved 6 June 2005 from http://www.icl.pku.edu.cn/icl_tr/papers_2000-2003/2002

Tabachnick, B. G., & Fidell, L. S. (1996). *Using multivariate statistics* (4th ed.). Boston, MA: Allyn & Bacon.

Teufel, S., Moens, M. (1997). Sentence extraction as a classification task. In *Proceedings of the ACL-97/EACL-97 Workshop on Intelligent and Scalable Text Summarization* (pp.58-65). Retrieved 4 June 2005 from http://acl.ldc.upenn.edu/W/W97/W97-0710.pdf

Teufel, S., Moens, M., (2002). Summarizing scientific articles: Experiments with relevance and rhetorical status. *Computational Linguistics, 28* (4), 409-445.

Tombros, A., & Sanderson, M. (1998). Advantage of query biased summaries in information retrieval. In *Proceedings of the 21st ACM SIGIR Conference on Research and Development in Information Retrieval* (pp.2-10). New York: ACM. Retrieved 6 June 2005 from http://portal.acm.org/citation.cfm?id=290947

Trochim, William M. K. (1999). *The research methods knowledge base.* Cincinnati, OH: Atomic Dog Publishing.

Vanderwende, L., Banko, M., & Nenezes, A. (2004). Event-centric summary generation. *In Proceedings of the Document Understanding Conference 2004.* Retrieved 2 June 2005 from http://www-nlpir.nist.gov/projects/duc/pubs.html

Van Rijsbergen, C. J. (1979). *Information Retrieval.* London: Butterworth.

Weber, R. P. (1990). *Basic content analysis* (2nd ed.). Newbury Park, CA: Sage Publications.

White, M., Korelsky, T., Cardie, C., Ng, V., Pierce, D., & Wagstaff, K. (2001). Multi-document summarization via information extraction. In *Proceedings of the 1st International Conference on Human Language Technology Research.* Retrieved 3 June 2005 from http://www.cse.buffalo.edu/faculty/drpierce/papers/hlt2001.html

Wollersheim, D., & Rahayu, W. (2002). Methodology for creating a sample subset of dynamic taxonomy to use in navigating medical text databases. In *Proceedings International Database Engineering and Applica-*

tions Symposium (pp. 276-284). Washington, DC: IEEE Computer Society. Retrieved 6 June 2005 from http://homepage.cs.latrobe.edu.au/lewisba/SPIRT/ideas02_wollersheim_d.pdf

Wu, H., Radev, D., & Fan, W. (2004). Towards answer-focused summarization using search engines. In M. T. Maybury (Ed.), *New Directions in Question Answering* (pp.227-236). Menlo Park, CA: AAAI.

Zajic, D., Dorr, B., & Schwartz, R. (2004). BBN/UMD at DUC-2004: Topiary. In *Proceedings of the Document Understanding Conference 2004.* Retrieved 3 June 2005 from http://www-nlpir.nist.gov/projects/duc/pubs.html

Zamir, O., & Etzioni, O. (1999). Grouper: A dynamic clustering interface to web search results. In *Proceedings of the 8th International World Wide Web Conference* (pp.283-296). Retrieved 3 June 2005 from http://www8.org/w8-papers/3a-search-query/dynamic/dynamic.html

Zhang, Z.., Blair-Goldensohn, S., & Radev, D. R. (2002). Towards CST-enhanced summarization. In *Proceedings of the 18th National Conference on Artificial Intelligence* (pp. 439-445). Menlo Park, CA: AAAI. Retrieved 5 June 2005 from http://portal.acm.org/citation.cfm?id=777092.777162

Zhang, Z. Otterbacher, J., & Radev, D. R. (2003). Learning cross-document structural relationships using boosting. In *Proceedings of the 12th International Conference on Information and Knowledge Management* (pp.124-130). New York: ACM. Retrieved 5 June 2005 from http://portal.acm.org/citation.cfm?id=956887

Appendix I:

An Example of Three Types of Summaries

Note: the three types of summaries are on the topic of "school crime" and have a compression rate of 20%.

1. SYSTEM 2

- Number in the brackets indicates the number of documents.
- Concepts highlighted in red are the more common concepts in sociology dissertation abstracts.

In these 10 dissertation abstracts, the following context relations were found:

perception (2), attitude(1), framework(1), hypothesis(1), model(1), perspective(1), theory(1), view(1)

In these 10 dissertation abstracts, the following research methods were found:

survey(4), case study(2), regression analysis(2), sampling(2), archival research(1), bivariate analysis(1), correlational research(1), empirical research(1), experiment(1), interview(1), multilevel analysis(1), multivariate analysis(1), questionnaire(1), secondary analysis(1)

These 10 dissertation abstracts were mainly about:

1. Education	2. Social and human sciences	3. Politics and law
4. Economics	5. General concepts	

1. Education

- **school(10),** including public school(5), high school(4), student and school(2), **daily school(1),** individual school(1), large school(1), **matching school(1),** middle school(1), **restructured school(1),** selected school(1), **serious school(1),** suburban school(1), school and community(1), school in the Camden(1), and more ...

Different aspects were investigated, including school crime(5), school district(4), school violence(3), **school campus(3),** school safety(2), school size(2), **area of school(1),** area of the school(1), **aspect of school(1),** behavior at school(1), **commitment to school(1),** disorder within the school(1), **officer in school(1),** and more ...

The following relationships were investigated:
- There may be an effect on school delinquency .
- There was no effect on retention and recruitment .

- It was affected by <u>number of areas for possible intervention by policy makers</u>, <u>administrator and school variables</u> .
- It may be affected by <u>school restructuring</u>, <u>juvenile offenses</u> .
- There was a relation with <u>number of students</u>, <u>school district</u>, <u>factors</u>, <u>principal tenure and teacher attendance</u>, <u>abolition of corporal punishment</u> .
- There may be a relation with <u>student extracurricular activity participation</u> .
- There was no relation with <u>average number of activities</u>, <u>school dropout rate and school size and rate of school crime and school violence</u> .

- **student(9)**, including student and school(2), individual student(1), serious student(1), student or teacher(1), violence and student(1), student in this school(1), and <u>more</u> ...

  Different aspects were investigated, including number of student(1), percent of the student(1), percentage of student(1), right of student(1), student attendance(1), student commitment(1), student crime(1), student delinquency(1), student dropout(1), student extracurricular activity(1), student involvement(1), student mobility(1), student respondent(1), student tardiness(1), and more ...

  The following relationships were investigated:
  - There was a relation with <u>school size</u> .
  - There may be a relation with <u>high school size</u> .

- **campus(4)**, including school campus(3), and <u>more</u> ...

  Different aspects were investigated, including officer on campus(1), and <u>more</u> ...

  The following relationships were investigated:
  - It may be affected by <u>juvenile offenses</u> .
  - There was a relation with <u>factors</u> .

2. Social and human sciences

- **crime(7)**, including school crime(5), serious crime(1), student crime(1), violent crime(1), crime and safety(1), crime and violence(1), crime in Texas(1), crime to law(1), crime on high school(1), and <u>more</u> ...

  Different aspects were investigated, including crime data(1), crime rate(1), number of crime(1), type of crime(1), and <u>more</u> ...

  The following relationships were investigated:
  - It was affected by <u>number of areas for possible intervention by policy makers</u> .
  - There was a relation with <u>factors</u>, <u>school district</u>, <u>principal tenure and teacher attendance</u>, <u>abolition of corporal punishment</u>, <u>disorder and lack of parent/student engagement</u>.
  - There may be a relation with <u>high school size</u> .
  - There was no relation with <u>school size</u> .

- **violence(3)**, including school violence(3), serious violence(1), crime and violence(1), violence and student(1), violence in the school(1), violence in their school(1), and <u>more</u> ...

  Different aspects were investigated, including prevalence of violence(1), and <u>more</u> ...

The following relationships were investigated:
- There was no effect on <u>retention and recruitment</u> .
- There was no relation with <u>school size</u> .

- **assault(3)**, including aggravated assault(2), sexual assault(2), simple assault(1), and <u>more</u> ...

3. Politics and law

- **law(3)**, including case law(1), weapon law(1).

  Different aspects were investigated, including attitude toward law(1), crime to law(1), law enforcement(1), law violation(1), and <u>more</u> ...

4. Economics

- **weapon(4)**, including gang and weapon(1).

  Different aspects were investigated, including fight with a weapon(1), increase in weapon(1), weapon law(1), and <u>more</u> ...

5. General concepts

- **safety(4)**, including school safety(2), crime and safety(1), safety and security(1), security and safety(1), and <u>more</u> ...

  Different aspects were investigated, including safety report(1), and <u>more</u> ...

- **security(4)**, including increased security(1), school security(1), officer and security(1), police or security(1), safety and security(1), security and safety(1), and <u>more</u> ...

  Different aspects were investigated, including security officer(2), security measure(1), security staff(1), and <u>more</u> ...

2. OBJECTIVE

- [1]The purpose of this research is to assess the perception of public school districts' human resources directors regarding the effects of serious school violence on teacher retention and recruitment. [2]In this study, serious school violence is defined as: homicides, shootings, rape or sexual assaults, robberies, aggravated assaults, and physical attacks or fights with a weapon, perpetrated against a student or teacher on school property. (<u>doc-id=1</u>)

- [3]This study addresses these questions through formal analysis of case law on forty-eight relevant cases published from 1974 through 1997 to determine how this legal authority is being defined by federal and state courts across the United States. (<u>doc-id=2</u>)

- [1]The purpose of this study was to determine the types and prevalence of violence in three high schools in the camden city public school district, as perceived by students, staff, and a gang abatement task force. (doc-id=3)

- [4]This study examined school administrator differences in reporting school crime based upon selected school and administrator variables. (doc-id=4)

- [1]The purpose of this study was to investigate the relationship between school size and the variables of school dropout rate, rate of school crime and violence and student extracurricular activity participation. [3]Multiple regression analyses and bivariate correlation procedures were utilized to determine if significant relationships existed between school size and the independent variables of student extracurricular activity participation, school dropout rate and rate of school crime and violence. [4]The additional independent variables of school socioeconomic status, distance from home to school and community size were also entered into the multiple regression analyses. (doc-id=5)

- [4]I examine the impact of high school restructuring on school delinquency using a broad conception of delinquency that considers both minor and serious juvenile disorders within the school setting. [5]My purpose here is to answer the following question: what are the effects of restructuring on school delinquency? [6]The theoretical framework links concepts and variables drawn primarily from social bonding and social disorganization theories of juvenile delinquency to address this problem. (doc-id=6)

- [6]This research posits a theoretical model of school crime based on family, home, economics and demography, in association with minority status and educational elements, exacerbated by drugs, gangs and weapons. [8]Scrupulous attention was paid to the recording of criminal incidents and their associated offenses in the sample districts. [9]A rare opportunity was afforded to analyze empirical data relating to actual criminal offenses on public school campuses. [10]Detailed descriptions are given of numbers of incidents, offenses, ages of offenders, place of offense, sex of offenders, involvement of drugs, gangs and weapons. (doc-id=7)

- [1]This study examines factors related to student-initiated serious crime on high school campuses. (doc-id=8)

- [1]This study proposes to answer three research questions; namely (1) were the observed frequencies of criminal incidences, per 1,000 students, within expected frequencies based upon school district size and district type (e.g., urban, suburban, non-metropolitan, and rural)? [2](2) Were certain categories of criminal incidences (crimes against persons, crimes against society, crimes against property, and crimes against self) more likely to occur in certain areas of the school campus? [3](3) Were individuals identified as 'repeat offenders' (having committed more than one offense over a three-month period), more likely to commit certain types of crimes? (doc-id=9)

- [7]This research focused on the identification of variables associated with variance in school crime rates, with an emphasis on identifying those that are manipulable. [8]If there are aspects of daily school operation that policy makers can manipulate, school crime rates might be influenced meaningfully. [9]Drawing upon a number of theoretical perspectives, hypotheses regarding school crime were postulated. [10]These hypotheses were tested by examining the cleveland public schools for a twenty-one year period, 1973-1993, using individual school buildings as the unit of measure. (doc-id=10)

190

3. MEAD

- [1]The purpose of this research is to assess the perception of public school districts' human resources directors regarding the effects of serious school violence on teacher retention and recruitment. [2]In this study, serious school violence is defined as: homicides, shootings, rape or sexual assaults, robberies, aggravated assaults, and physical attacks or fights with a weapon, perpetrated against a student or teacher on school property. [3]This qualitative, issues-oriented case study was assessed through an analysis of a public school district's human resource department's policies and archival records, and responses on surveys from public school district human resources directors. [6]The human resources directors believe that serious school violence is increasing across the nation, however, 94% believe serious school violence has not effected retention and recruitment in underline>their /underline> district and 92% indicated that their schools were safe to very safe. (doc-id=1)

- [1]The alarming escalation of school crime and violence in recent years is being countered more and more frequently with the establishment of police and security programs within troubled public schools. (doc-id=2)

- [1]The publicity surrounding a number of well publicized and tragic school shootings in the late 1990's has brought a national focus on the school safety issue and has left the impression that america's schools are unsafe. [3]One concern that has emerged from a review of crane reports collected by law enforcement agencies is what many believe may be an underreporting of school crane by school administrators. many factors exist that may effect the accurate reporting of crime to law enforcement by school administrators. [4]This study examined school administrator differences in reporting school crime based upon selected school and administrator variables. [8]Significant differences were found between schools located in cities and towns, schools with and without police or security officers on campus, school administrators who believe reporting crime impacts school safety and those who don't, and those who perceive having district administrative support in reporting school crime and those not perceiving this support. (doc-id=4)

- [1]The purpose of this study was to investigate the relationship between school size and the variables of school dropout rate, rate of school crime and violence and student extracurricular activity participation. [3]Multiple regression analyses and bivariate correlation procedures were utilized to determine if significant relationships existed between school size and the independent variables of student extracurricular activity participation, school dropout rate and rate of school crime and violence. [7]The relationships between school size and school dropout rate and school size and rate of school crime and violence were not statistically significant. (doc-id=5)

- [1]Recent years have seen extensive debate on the multitude of problems plaguing secondary education in the united states, and the problem of school crime and deviance is gaining a sizable share of the attention. [4]I examine the impact of high school restructuring on school delinquency using a broad conception of delinquency that considers both minor and serious juvenile disorders within the school setting. (doc-id=6)

- [1]This study examines factors related to student-initiated serious crime on high school campuses. [5]Using bivariate and multivariate analysis of data drawn from the responses of 889 high school principals, it was found that disorder and lack of parent/student engagement (commitment to school values) displayed the strongest relationship to serious crime. (doc-id=8)

- [1]This study proposes to answer three research questions; namely (1) were the observed frequencies of criminal incidences, per 1,000 students, within expected frequencies based upon school district size and district type (e.g., urban, suburban, non-metropolitan, and rural)? [2](2) Were certain categories of criminal incidences (crimes against persons, crimes against society, crimes against property, and crimes against self) more likely to occur in certain areas of the school campus? null (doc-id=9)

Appendix II:

Questionnaire For User Evaluation

Topic 1: social support

Number of dissertation abstracts: 200

Submitted by: XXX

Institution: XXXXXXX

The purpose of this evaluation is to evaluate the quality and usefulness of the multi-document summaries of sociology dissertation abstracts. The set of dissertation abstracts retrieved for your topic is condensed into a summary. Four different summaries have been constructed with two kinds of structures: (1) focusing on research variables and their relationships, and (2) focusing on important sentences.

- **Summary 1** focuses on research variables and their relationships, as well as research methods and context relations.

- **Summary 2** also focuses on research variables and their relationships. Furthermore, similar concepts are grouped and categorized. In addition, important sociology concepts are highlighted in red.

- **Summary 3** consists of sentences that are mainly problem statements identified in each dissertation abstract.

- **Summary 4** consists of sentences that are ranked as important, according to certain sentence features, in the set of dissertation abstracts.

A. Evaluation of summary readability

1. Does the summary contain vacuous or very general information?
   - Summary 1: ☐ None ☐ A Little ☐ Some ☐ A lot
   - Summary 2: ☐ None ☐ A Little ☐ Some ☐ A lot
   - Summary 3: ☐ None ☐ A Little ☐ Some ☐ A lot
   - Summary 4: ☐ None ☐ A Little ☐ Some ☐ A lot

2. Does the summary contain duplicate information?
   - Summary 1: ☐ None ☐ A little ☐ Some ☐ A lot
   - Summary 2: ☐ None ☐ A little ☐ Some ☐ A lot
   - Summary 3: ☐ None ☐ A little ☐ Some ☐ A lot
   - Summary 4: ☐ None ☐ A little ☐ Some ☐ A lot

3. Does the summary contain dangling anaphora (e.g. unresolved pronouns)?
   - Summary 1: ☐ None ☐ A little ☐ Some ☐ A lot
   - Summary 2: ☐ None ☐ A little ☐ Some ☐ A lot
   - Summary 3: ☐ None ☐ A little ☐ Some ☐ A lot
   - Summary 4: ☐ None ☐ A little ☐ Some ☐ A lot

4. Is the summary fluent?
   - Summary 1: ☐ Not at all ☐ A little ☐ Quite fluent ☐ Very fluent
   - Summary 2: ☐ Not at all ☐ A little ☐ Quite fluent ☐ Very fluent
   - Summary 3: ☐ Not at all ☐ A little ☐ Quite fluent ☐ Very fluent
   - Summary 4: ☐ Not at all ☐ A little ☐ Quite fluent ☐ Very fluent

5. Is the summary concise?
   - Summary 1: ☐ Not at all ☐ A little ☐ Quite concise ☐ Very concise
   - Summary 2: ☐ Not at all ☐ A little ☐ Quite concise ☐ Very concise
   - Summary 3: ☐ Not at all ☐ A little ☐ Quite concise ☐ Very concise
   - Summary 4: ☐ Not at all ☐ A little ☐ Quite concise ☐ Very concise

6. Is the summary coherent?
   - Summary 1: ☐ Not at all ☐ A little ☐ Quite coherent ☐ Very coherent
   - Summary 2: ☐ Not at all ☐ A little ☐ Quite coherent ☐ Very coherent
   - Summary 3: ☐ Not at all ☐ A little ☐ Quite coherent ☐ Very coherent
   - Summary 4: ☐ Not at all ☐ A little ☐ Quite coherent ☐ Very coherent

7. Please rate the <u>overall readability</u> of each summary in terms of the above aspects.

Table 1: Rating of readability

Summaries	Rating Score						
	Very bad ──────────────────────────────▶ Very good						
	1	2	3	4	5	6	7
Summary 1							
Summary 2							
Summary 3							

Summary 4							

B. Evaluation of summary comprehensibility

8. Is the summary easy or hard to understand?
   - Summary 1: ☐ Very hard ☐ Quite hard ☐ Quite easy ☐ Very easy
   - Summary 2: ☐ Very hard ☐ Quite hard ☐ Quite easy ☐ Very easy
   - Summary 3: ☐ Very hard ☐ Quite hard ☐ Quite easy ☐ Very easy
   - Summary 4: ☐ Very hard ☐ Quite hard ☐ Quite easy ☐ Very easy
9. Does the summary give a clear indication of the main ideas of the topic?
   - Summary 1: ☐ Not at all ☐ A little ☐ Some ☐ A lot
   - Summary 2: ☐ Not at all ☐ A little ☐ Some ☐ A lot
   - Summary 3: ☐ Not at all ☐ A little ☐ Some ☐ A lot
   - Summary 4: ☐ Not at all ☐ A little ☐ Some ☐ A lot

10. Please rate the <u>overall comprehensibility</u> of each summary in terms of the above aspects.

Table 2. Rating of comprehensibility

Summaries	Rating Score						
	Very bad						Very good
	1	**2**	**3**	**4**	**5**	**6**	**7**
Summary 1							
Summary 2							
Summary 3							
Summary 4							

C. Evaluation of summary usefulness

11. Please select your purpose for reading the dissertation abstracts.
    - ☐ For your PhD project
    - ☐ For your Master project
    - ☐ For your coursework
    - ☐ For teaching

    If your purpose is not found above, please indicate: _____

12. In what ways is each summary useful for your purpose? Please select one or more.
    Summary 1:
    - ☐ Give you an overview of the research area;
    - ☐ Help you identify research gaps in the area easily;
    - ☐ Help you identify the documents of interest easily;
    - ☐ Indicate research trends in the area;
    - ☐ Indicate similarities among previous studies;
    - ☐ Indicate differences among previous studies;
    - ☐ Indicate important concepts in the area;
    - ☐ Indicate important theories, views, or ideas in the area;
    - ☐ Indicate important research methods used in the area;

    Please list other ways, if any:

Summary 2:

☐ Give you an overview of the research area;
☐ Help you identify research gaps in the area easily;
☐ Help you identify the documents of interest easily;
☐ Indicate research trends in the area;
☐ Indicate similarities among previous studies;
☐ Indicate differences among previous studies;
☐ Indicate important concepts in the area;
☐ Indicate important theories, views, or ideas in the area;
☐ Indicate important research methods used in the area;

Please list other ways, if any:

Summary 3:

☐ Give you an overview of the research area;
☐ Help you identify research gaps in the area easily;
☐ Help you identify the documents of interest easily;
☐ Indicate research trends in the area;
☐ Indicate similarities among previous studies;
☐ Indicate differences among previous studies;
☐ Indicate important concepts in the area;
☐ Indicate important theories, views, or ideas in the area;
☐ Indicate important research methods used in the area;

Please list other ways, if any:

Summary 4:

☐ Give you an overview of the research area;
☐ Help you identify research gaps in the area easily;
☐ Help you identify the documents of interest easily;
☐ Indicate research trends in the area;
☐ Indicate similarities among previous studies;
☐ Indicate differences among previous studies;
☐ Indicate important concepts in the area;
☐ Indicate important theories, views, or ideas in the area;
☐ Indicate important research methods used in the area;

Please list other ways, if any:

13. Please rate the <u>overall usefulness</u> of each summary for your purpose.

Table 3: Rating of usefulness for your purpose

Summaries	Rating Score						
	Not useful						Very useful
	1	2	3	4	5	6	7
Summary 1							
Summary 2							
Summary 3							
Summary 4							

D. Overall Evaluation

14. Please rank the four summaries in order of your preference.
    - **No. 1 :** _____
    - **No. 2 :** _____
    - **No. 3 :** _____
    - **No. 4 :** _____

    Please explain.

15. If the four summaries are readily available for you, which summaries are you likely to use for your purpose? You can select one or more.
    ☐ Summary 1
    ☐ Summary 2
    ☐ Summary 3
    ☐ Summary 4
    ☐ None

E. In-depth Questions

16. Two types of summary structure are used in the summaries. Summary 1 and 2 focus on research variables, whereas summary 3 and 4 focus on important sentences. Which type of structure do you prefer?
    ☐ Variable-based
    ☐ Sentence-based

    Please explain.

17. Summary 1 & 2 both focus on research variables and relationships. However, in summary 2, the concepts are categorized, and important concepts are highlighted. Do you find concept categorization in summary 2 useful?
    ☐ Not useful at all
    ☐ A little useful
    ☐ Quite useful
    ☐ Very useful

    Please explain.

18. Do you find concept highlighting in summary 2 useful?
    ☐ Not useful at all
    ☐ A little useful
    ☐ Quite useful
    ☐ Very useful

    Please explain.

19. Summary 3 & 4 both focus on important sentences. However, summary 3 mainly contains problem statements, whereas summary 4 contains sentences that are ranked as important. Which do you prefer?
    ☐ Mainly problem statements
    ☐ Sentences ranked as important

    Please explain.

F. Suggestions

20. What improvements would you suggest for the summaries, if any?

Appendix III:

Data from Questionnaire for Researchers

(1) Readability

Q1-7: Frequency (percentage) of the researchers selecting the different aspects of readability for the four types of summaries

Readability criteria	Degree	SYSTEM 1	SYSTEM 2	OBJECTIVES	MEAD
1. Vacuous or general information	None	3 (15%)	2 (10%)	4 (20%)	4 (20%)
	A little	9 (45%)	11(55%)	6 (30%)	3 (15%)
	Some	7 (35%)	5 (25%)	6 (30%)	6 (30%)
	A lot	1 (5%)	2 (10%)	4 (20%)	7 (35%)
	Total	20 (100%)	20 (100%)	20(100%)	20(100%)
2. Duplicate information	None	2 (10%)	4 (20%)	9 (45%)	9 (45%)
	A little	8 (40%)	8 (40%)	8 (40%)	8 (40%)
	Some	9 (45%)	7 (35%)	3 (15%)	2 (10%)
	A lot	1 (5%)	1 (5%)	0	1 (5%)
	Total	20 (100%)	20(100%)	20(100%)	20(100%)
3. Dangling anaphor	None	3 (15%)	4 (20%)	10 (50%)	11 (55%)
	A little	8 (40%)	8 (40%)	7 (35%)	6 (30%)
	Some	8 (40%)	7 (35%)	3 (15%)	2 (10%)
	A lot	1 (5%)	1 (5%)	0	1 (5%)
	Total	20(100%)	20(100%)	20(100%)	20(100%)
4. Fluent	Not at all	3 (15%)	1 (5%)	0	1 (5%)
	A little	6 (30%)	7 (35%)	2 (10%)	4 (20%)
	Quite fluent	9 (45%)	8 (40%)	8 (40%)	6 (30%)
	Very fluent	2 (10%)	4 (20%)	10 (50%)	9 (45%)
	Total	20(100%)	20(100%)	20(100%)	20(100%)
5. Concise	Not at all	1 (5%)	0	0	0
	A little	2 (10%)	3 (15%)	5 (25%)	13 (65%)
	Quite concise	10 (50%)	9 (45%)	15 (75%)	5 (25%)
	Very concise	7 (35%)	8 (40%)	0	2 (10%)
	Total	20(100%)	20(100%)	20(100%)	20(100%)
6. Coherent	Not at all	4 (20%)	4 (20%)	1 (5%)	3 (15%)
	A little	2 (10%)	1 (5%)	2 (10%)	2 (10%)
	Quite coherent	6 (30%)	8 (40%)	10 (50%)	10 (50%)
	Very coherent	8 (40%)	7 (35%)	7 (35%)	5 (25%)
	Total	20(100%)	20(100%)	20(100%)	20(100%)
Overall readability	Average score	4.40	5.20	5.70	5.00
	Std. Deviation	1.818	1.576	1.342	1.556

(2) Comprehensibility

Q8-10: Frequency (percentage) of the researchers selecting the different aspects of comprehensibility for the four types of summaries

Comprehensibility criteria	Degree	SYSTEM 1	SYSTEM 2	OBJECTIVES	MEAD
1. Understandability	Very hard	3 (15%)	1 (5%)	1 (5%)	1 (5%)
	Quite hard	6 (30%)	4 (20%)	3 (15%)	3 (15%)
	Quite easy	6 (30%)	9 (45%)	9 (45%)	10(50%)
	Very easy	5 (25%)	6 (30%)	7 (35%)	6 (30%)
	Total	20(100%)	20(100%)	20(100%)	20(100%)
2. Indication of the main ideas of the topic	Not at all	1 (5%)	1 (5%)	0	1 (5%)
	A little	7 (35%)	4 (20%)	5 (25%)	5 (25%)
	Some	5 (25%)	7 (35%)	5 (25%)	7 (35%)
	A lot	7 (35%)	8 (40%)	10 (50%)	7 (35%)
	Total	20(100%)	20(100%)	20(100%)	20(100%)
Overall comprehensibility	Average score	4.75	5.10	5.60	4.95
	Std. Deviation	1.832	1.774	1.095	1.572

(3) Usefulness

Q12-13: Frequency (percentage) of the researchers selecting the different aspects of usefulness for the four types of summaries

Usefulness criteria		SYSTEM 1	SYSTEM 2	OBJECTIVES	MEAD
1. Give you an overview of the research area		11 (55%)	14 (75%)	11 (55%)	10 (50%)
2. Help you identify research gaps in the area easily		5 (25%)	6 (30%)	4 (20%)	3 (15%)
3. Help you identify the documents of interest easily		10 (50%)	10 (50%)	13 (65%)	13 (65%)
4. Indicate research trends in the area		10 (50%)	9 (45%)	8 (40%)	8 (40%)
5. Indicate similarities among previous studies		10 (50%)	12 (60%)	3 (15%)	2 (10%)
6. Indicate differences among previous studies		3 (15%)	5 (25%)	5 (25%)	2 (10%)
7. Indicate important concepts in the area		14 (70%)	15 (75%)	9 (45%)	8 (40%)
8. Indicate important theories, views, or ideas in the area		5 (25%)	7 (35%)	10 (50%)	10 (50%)
9. Indicate important research methods used in the area		14 (70%)	11 (55%)	6 (30%)	5 (25%)
Overall usefulness	Average score	5	5.70	5.65	4.9
	Std. Deviation	1.864	1.418	1.137	1.714

(4) Overall evaluation

Q14-15: Frequency (percentage) of the researchers for overall evaluation for the four types of summaries

Rank	SYSTEM 1	SYSTEM 2	OBJECTIVES	MEAD	Total
No.1(weight=4)	3 (15%)	11 (55%)	6 (30%)	0	20 (100%)
No.2 (weight=3)	5 (25%)	2 (10%)	7 (35%)	6 (30%)	20 (100%)
No.3 (weight=2)	5 (25%)	6 (30%)	5 (25%)	4 (20%)	20 (100%)
No.4 (weight=1)	7 (35%)	1 (5%)	2 (10%)	10 (50%)	20 (100%)
Weighted rank score	2.15	3.15	2.85	1.8	-
Preference	6 (30%)	14 (70%)	11 (55%)	5 (25%)	-

(5) In-depth questions

Q16: Frequency (percentage) of the researchers for comparing the variable-based structure and the sentence-based structure

Preference	Variable-based structure	Sentence-based structure	Total
Frequency	14 (70%)	6 (30%)	20 (100%)

Q17-18: Frequency (percentage) of the researchers for usefulness of the taxonomy

	Not useful at all	A little useful	Quite useful	Very useful	Total
Concept categorization	3 (15%)	3 (15%)	8 (40%)	6 (30%)	20 (100%)
Concept highlighting	0	5 (25%)	5 (25%)	10(50%)	20 (100%)

Q19: Frequency (percentage) of the researchers for comparing OBJECTIVES and MEAD summary

Preference	OBJECTIVES	MEAD	No difference	Total
Frequency	14 (70%)	5 (25%)	1 (5%)	20 (100%)

Appendix IV:

Data from Questionnaires for General Users

(1) Readability

Q1-7: Frequency (percentage) of the general users selecting the different aspects of readability for the four types of summaries

Readability criteria	Degree	SYSTEM 1	SYSTEM 2	OBJECTIVES	MEAD
1. Vacuous or general information	None	5(12.5%)	7(17.5%)	6(15.0%)	6(15.0%)
	A little	19(47.5%)	13(32.5%)	10(25.0%)	11(27.5%)
	Some	11(27.5%)	13(32.5%)	18(45.0%)	17(42.5%)
	A lot	5(12.5%)	7(17.5%)	6(15.0%)	6(15.0%)
	Total	40(100%)	40(100%)	40(100%)	40(100%)
2. Duplicate information	None	14(35.9%)	13(33.3%)	16(41.0%)	17(43.6%)
	A little	12(30.8%)	14(35.9%)	14(35.9%)	11(28.2%)
	Some	8(20.5%)	8(20.5%)	9(23.1%)	11(28.2%)
	A lot	5(12.8%)	4(10.3%)	0	0
	Total	39(100%)	39(100%)	39(100%)	39(100%)
3. Dangling anaphor	None	15(44.1%)	15(44.1%)	15(45.5%)	17(51.5%)
	A little	10(29.4%)	10(29.4%)	11(33.3%)	10(30.3%)
	Some	7(20.6%)	7(20.6%)	6(18.2%)	4(12.1%)
	A lot	2(5.9%)	2(5.9%)	1(3.0%)	2(6.1%)
	Total	34(100%)	34(100%)	33(100%)	33(100%)
4. Fluent	Not at all	6(15.0%)	4(10.0%)	5(12.5%)	4(10.0%)
	A little	15(37.5%)	12(30.0%)	8(20.0%)	10(25.0%)
	Quite fluent	16(40.0%)	21(52.5%)	24(60.0%)	23(57.5%)
	Very fluent	3(7.5%)	3(7.5%)	3(7.5%)	3(7.5%)
	Total	40(100%)	40(100%)	40(100%)	40(100%)
5. Concise	Not at all	6(15.0%)	4(10.0%)	11(27.5%)	10(25.6%)
	A little	12(30.0%)	6(15.0%)	7(17.5%)	7(17.9%)
	Quite concise	17(42.5%)	23(57.5%)	18(45.0%)	20(51.3%)
	Very concise	5(12.5%)	7(17.5%)	4(10.0%)	2(5.1%)
	Total	40(100%)	40(100%)	40(100%)	40(100%)
6. Coherent	Not at all	6(15.8%)	1(2.6%)	5(13.2%)	5(13.2%)
	A little	14(36.8%)	13(34.2%)	14(36.8%)	11(28.9%)
	Quite coherent	18(47.4%)	21(55.3%)	16(42.1%)	17(44.7%)
	Very coherent	0	3(7.9%)	3(7.9%)	5(13.2%)
	Total	38(100%)	38(100%)	38(100%)	38(100%)
Overall readability	Average score	3.90	5.00	3.78	3.80
	Std. Deviation	1.482	1.536	1.672	1.620

(2) Comprehensibility

Q8-10: Frequency (percentage) of the general users selecting the different aspects of comprehensibility for the four types of summaries

Comprehensibility criteria	Degree	SYSTEM 1	SYSTEM 2	OBJECTIVES	MEAD
1. Understandability	Very hard	7(17.5%)	3(7.5%)	5(12.5%)	6(15.0%)
	Quite hard	15(37.5%)	8(20.0%)	17(42.5%)	15(37.5%)
	Quite easy	18(45.0%)	21(52.5%)	15(37.5%)	15(37.5%)
	Very easy	0	8(20.0%)	3(7.5%)	4(10.0%)
	Total	40(100%)	40(100%)	40(100%)	40(100%)
2. Indication of the main ideas of the topic	Not at all	6(15.0%)	2(5.0%)	5(12.8%)	8(20.5%)
	A little	18(45.0%)	11(27.5%)	14(35.9%)	10(25.6%)
	Some	11(27.5%)	15(37.5%)	15(38.5%)	12(30.8%)
	A lot	5(12.5%)	12(30.0%)	5(12.8%)	9(23.1%)
	Total	40(100%)	40(100%)	40(100%)	40(100%)
Overall comprehensibility	Average score	3.88	4.58	3.85	3.73
	Std. Deviation	1.636	1.738	1.642	1.754

(3) Usefulness

Q12-13: Frequency (percentage) of the general users selecting the different aspects of usefulness for the four types of summaries

Usefulness criteria	SYSTEM 1	SYSTEM 2	OBJECTIVES	MEAD
1. Give you an overview of the research area	15 (37.5%)	18(45%)	23(57.5%)	23(57.5)
2. Help you identify research gaps in the area easily	6(15%)	8(20%)	4(10%)	5(12.5%)
3. Help you identify the documents of interest easily	16(40%)	16(40%)	16(40%)	12(30%)
4. Indicate research trends in the area	10(25%)	11(27.5%)	8(20%)	8(20%)
5. Indicate similarities among previous studies	9(22.5%)	10(25%)	4(10%)	5(12.5%)
6. Indicate differences among previous studies	6(15%)	7(17.5%)	4(10%)	2(5%)
7. Indicate important concepts in the area	16(40%)	18(45%)	13(32.5%)	14(35%)
8. Indicate important theories, views, or ideas in the area	10(25%)	9(22.5%)	10(25%)	11(27.5%)
9. Indicate important research methods used in the area	15(37.5%)	14(35%)	6(15%)	6(15%)

Overall usefulness		SYSTEM 1	SYSTEM 2	OBJECTIVES	MEAD
Overall usefulness	Average score	3.73	4.57	3.73	3.76
	Std. Deviation	1.557	1.708	1.627	1.817

(4) Overall evaluation

Q14-15: Frequency (percentage) of the general users for overall evaluation for the four types of summaries

Rank	SYSTEM 1	SYSTEM 2	OBJECTIVES	MEAD	Total
No.1 (weight=4)	4(10%)	22(55.0%)	6(15.0%)	8(20.0%)	40(100%)
No.2 (weight=3)	19(47.5%)	6(15.0%)	10(25.0%)	5(12.5%)	40(100%)
No. 3 (weight=2)	9(22.5%)	4(10.0%)	15(37.5%)	12(30.0%)	40(100%)
No. 4 (weight=1)	8(20.0%)	8(20.0%)	9(22.5%)	15(37.5%)	40(100%)
Weighted rank score	2.475	3.05	2.325	2.15	-
Preference	7(17.9%)	25(64.1%)	12(30.8%)	13(33.3%)	-

(5) In-depth questions

Q16: Frequency (percentage) of the general users for comparing the variable-based structure and the sentence-based structure

Preference	Variable-based structure	Sentence-based structure	Total
Frequency	24(61.5%)	15(38.5%)	39 (100%)

Q17-18: Frequency (percentage) of the general users for usefulness of the taxonomy

Function of taxonomy	Not useful at all	A little useful	Quite useful	Very useful	Total
Concept categorization	3 (7.7%)	8(20.5%)	14(35.9%)	14(35.9%)	39 (100%)
Concept highlighting	4(10.3%)	11(28.2%)	15(38.5%)	9(23.1%)	39 (100%)

Q19: Frequency (percentage) of the general users for comparing OBJECTIVES and MEAD summary

Preference	OBJECTIVES	MEAD	No difference	Total
Frequency	21 (52.5%)	16(40%)	3 (7.5%)	40 (100%)

www.ingramcontent.com/pod-product-compliance
Lightning Source LLC
La Vergne TN
LVHW042333060326
832902LV00006B/147